# ΛΟΓΟΙ ΙΗΣΟΥ
## Studies in Q

University of South Florida
# INTERNATIONAL STUDIES IN FORMATIVE CHRISTIANITY AND JUDAISM

EDITORIAL BOARD

FOR THE UNITED STATES
Jacob Neusner, University of South Florida and Bard College
James Strange, University of South Florida
William Scott Green, University of Rochester
Bruce Chilton, Bard College
Alan J. Avery-Peck, College of the Holy Cross

FOR ISRAEL
Ithamar Gruenwald, University of Tel Aviv
Mayer Gruber, Ben Gurion University of the Negev

FOR SCANDINAVIA
Karl-Gustav Sandelin, Åbo Akademi
Heikki Räisänen, University of Helsinki
Karl-Johan Illman, Åbo Akademi

FOR ITALY
Mauro Pesce, University of Bologna
Adriana Destro, University of Bologna
Pier Cesare Bori, University of Bologna

FOR GERMANY
Gerd Lüdemann, University of Göttingen

FOR AUSTRIA
Günther Stemberger, University of Vienna

FOR NEW ZEALAND
Gregory W. Dawes, University of Otago

FOR CANADA
Herbert Basser, Queens University
Craig Evans, Trinity Western University

FOR EASTERN AND SOUTHEASTERN EUROPE
Petros Vassiliadis, Aristotle University of Thessaloniki
Nikolai Schivarov, University of Sofia, Bulgaria
Vasile Mihoc, University of Sibiu, Romania
January Ivlief, Theological Academy, St. Petersburg, Russia
Dimitrios Passakos, Aristotle University of Thessaloniki

FOR FRANCE
Jean Magne, Paris

# ΛΟΓΟΙ ΙΗΣΟΥ
## STUDIES IN Q

PETROS VASSILIADIS

Scholars Press
Atlanta, Georgia

# ΛΟΓΟΙ ΙΗΣΟΥ
## Studies in Q
### by
### Petros Vassiliadis

Published by Scholars Press for the University of South Florida

Copyright © 1999 by the University of South Florida

All rights reserved. No part of this work may be reproduced or transmitted in any form or by any means, electronic or mechanical, including photocopying and recording, or by means of any information storage or retrieval system, except as may be expressly permitted by the 1976 Copyright Act or in writing from the publisher. Requests for permission should be addressed in writing to the Rights and Permissions Office, Scholars Press, P.O. Box 15399, Atlanta, GA 30333-0399, USA.

Library of Congress Cataloging in Publication Data

Vassiliadis, Petros.
    Logoi Iēsou : studies in Q / Petros Vassiliadis.
      p.   cm. — (University of South Florida international studies in formative Christianity and Judaism ; v. 8)
    Includes bibliographical references.
    ISBN 0-7885-0567-X (cloth : alk. paper)
    1. Q hypothesis (Synoptics criticism) 2. Bible. N.T. Gospels—Criticism, interpretation, etc. I. Title. II. Title: Studies in Q. III. Series.
BS2555.2.V295 1999
226'.066—dc21                           99-24288
                                                  CIP

Printed in the United States of America
on acid-free paper

*To my father Basil
in memoriam*

# TABLE OF CONTENTS

| | |
|---|---|
| Preface | ix |
| 1. Did Q Exist? | 1 |
| 2. The Nature and Extent of the Q-Document | 39 |
| 3. The Original Order of Q. Some Residual Cases | 61 |
| 4. Prolegomena to a Discussion on the Relationship Between Mark and the Q-Document | 71 |
| 5. The Text of Q. A Basic Reconstruction of the Q-Document | 85 |
| 6. Eucharist and Q | 117 |
| 7. The Function of John the Baptist in Q and Mark | 133 |
| 8. The Challenge of Q. The Cynic Hypothesis | 141 |
| 9. EXCURSUS: Behind Mark. Towards a Written Source | 153 |

# PREFACE

One of the major issues, which will most probably occupy biblical research during the coming decades, is the study of Q. Not so much as a solution to the Synoptic problem, but because of the effects it will cause to the conventional picture of Christian origins, which dominated biblical scholarship for almost a century. This well-known to scholarly circles second source of the Synoptic tradition, now lost, seems to expound a radically different theological view from the mainstream kerygmatic expression of the early Church. It is not surprising, therefore, that Q—even when it is accepted as a solution to the Synoptic problem—caused many problems and creates an unprecedented polarity of views, any time it comes to terms with Christian origins.

An answer to this problem with all honesty is being attempted in this volume by a Greek Orthodox biblical scholar, who simply wants to add his voice to those undertaken by other scholars in the search for Christian origins. The volume offers an overall treatment to this most important and at the same time highly controversial issue of modern biblical scholarship. It consists of nine studies on Q carried out during the last three decades. Some of these studies have already been published in widely known scholarly biblical journals, others in less known local ones—and therefore hardly available—and still others are not published yet.

These nine studies, presented here with only minor editorial modifications, are not classified according to their chronological appearance, but according to a logical scheme. Thus, the first studies deal with literary questions, whereas the last ones are devoted to theological issues of Q.

Chapter 1 "Did Q Exist?" deals with the problem of Q's existence, focusing on a critical examination of the arguments against the existence of the Q-Document since the time of Streeter. It was first published in English in Θεολογία καὶ Ἐκκλησία (=Theologia and Ecclesia), a journal of general theological studies (London 1980ff). It appeared in vol. 1 (1980), pp. 287-328.

Chapter 2 "The Nature and Extent of the Q-Document" is self-evident, dealing mainly with the procedural principles for reconstructing the Q-Document. It first appeared in English in *Novum Testamentum* vol. 20 (1978), pp. 49-73.

Chapter 3 further takes up the problem of the original order of the Q-Document. It first appeared as "The Original Order of Q. Some Residual Cases", in J. Delobel (ed.), *Logia. Les Paroles de Jésus - The sayings of Jesus: Memorial Joseph Coppens*, BETL 59 Leuven 1982, pp. 379-387.

Chapter 4 touches the Q-Marcan relations. It was originally published under the title: "Prolegomena to a Discussion on the Relationship Between Mark and the Q-Document", in Δελτίον Βιβλικῶν Μελετῶν vol. 4 (1975), pp. 31-46. Δελτίον Βιβλικῶν Μελετῶν (Deltion Biblikôn Meletôn=Bulletin of Biblical Studies, Athens 1972ff.) is the only Orthodox scholarly biblical journal.

Chapter 5 "The Text of Q" appears for the first time here, and is a basic reconstruction of the original Greek text of Q.

The following three chapters all deal with theological problems of the Q-Document. Chapter 6 "Eucharist and Q" was first published in the *Scholarly Annual of the Department of Theology at the Aristotle University of Thessaloniki*, n.s. 6 (1996) pp. 111-130.

Chapter 7 "The Function of John the Baptist in Q and Mark" was published in Θεολογία, a journal of general theological studies (Athens 1929ff). It appeared in vol. 46 (1975) pp. 405-413.

Chapter 8 "The Challenge of Q. The Cynic Hypothesis" appeared in the *Atti del V Simposio di Tarso su S. Paolo Apostolo*, edited by L. Padovese, Rome 1998, pp. 41-60.

Finally, chapter 9 is an excursus under the title "Behind Mark. Towards a Written Source," which was first published in *NTS* vol. 20 (1974) pp. 155-160.

Thessaloniki, June 1998                                         Petros Vassiliadis

# 1
# DID Q EXIST ?*

The era of Literary Criticism culminated in 1924 with Streeter's *Four Gospels*. This book has led, among other things, to the general acceptance of the Q-Hypothesis. So widespread was the acceptance, at least in Great Britain, of the existence of a common source behind Matthew and Luke besides Mark, that within two years of the publication of this major work, E. W. Lummis, one of the rare dissentients, asked "why so many critics refuse to read and listen to a word against the dogma known as 'Q'."[1] He was astonished in particular by the readiness with which the Q-Hypothesis was "taught and accepted as established and fundamental truth."[2] J. H. Ropes, on the other hand, though holding the Priority of Mark insisted ten years later that "the grounds on which Q's existence is inferred by modern scholars are far less secure than is commonly represented or supported."[3]

Ironically enough, nearly all studies on Q which have been published in the last decade or so, important as they are, have paid little or no attention to literary questions. M. Hooker has rightly criticized this attitude of writing on the theology of Q "without really considering the

---

*This article covers the period up to 1974. For reasons beyond my wish I have been able to publish it in English only in 1981 under the title "Did Q Exist? A Critical Examination of the Arguments against the Existence of the Q-Document since the Time of Streeter." However, a modified version had already appeared in Greek as ch. I of my doctoral dissertation, Ἡ περὶ τῆς Πηγῆς τῶν Λογίων θεωρία (Athens, 1977).

Apart from the usual abbreviations a few more are used which may not be familiar to all readers:

    OSSP    :*Oxford Studies in the Synoptic Problem*, ed. by W. Sanday (Oxford, 1911).
    SE vol. I  : *Studia Evangelica*, ed. by F. L. Cross (Berlin, 1959).
    SG       : *Studies in the Gospels. Essays in Memory of R. H. Lightfoot*, ed. by D. E. Nineham (Oxford, 1955).
    INT     :A. Robert-A. Feuillet, *Introduction to the New Testament*, (ET, New York, 1965).
    *Trajectories* : J. M. Robinson-H. Koester, *Trajectories through Early Christianity* (Philadelphia, 1971).
    *Jesus I*   :*Jesus and Man's Hope, I.* ed. by D. G. Buttrick (Pittsburgh, 1970).
    *Jesus II*  :*Jesus and Man's Hope, II.* ed. by D. G. Miller and D. Y. Hadidian (Pittsburgh, 1971).

[1] "A Case against Q," *HJ* 24 (1926), pp. 755-65, esp. p. 757.
[2] Ibid., p. 765.
[3] *The Synoptic Gospels* (Massachusetts, 1934), p. 37.

question whether Q ever existed."[4] For the Q-Hypothesis and the existence of the Q-Document itself have come under heavy criticism both within the context of discussion of the Two-Document theory, and on its own. Even among those who did not attack the Q-Hypothesis directly not a few have been becoming in the course of time more skeptical or reluctant. This, however, is hardly surprising; for apart from the serious challenges to the Two-Document theory in the last two decades, there are certain reasons, both negative and positive, which explain why a number of scholars are deeply suspicious or even hostile toward Q. Two kinds of criticism are directed against Q: some scholars insist that the Q-Hypothesis falls short of absolute certainty; others refer to alternative solutions, stressing that a number of the arguments which were advanced during the literary-critical era (especially by Streeter) are inconclusive. The importance of these attacks on Q lies not so much on the force of the criticism directed against Q, but on the way alternative hypotheses (e.g. the use of Matthew by St. Luke) can plausibly be advanced. We shall now turn to these criticisms, starting with those which attack or reject the Two-Document theory as a whole.

## 1. The challenge to the Two-Document theory as a whole

The Q-Hypothesis constitutes without doubt an inseparable part of the Two-Document theory.[5] For it cannot be held unless the Priority of Mark be assumed;[6] and if either the entire theory, or the Marcan Priority alone, is shaken, the Q-Hypothesis collapses, too.

Some scholars have recently drawn attention to the *indecisiveness of the criteria* which have been employed for the generally accepted solution to the Synoptic Problem, i.e. the Two-Document theory.[7] N. H. Palmer was the first to question the theory by critically examining the criteria, methods, and general arguments used by Gospel criticism, including Source-criticism. He did not attack the Two-Document theory openly, but made valuable observations; he pointed out, for instance, that "the critic's 'best

---

[4] "In his own Image," in *What about the New Testament? Festschrift to C. F. Evans* (Cambridge, 1975), pp. 28-44, esp. p. 30.

[5] It is not accidental that in his attempt to establish the Priority of Matthew, B. C. Butler, *The Originality of St. Matthew: A Critique of the Two-Document Hypothesis* (Cambridge, 1951), started with an attack on the Q-Hypothesis (cf. chs. I & II, pp. 1ff).

[6] T. R. Rosché, "The Words of Jesus and the Future of the 'Q' Hypothesis," *JBL* 79 (1960), pp. 210-20, made this point quite clear (pp. 210f.). This was also confirmed by C. E. Carlston-D. Norlin, "Once more-Statistics and Q," *HTR* 64 (1971), pp. 59-78, esp. p. 77.

[7] It is to be noted that the theory as a whole was originally put forward to account for the apparently existing Synoptic relationships by means of certain criteria which have now lost, if not their validity, at least much of their credibility and strength.

explanation'...may not be good enough for the historian;"[8] and that we cannot argue that "a relationship apparent in one passage must hold throughout that document. Proving in one place only shows it possible elsewhere."[9] Palmer admitted that a close literary relationship exists between the first three Gospels, but he doubted the degree of certainty with which the direction of borrowing has been so far determined.[10]

The following year E. P. Sanders made a more direct criticism from quite a different angle. He sought criteria from the Synoptic tradition neither from the pre-canonical tradition, nor from literature contemporary with the Gospels, but from the post-canonical tradition; he examined statistically as possible tendencies of the tradition its increasing length, its increasing detail, and its diminishing Semitisms. He concluded that "the evidence does not seem to warrant the degree of certainty with which many scholars hold the Two-Document hypothesis."[11] Sanders, therefore, suggested that "with all due respect for scientific preference for the simpler view, the evidence seems to require a more complicated one."[12]

On the question of the *Priority of Mark,* on the other hand, H. G. Wood rightly pointed out that "we are so accustomed to regarding (it) as the most assured result of the critical study of the Synoptic Problem, that we have almost forgotten the evidence that established the conclusion."[13] It is hardly surprising, therefore, that in modern commentaries "it is no longer necessary to prove the Priority of Mark.[14] This is thought to have been convincingly established by Streeter who gave in the syllabus of ch. VII of his book the following five reasons for accepting it:

"(1) Matthew reproduces 90% of the subject matter of Mark in language very largely identical with that of Mark; Luke does the same for rather more that half of Mark.

(2) In any average section, which occurs in the three Gospels, the majority of the actual words used by Mark are reproduced by Matthew and Luke, either alternately or both together.

---

[8] N. H. Palmer, The *Logic of Gospel Criticism* (Cambridge, 1969), pp. 151, 167f.

[9] Ibid., p. 139.

[10] Ibid., p. 161.

[11] *The Tendencies of the Synoptic Tradition* (Cambridge, 1969), p. 278.

[12] Ibid., p. 279; this last observation is something which has been also made earlier by E. Schweizer when he stated that "the process of the origin of our Synoptic Gospels was certainly more complex than the oversimplifying abstraction of the Two-Source theory describes it" ("Eine hebraisierende Sonderquelle des Lukas?" *TZ* 11 (1951), pp. 161ff:, esp. p. 161). This criticism might be valid, but it is doubtful whether it affects the theory fundamentally. On the other hand, Sanders' study, important as it is, appears quite limited in scope; cf. J. A. Fitzmyer, "The Priority of Mark and the 'Q' Source in Luke," *Jesus I*, pp. 131-170, esp. p.142; cf. also H. F. D. Sparks' penetrating review of Sanders' book in *JTS* n.s. 21 (1970), pp. 469-73.

[13] "The Priority of Mark," *ExpT* 65 (1953), pp. 17-19, esp. p. 17.

[14] V. Taylor, *The Gospel According to St. Mark* (London, 1969²), p.11.

(3) The relative order of incidents and sections in Mark is in general supported by both Matthew and Luke; where either of them deserts Mark, the other is usually found supporting him.

This conjunction and alteration of Matthew and Luke in their agreement with Mark as regards (a) content, (b) wording, (c) order, is only explicable if they are incorporating a source identical, or all but identical with Mark.

(4) The primitive character of Mark is further shown by (a) the use of phrases likely to cause offense, which are omitted or toned down in the other Gospels, (b) roughness of style and grammar, and the preservation of Aramaic words.

(5) The way in which Marcan and non-Marcan material is distributed in Matthew and Luke respectively looks as if each had before him the Marcan material in a single document, and was faced with the problem of combining this with material from the other sources."[15]

It is not known (nor is it discernible) whether Streeter deliberately put the argument from order in third place. There is no question that this is the basic argument for the hypothesis of the Marcan Priority, as the case was stated in K. Lachmann's epoch-making article.[16] But Lachmann believed in the existence of a *Grundschrift* (a common written source from which all three Synoptists derived their material) to which *Mark simply stands nearest*. However if the existence of a *Grundschrift* together with the various *Ur-Markus* theories is dispensed with, as by Streeter[17] and almost all subsequent critics,[18] the whole matter appears in a new light.[19] And further, if we examine the narrative sequence on its merits,[20] then the outcome does not emerge as easily as had usually been supposed. On these grounds, a number of scholars supporting the Priority of Matthew, with B.

---

[15] *The Four Gospels: A Study of Origins* (London, 1924), pp. 151f. As to the Augustinian view that Mark was the abbreviator of Matthew, Streeter pointed out that "it is usually Matthew who does the abbreviation" (ibid., p.158).

[16] "De ordine narrationum in evangeliis synopticis", *TSK* 8 (1835), pp. 570ff. An English, translation of most of Lachmann's study, which was written in Latin, is given in N. H. Palmer "Lachmann's Argument," *NTS* 13 (1967), pp. 368-78.

[17] *Op. cit.,* pp. 168ff., 331.

[18] Although A. M. Hunter was quite categorical that this theory has been given its 'quietus' by Streeter *(Interpreting the N.T.: 1900-1950* (London, 1951), p. 41), the fact that Bultmann *(Form Criticism: A New Method of N.T. Research* (Chicago, 1934), pp. 13ff.) and G. Bornkamm *(Jesus of Nazareth,* (ET London, 1962³), p. 2I7) still make use of it suggests that the hypothesis has not quite died. Fitzmyer has most recently stated that "the, possibility of Ur-Markus is still admissible" *(art. cit.,* p. 147) Marxsen, on the other hand regards it as unnecessary *(Introduction to the New Testament: An Approach to its Problems,* (ET Philadelphia, 1968), p.116).

[19] Even E. B. Redlich's point that the first three arguments only together furnish decisive evidence for the Marcan Priority, no matter whether they may not hold true separately *(The Student's Introduction to the Synoptic Gospels* (London, 1936), p. 31), cannot be held since "wording" and "content" can easily turn to support the Priority of Matthew, once the argument from order is considered as invalid.

[20] Cf. E. P. Sanders, "The Argument from Order and the Relationship between Matthew and Luke," *NTS* 15 (1969), pp. 249-61. About his arguments see below.

C. Butler leading the way, began to speak of the *Lachmann Fallacy*,[21] and to claim that it demolished the Two-Document Hypothesis. Similarly scholars from the opposite side, such as G. M. Styler, who eventually insists that "however insecure the argument used in the past, the reasons for accepting the priority of Mark are in fact strong,"[22] acknowledged the shock that was felt by many N.T. critics who take seriously into account literary critical issues.[23]

Furthermore, the Two-Document theory seemed to have lost in the last two decades considerable ground as a result of two important studies by B. C. Butler and W. R. Farmer. The importance of the former's work[24] lies not so much on its final conclusion - it was intended to restore the Priority of Matthew in the Augustinian form- but on the way it attacked Streeter's "fundamental solution" on its own ground, i.e. by the use of his old arguments. Similarly, the achievement of the latter's work[25] is not to be sought in the revival of the Griesbach Hypothesis;[26] it lies on the way it uncovered the defects of the Two-Document theory from the historical point of view, i.e. by an astonishingly detailed historical survey of the

---

[21] B. C. Butler, *op. cit.,* pp. 62ff. W. R. Farmer, *The Synoptic Problem: A Critical Analysis* (New York, 1964), in addition, tried to manifest this fallacy by giving a full account of the different stages from Holtzmann to Streeter through which the Two-Document theory has proceeded (pp. 48-117).

[22] "The Priority of Mark", *Excursus* in C. F. Moule, *The Birth of the New Testament* (London, 1962), pp. 215-32, esp. p, 232 n. 3.

[23] Cf. H. G. Wood, "The Priority of Mark," p.17.

[24] B. C. Butler's *The Originality of St. Matthew* has rightly been assessed by A. M. Farrer as "the most important discussion... of the essentials of the two document hypothesis since Streeter's *Four Gospels" (JTS* n.s. 3 (1952) pp. 102-06, esp. p.102).

[25] Farmer's major critical study is *The Synoptic Problem,* but his views have been consistently stated in a number of articles too; cf. "A 'Skeleton in the Closet' of the Gospel Research," *BR* 6 (1961), pp. 18-42 (Kümmel was misled by this article and classified Farmer under the Augustinians); "The Two-Document Hypothesis as a Methodological Criterion in Synoptic Research," *ATR* 48 (1966), pp. 380-96, in which Farmer on a remark by Bultmann on Mt 16.17-19, drew attention to Form-Criticism's unwilling challenge to Marcan Priority; there Farmer also opposed the idea of the Two-Document theory's being a methodological presupposition from which to derive criteria for Jesus' authentic teaching. Cf. further "The Synoptic Problem and the Contemporary Theological Chaos," *Christian Century* 83 (1966), pp. 1204-06; "Some Thoughts on the Provenance of Matthew," in *The Teacher's Yoke: Studies in Memory of H. Trantham* (Texas, 1964), pp. 109-16; "The Lachmann Fallacy," *NTS* 14 (1968), pp. 411-13.

[26] *The Synoptic Problem*; p. 277. For a detailed presentation of the strongest arguments of this theory see D. L. Dungan, "Mark - The Abridgment of Matthew and Luke," in *Jesus I,* pp. 51-97, in which Dungan fully endorses the Griesbach Hypothesis. C. H. Talbett - E. V. McKnight, "Can the Griesbach Hypothesis be Falsified?" *JBL* 91 (1972), pp. 338-68, have attempted to falsify, or at least to cast doubt upon the Griesbach hypothesis. G. W. Buchanan, however, found their arguments inconclusive without thereby accepting the hypothesis as such ("Has the Griesbach Hypothesis been Falsified," *JBL* 93 (1974), pp. 550-72).

process of Synoptic research from the rise of Source-criticism down to Streeter.

These are the most important issues involved in the Two-Document theory, either as a whole, or with reference to the Priority of Mark. In the face of such criticisms, especially those referring to the validity of principles employed, a working hypothesis has certainly to be checked by means of secure tests. After all we cannot hope for a definite and certain solution to the Synoptic Problem, since the data to its solution are "scarcely adequate or available to us."[27]

One of the most secure tests in this case is certainly Statistics. B. de Solages was the first in recent times to undertake such a task with relation to the Synoptic tradition.[28] Using as sampling units Synoptic pericopes, he claimed to have systematically established the Two-Document hypothesis. His laborious work[29] - a 1128-page study - proceeded both by checking the relations between Matthew, Mark, Luke, and by comparing the texts by the number of words common to Matthew-Mark-Luke, Matthew-Mark alone, Matthew-Luke alone, and Mark-Luke alone. This procedure, however, though it involves statistical analysis, combinatory analysis, and the calculus of probability of causes to word occurrences within pericopes, met with a reasonable objection. W. R. Farmer rightly points out that "what Solages has actually done is to document in exhaustive detail the fact that Mark is in some sense the middle term between Matthew and Luke."[30]

What, however, de Solages had failed to establish convincingly, was undertaken some years later by A. M. Honoré[31] who engaged in more austere statistical study on the following lines. He first divided the entire

---

[27] J. A. Fitzmyer, *art. cit.*, p.137.

[28] The pioneer in this field is of course J. C. Hawkins with his *Horae Synopticae* (Oxford, 1899, 1909²). The difference, however, between Hawkins' statistical approach, and the more recent use of this method, is that the former seeks a solution, whereas the latter tries to establish one. P. N. Harrison and R. Morgenthaler had, of course, used similar methods earlier, but they worked on the Pauline Epistles, and in addition used only vocabulary items as sampling units.

[29] *A Greek Synopsis of the Gospels: A New Way of Solving the Synoptic Problem* [ET, Leiden, 1959). Solages has recently published another work, *La Composition des évangiles de Luc et de Matthieu et leurs sources* (Leiden, 1973), which deals with those related issues that remained untouched in his first study. His conclusion is that Matthew and Luke depend on Mark but are independent of each other.

[30] *The Synoptic Problem,* p. 197. Farmer also noticed that Solages deliberately by-passed the minor agreements, and he judged that his statistics had been made on "unrealistic terms" (ibid.).

[31] "A Statistical Study on the Synoptic Problem," *NT* 10 (1968), pp. 95-147. A. G. Morton and G. H. C. McGregor had earlier undertaken a similar task *(The Structure of Luke and Acts,* London, 1965), using essentially stylistic techniques; their study, however, was confined to the Lucan phenomena only, and their result was the Streeterian theory of the existence of a Proto-Luke.

tradition into single, double, and triple tradition material with regard to their verbal agreements; in the triple tradition 1852 words were found in close verbal agreement. Then, using mainly these 1852 verbal agreements as well as other elements, he attempted the following six independent studies: (i) Double-link analysis, (ii) Triple-link analysis, (iii) Statistics on the sequence of the pericopes, (iv) Comparison of lengths and verbal agreements in Double and Triple traditions, (v) Statistics on the quantitative use of sources, and (vi) Statistics on variations in distribution of common material. His conclusions[32] were based, with one exception, on two of his studies; "it is therefore safe to accept them,"[33] especially in the light of his declaration that "during most of the investigation. (he) was inclined to believe that the received critical opinion was wrong."[34]

However, in such studies, as Honoré himself admitted, certain limitations are inevitable,[35] since they are all dependent on certain presuppositions.[36] It is advisable, therefore, despite the fact that all criticisms of the Two-Document theory have been subject to the same or similar limitations,[37] to consider, in addition, the relation of the Two-

---

[32] Honoré's conclusions were: (a) Mark is the main link between Matthew and Luke;proved by studies I & III; (b) Both St. Matthew and St. Luke used Mark (studies IV & V); (c) St. Matthew did not use Luke (II & V); (d) St. Luke did not use Matthew (IV & V); (e) They consequently used other sources (deduced from c & d); (f) Q was not a single document (only from III *(op. cit.,* p. 135). On the last conclusion see my article "The Nature and Extent of the Q-Document," *NT* 10 (1978), pp. 49-73, esp. pp. 59f.

[33] Ibid.

[34] Ibid. It is also significant that one of his advisors was E. P. Sanders (p. 95 n.).

[35] "One limitation", says Honoré, "is that the Studies are dependent on certain assumptions about the way in which the authors and editors behave... Another limitation is that the study is concerned with the interrelations of the gospels as we have them and tells us nothing (or not much) about the documents which lie behind them" *(art. cit.,* p. 135).

[36] J. J. O'Rourke went even further: after considering some principles of the above statistical studies he concluded that "it is difficult to have any confidence on the application of (their) results to the study of the sources of the Synoptics" ("Some Observations on the Synoptic Problem and the Use of Statistical Procedures," *NT* 16 (1974), pp. 272-77, esp. p. 277).

[37] It is necessary, in addition, to take note of those scholars whose attitude to the Q-Hypothesis has been determined by their belief in the priority of Matthew (or Luke). Neither P. Parker, *The Gospel before Mark* (Chicago, 1953), nor H. Meynell, "The Synoptic Problem: Some Unorthodox Solutions," *Theology* 70 (1967), pp. 386-97 (who seems to have adopted Parker's solution in its general outlines, and have advanced the tentative suggestion that Mark was rearranged when Matthew and Luke became known in Rome), disavow the Q-Hypothesis; on the contrary, Parker's linguistic evidence has rather increased the credibility of Q *(op. cit.,* pp. 30f. More about his arguments below). Nor does R. L. Lindsey ("A Modified Two-Document Theory of the Synoptic Dependence and Interdependence," *NT* 6 (1963), pp. 239-63 ; also idem, *A Hebrew Translation of the Gospel of Mark,* Jerusalem, no date), among the "Luke-Priorists". The same is also true of L. Vaganay's solution *(Le Problème synoptique* (Paris, 1954), since his "S" (Aramaic Logia), and "Sg" (its translation into Greek) are practically

Document theory to *theological* issues. To the extent that contemporary Synoptic scholarship, and especially Redaction-Criticism, which presupposes the Two Document theory, is successful, it lends verification to this theory, so that "it establishes itself beyond *reasonable* doubt."[38]

---

identical with Q of the Two-Document theory. A. Caboury's theory, on the other hand, which like those of W. L. Knox, L. Cerfaux and X. Léon-Dufour, looks towards a solution of multiple documentation, despite its ingenuity and originality, it complicates the problem rather than solves it *(La Structure des Evangiles synoptiques,* Leiden, 1970). We do not need to examine these hypotheses in detail; none offers a more plausible solution.

Since, however, Butler and Farmer's views made a powerful impact on contemporary Synoptic scholarship, it is worth referring to criticisms of them which have been made from time to time. Thus, H. G. Wood, dealing with Butler's thesis noticed an important error in method in his book: "Dom Butler contends that Mark is a source only for St. Luke, and the knowledge of Matthew's order comes to St. Luke through Mark. This is very strange because Dom Butler claims to have proved that Luke is also dependent on Matthew" ("The Priority...," pp. 17f.); his further point, however, "that the argument based on a comparison of the order and arrangement of incidents in Mark and Matthew still holds good," is, as we have seen, questionable. G. M. Styler, too, noted that "although Butler naturally gives most space to the passages that seem to tell in his favour, he does not attempt to conceal the fact that there are strong arguments on the other side... Until some less incredible explanation (than that given by Butler i.e. that St. Peter had access to a copy of Matthew) is forthcoming, the natural conclusion that Mark is prior to Matthew will continue to hold the field" ("The Priority...," p. ?32). So F. W. Beare who reviewing Farmer made the following significant remark which can also apply to Butler: "It is hard to imagine why Mark should have been written if it was designed for the use of churches which already possessed and were using Matthew and Luke" *(JBL* 84 (1965), pp. 295-97). N. Perrin, on the other hand, referring to all attacks directed against the Two-Document theory, rightly points out that "if Farmer and others wish to return to the hypothesis of the Priority of Matthew, then they must show us that this contemporary work is producing false results, and that better results would be attained on the basis of their hypothesis" *(Rediscovering the Teaching of Jesus* (London, 1967), p. 35). This, of course, is not without exception. Thus, in the report from the working section on Mark at the Pittsburgh Festival on the Gospels given by W. R. Farmer, D. L. Dungan is said to have pointed out that "the Griesbach hypothesis was useful in offering an explanation for the gnostic proclivities of Mark" *(Jesus II,* p. 344). This sole remark, however, cannot be compared with the cumulative evidence of the Two-Document hypothesis. Similarly, W. Schmithals in his review of Farmer's book noted among others that no consideration was made of the way Redaction-Criticism has confirmed the Two-Document hypothesis *(TLZ* 92 (1967), pp. 424f.). Even A. M. Farrer who rejoiced in reviewing Butler at his "demolition of the Q-Hypothesis" criticized "his attempt to place Mark after Matthew in a *tour de force* which would hardly survive a balanced consideration of all the evidence" *(JTS* n.s. 3 (1952), pp. pp. 102-06, esp. p.106.).

In general, apart from the Two-Document hypothesis no other solution to the Synoptic Problem has carried conviction, at least up to the present, mainly because *they all start from doubtful, or inadequately explained points in the established solution, without facing the Synoptic Problem as a whole.*

[38] N. Perrin, *op. cit.,* p. 35 (the italics mine).

*Did Q Exist?*

We may, therefore, conclude in the light of this brief discussion that the Two-Document theory is a reasonably based and sound one; for when a working hypothesis is successfully tested both statistically and by means of theological works done on the basis of it, then the hypothesis falls short only of *utmost* certainty.[39]

*2. The disappearance of the Q-Document and the lack of any external evidence for it.*

Opponents of the Q-Hypothesis have always stressed that the Q-Document is lost. This is undoubtedly not a very encouraging observation to start with. Of course it has been argued since Schleiermacher that Papias' controversial note on Matthew[40] was positive evidence for the existence of Q. Whether, however, *logia* designates a collection of sayings, like Q,[41] and not a Gospel-type writing,[42] or even our canonical Matthew,[43] is still argued.[44] To avoid in future any kind of Schleiermacher Fallacy[45] (!) it is advisable to leave Papias' notice, in spite of its great age, out of consideration with regard to the Q-Hypothesis.[46] With this in mind, and granted that Q is by no means covered by Luke's prologue (1.1), Farrer argued that "there is no independent evidence for anything like Q. To postulate Q is to postulate the unevidenced and unique."[47] But Farrer was not the only scholar to make this point; before him J. Chapman among others considered Q as something "paradoxical," "undefined" and "elusive,"[48] whereas Butler contested that "the appeal to Q is unnecessary and embarrassing."[49]

---

[39] Half a century ago Streeter considered the Q-Hypothesis as "one which, though highly probable, falls just short of certainty" *(op. cit.,* p.184).

[40] "So then Matthew composed the logia in the Hebrew language, and each one interpreted them as he could" (Eusebius, *H.E.,* iii 39).

[41] Cf. H. Koester, "One Jesus and Four Primitive Gospels," *HTR* 61 (1968), pp. 203-47; also in *Trajectories,* pp. 158-204 to which all references hereafter.

[42] Cf. J. Kürzinger, "Das Papiaszeugnis und die Erstgestalt des Mt," *BZ* n.s. 4 (1960), pp. 19-38.

[43] Cf. A. M. Farrer, *A Study in Mark* (London, 1951), pp. 13ff.

[44] J. Jeremias, *New Testament Theology. Vol. I: The Proclamation of Jesus* (ET, London, 1972²), arguing against Q writes: "What was once the main support of the Q hypothesis, the witness of Papias...can no longer bear the burden" (p.38).

[45] It is at least clear that Papias' logia "is not accepted in Schleiermacher's sense" (cf. E. W. Lummis, "A Case against Q," p. 757).

[46] Cf. W. G. Kümmel, *Introduction to the New Testament* (ET, London, 1970²), p. 44.

[47] A. M. Farrer, "On Dispensing with Q," *SG,* pp. 55-88, esp. p. 58. To Farrer "the postulation of unevidenced writing of an undeterminable sort is a hazardous proceeding" (ibid., p. 61).

[48] *Matthew, Mark, and Luke* (London, 1937), pp. 95ff.

[49] *Op. cit.,* p. 22; cf. also E. W. Lummis who spoke of the "fallacious superfluity of Q"*(art. cit.,* p. 765).

Against all these it may be argued that the existence of a written source can be asserted in literary terms with a good deal of assurance even if its fate remains uncertain. J. M. Robinson made this point quite clear when he insisted that "the mere fact that a source is no longer extant should not be taken as an argument against its existence... Rather one should seek, within the period leading up to the emergence of the canon, tendencies making intelligible the preservation of what survived and the non preservation of what did not survive."[50] However, if we are not to abandon the Q-Hypothesis, we have to give an answer to the vital question: Why has a document important enough to be incorporated in two of our canonical Gospels disappeared? It has been, of course, postulated that "its incorporation did not destroy its independent circulation,[51] and perhaps traces of it "can be found in some of the apocryphal gospels (e.g. the Gospel Καθ' 'Εβραίους)"[52] or that it ceased to exist after its incorporation.[53] But the crucial question why it has entirely disappeared still remains.

The question has in fact been treated in a short article by G. D. Kilpatrick, who came to the conclusion that "at an early date Mark and Q were used together over a wide area, Q being anonymous, rather amorphous and without a passion narrative. Next either Matthew or Luke was associated with these two documents in the use of the church and Q dropped out of use."[54] In this explanation, Q was lost simply because it was entirely (or almost entirely) embodied in one of the church's canonical books.[55] This view has since generally accepted among Q supporters without modification.[56] J. M. Robinson, however, has recently challenged this view in the course of his suggestions about the *Gattung* of Q; the reason for Q's disappearance, he appears to maintain, is rather to be sought in the fact that "perhaps Q was becoming suspect of heresy at the

---

[50] "The Johannine Trajectory", in *Trajectories,* pp. 232-68, esp. p. 239.

[51] J. Moffatt, *An Introduction to the Literature of the New Testament* (Edinburgh, 1911), p. 204.

[52] Ibid.

[53] So R. C. Heard; see C. F. D. Moule-A. M. G. Stephenson, "R. G. Heard on Q," *NTS* 2 (1955), pp. 114-18.

[54] "The Disappearance of Q," *JTS* 42 (1941), pp. 182-84, esp. p.184. Cf. also H. von Soden, *Early Christian Literature* (ET, London, 1906), p.142.

[55] Why Mark, which was also embodied in Matthew and Luke, escaped this fate is explained by Kilpatrick as follows: "In the third stage, in addition to Mark, Matthew and Luke were together in use in the church, and Mark was falling into background. Its disappearance, though not its disuse, were prevented by its apostolic connections and the late date of its fall from favour" *(art. cit. ,* p.184).

[56] Cf. W. H. Blyth Martin, "The Indispensibility of Q," *Theology* 59 (1956), pp. 182-88, esp. p. 182; also F. G. Downing, "Towards the Rehabilitation of Q," *NTS* 11 (1965), pp. 169-81, esp. p.181.

time when its gattung was being exploited by Gnostics;[57] nonetheless this "gnosticizing proclivity (was) blocked by St. Matthew and Luke by embedding Q in the Marcan gospel form,"[58] and thus Q continued to "be acceptable in the orthodox church only in the context of this other gattung, that of 'Gospel'."[59] Therefore, according to Robinson's suggestion, it was not its incorporation into Matthew and Luke that made the Q-Document disappear, but rather the gnosticizing proclivity of its *Gattung*.[60]

It is difficult to decide which of these two suggestions is the more plausible. However, in view of a number of apocryphal and other early Christian writings with evident similarities with Q which were kept outside the canon, and nearly disappeared (most notably the *Gospel of Thomas*), it is Robinson's suggestion that seems the more likely. Nevertheless, to endorse his view need not discard altogether Kilpatrick's explanation. There must be some reason beside Q's gnosticizing orientation which led to its complete disappearance. After all *Didache*, a document also of great age, and very similar to Q, did survive.

In the light, therefore, of these observations the argument that Q disappeared lacks force.

## 3. The alleged literary uniqueness of the Q-Document

Several scholars insist that the absence of any similar document from the same literary genre as Q (i.e. consisting almost entirely of sayings) in the early Christian literature makes a firm decision in favor of the Q-Hypothesis somewhat difficult. Farrer was again the scholar who most forcibly drew attention to this: "If we were dealing with a rich and various literature it might be tolerable...But what did the primitive Christians write, beside letters and homilies and gospels? Q was neither a letter nor a homily, nor was it a gospel."[61] To this argument another one was added: the strange manner in which the Q-Document was constructed. "After a (narrative) exordium so full of dogmatic weight and historical interest, is it credible, asked Farrer, that the book should peter out in miscellaneous oracles, and conclude without any account of those events which, to a

---

[57] "The Johannine Trajectory," p. 239.
[58] "The Problem of History in Mark Reconsidered," *USQR* 20 (1965), pp. 131-147, esp. p. 135.
[59] "LOGOI SOPHON: On the Gattung of Q', in *Trajectories,* pp. 71-117, esp. p.13.
[60] "Whereas Q", says Robinson, "may have been no more than an innocent use of a Gattung familiar from wisdom literature, it could when transmitted in increasingly gnosticizing times and places come to require for safety's sake, such a fleshing-out as the Marcan text would provide" ("The Literary Composition of Mark", in M. Sabbe (ed.), *L'Evangile selon Marc: Tradition et rédaction* (Gembloux, 1974), pp. 11-19, esp. p.15).
[61] "On Dispensing with Q", p. 61.

Christian faith, are supremely significant?"[62] On this ground it is of course difficult to visualize such a document; but to Farrer even more difficult to believe was why the writer of such a document "should supply the exordium, while omitting the conclusion."[63]

To all these objections, however, it has been argued since Streeter[64] that the Q-Document was written on the pattern of the O.T. prophetic books, like Jeremiah or Isaiah, in which exactly the same phenomenon occurs; Jeremiah e.g. starts with narratives, and then gradually peters out to discourse material; the prophet Isaiah, on the other hand, is believed to have suffered under Manasseh (as Jesus suffered under Pontius Pilate), and yet the book of Isaiah does not record his death. To these Farrer countered: "Christ was no mere prophet... The divine act in Isaiah is his call, not his death. It is otherwise with Christ."[65] This last observation, however, presupposes the orthodoxy of the community which lies behind Q;[66] and further, takes for granted a certain uniformity in Primitive Christianity.[67] But Christian origins are so obscure, that it would be an *a priori* statement to say that the first Christians wrote only letters, homilies, and gospels, and that they all preached the same standard "Gospel."[68] In the opinion e.g. of W. Bauer and others[69] considerable diversity is to be found in early Christianity, even if Bauer's maxim that Catholic Orthodoxy is only the most successful heresy be regarded as extreme. H. E. Tödt, on the other hand, successfully argued that the passion kerygma was

---

[62] Ibid., p. 60; cf. also A. W. Argyle, "Agreements between Matthew and Luke", *ExpT* 73 (1963), pp. 19-22, who, in addition, pointed out that Q reveals a "solid narrative frame work" on the examination of Mt 5.1f. par., and Mt 7. 28f. par. (pp. 19f.).

[63] "On Dispensing....," p. 60.

[64] *The Four Gospels*, p. 291.

[65] "On Dispensing....," p. 60.

[66] On this see further discussion in my dissertation, Ἡ περί τῆς Πηγῆς τῶν Λογίων θεωρία, (Athens, 1977). p. 119ff.

[67] As M. J. Suggs, *Wisdom, Christology and Law in Matthew's Gospel* (Massachusetts, 1970) points out, this sort of objection is "no doubt intensified by the idea of a normative primitive kerygma (a first century orthodoxy derived from Paul and Acts)" (p.6).

[68] Cf., however, Gal 1.6f., Col 1.23 etc.

[69] W. Bauer, *Orthodoxy and Heresy in Earliest Christianity* (ET, London, 1972); cf. also H. E. W. Turner, *The Pattern of Christian Truth: A Study in the Relations between Orthodoxy and Heresy in the Early Church* (London, 1954); A. Ehrhardt, "Christianity before the Apostles' Creed," *HTR* 55 (1962), pp. 73-119, and also in *The Framework of the New Testament Stories* (Manchester, 1964), pp. 151-99; H. Koester, "GNOMAI DIAFOROI: The Origin and Nature of Diversification in the History of Early Christianity," *HTR* 58 (1965), pp. 279-318, and also in *Trajectories*, pp. 114-157 to which all references hereafter.

not proclaimed by the Q-Community at all (so G. N. Stanton on different grounds).[70]

As to the main objection regarding the literary uniqueness of Q, this has been met in part by a comparison with contemporary writings such as *Ethiopic Enoch,* and in particular with *Didache,* which both, like Q, contained "paraenesis, eschatological prophecy, and clearly ended in eschatological prognosis."[71] T. W. Manson, in addition, has shown that Q and *Didache* bear striking resemblance so far as their structural divisions are concerned.[72] But the *Didache* cannot provide by itself determinative support to the Q-Document because of its special character,[73] and *Enoch* is from an altogether different realm, that of Apocalypticism, and can only account for the last part of the Q-Document, which clearly orientates toward the End. With regard to its first part, especially the Sermon on the Mount/Plain, the Q-Document has a close parallel in the *Pirqê Aboth,* a collection of sayings of Jewish Rabbis before and after the first century AD., which, unlike the rest of *Mishna* contained no legal advice *(halakah).* *Pirqê Aboth* may have, in addition, an important bearing on the question why the community behind Q had been urged to preserve Jesus' teaching.[74]

Recently a much more appropriate appeal has been made to the Coptic document, discovered in the Gnostic library at Nag-Hammadi, known as the *Gospel of Thomas.*[75] This document is a collection of sayings of Synoptic type with negligible narrative material. Kümmel provides in his *Introduction* a summary of the debate on the relationship between the Gospel of Thomas and Q, up to the early sixties,[76] and concludes that "the Gospel of Thomas presupposes the meaning of Jesus' person in the role of the Gnostic revealer, and thereby shows itself as a literary from of a later

---

[70] More about their views in my dissertation, Ἡ περί τῆς Πηγῆς τῶν Λογίων θεωρία, p. 119ff.

[71] R. Bultmann, *The History of the Synoptic Tradition* (ET, Oxford, 1970²), p. 373

[72] *The Sayings of Jesus* (London, 1950²), p. 23 n. 1, first published as Part II of *The Mission and Message of Jesus* (London 1937), pp. 299-639.

[73] Cf. M. J. Suggs, *op. cit.,* p. 6. On the special character of the Didache, see H. Koester, *Synoptische Überlieferung bei den apostolischen Vätern* (Berlin, 1957), pp. 217ff.; also J.-P. Audet, *La Didache: Instructions des Apôtres* (Paris, 1958); R. Glover, "The Didache's Quotations and the Synoptic Gospels," *NTS* 5 (19S8), pp. 12-29; B. C. Butler, "The Literary Relations of Didache ch. XVI," *JTS* n.s. 11 (1960), pp. 265-83; and more recently B. Layton, "The Sources, Date, and Transmission of Didache 1.3b-2.1," *HTR* 61 (1968), pp. 343-83.

[74] Cf. the interesting discussion about *Pirqê Aboth* by W. D. Davies, "Reflections on Traditions: The Aboth Revisited," in *Christian History and Interpretation. Studies Presented to John Knox,* ed. by W. R. Farmer, C. F. D. Moule, R. R. Niebuhr (Cambridge, 1967), pp. 127-59.

[75] Downing e.g. recognizes in Q something which "is formally very like the gnostic Gospel of Thomas" *(art. cit.,* p.180).

[76] Pp. 57f.; cf. also H. Koester, "GNOMAI DIAFOROI...," pp. 128ff.

time."[77] It can, therefore, teach us nothing about the origin and literary character of Q.[78] Robinson's attempt, however, to show that they both belong to the same Gattung[79] has to a certain extent proved false Kümmel's last conclusion, and consequently "effectively eliminated any reason for doubting the existence of Q *on the grounds of its literary uniqueness.*"[80] Furthermore, in the following years H. Koester provided convincing evidence for the view that the Gospel of Thomas "represents the eastern branch of the gattung logoi, the western being represented by the synoptic *logoi* of Q."[81]

As Robinson and Koester's tentative but well documented views will not be accepted by all critics, Kümmel's observation still has some validity. However, the close connection of the *Gospel of Thomas* with the Oxyrhynchus Papyri 1, 654, 655, which apparently come from a comparatively early stage in the tradition, and which Kümmel does not take seriously into account, provides convincing evidence for the circulation in Early Christianity of documents like Q, i.e. consisting almost exclusively of sayings. On the whole, this objection to the Q-Hypothesis, as Fitzmyer rightly points out, "stems from a modern, preconceived idea of what *euaggelion* was in the early church."[82] In addition, the title of the Gospel of Thomas *(Peuaggelion pkata Thôman)* "shows us at least that the argument against Q drawn from its content is not necessarily valid."[83]

Thus, the argument from the literary uniqueness of Q, though strong, breaks down.[84] It stems from the special kerygmatic(?) character of the speeches in Acts, as well as of the other N.T. writings, which, however, are not necessarily a model of all Christian writings about Jesus; after all some important hints in Paul and in Acts do suggest the existence of "another Gospel(s)"[85] in the primitive church. On the other hand, writings like those

---

[77] *Introduction...*, p. 58.
[78] Ibid.
[79] "LOGOI SOPHON...", *passim*.
[80] M. J. Suggs, *op. cit.*, p. 8.
[81] "GNOMAI DIAFOROI...," p. 136; also idem, "One Jesus...," pp. 186f. Cf. also R. North, "Chenoboskion and Q," *CBQ* 24 (1962), pp. 154-70, who postulated on the basis of logia 65 and 16 of the Gospel of Thomas a hypothetical Proto-Thomas to have been the common source for both Q and Thomas, but concluded that "the identity of Proto-Thomas with Q is roughly as much an open question as the existence of any genuine univocal (sic) Q at all" (p.170).
[82] *Art. cit.*, p. I55. To Fitzmyer "none will deny that *euaggelion* was related to kerygma, but the two are not necessarily co-extensive terms" (ibid.).
[83] Ibid.
[84] F. V. Filson is also of the opinion that the Gospel of Thomas confirms the Q-Hypothesis ("New Greek and Coptic Gospel Manuscripts," *Bibl.Arch.* 24 (1961), pp. 1-18).
[85] Cf. A. Ehrhardt, who came to the conclusion that "we have to allow for at least another Gospel, the Galilean Gospel" *(art. cit.,* p.161), in contrast to that of Jerusalem,

*Did Q Exist?* 15

which have in the course of time been appealed to, namely the *Ethiopic Enoch,* the *Didache,* the *Pirquê Aboth,* and above all the *Gospel of Thomas,* all of which can be paralleled in one at least aspect to the Q-Document, are not insufficient evidence for the literary character of Q.

*4. The variety of opinions among scholars with regard to the Q-Hypothesis*

The lack of consensus with regard to the form and content of the Q-Document is another reason for refusal by a number of scholars to accept the Q-Hypothesis. "Authors," wrote H. Höpfl, "are not agreed about the scope or origin, the time (of composition) or the historical value of the source Q, nor are they agreed concerning the manner in which the first and third evangelists made use of it."[86] The variety of opinions, especially with regard to the contents of Q can be seen at a glance in the sixteen reconstructions given by Moffatt.[87]

However, it has been a change since, and more recent writers who maintain the Q-Hypothesis have inclined towards a general agreement[88] differing only in secondary and mostly unimportant features. This has not prevented those who oppose the theory from speaking of "he prevailing uncertainty about the original shape, content, and very existence of Q,"[89] which in that case "remains a literary ghost needed to explain the material common to Matthew and Luke."[90] Moreover, even among those who take seriously the hypothesis, it is acknowledged that "there are almost as many Q-theories as scholars involved in the problem."[91] This criticism has been presented even in the form of ridicule by S. Petrie, who describes Q as

---

and who saw traces for at least three others: Alexandrine, Samaritan, and the Nicolaitan (pp. 157ff.).

[86] H. Höpfl-B. Gut, *Introductionis in s. utriusque Testamenti libros compendium,* vol. III (Rome, 1931³), p. 123.

[87] *Op. cit.,* pp. 197-202. For Farrer, too, the fact that "Q cannot be convincingly reconstructed" ("On Dispensing...", p. 59), is a strong argument against the hypothesis.

[88] V. Taylor, "The Elusive Q", *ExpT* 46 (1934), pp. 68-74, noted that "at first sight the existing position in relation to the Q hypothesis appears to be one of confusion... (but) closer study reveals lines of connection between the most discordant hypotheses" (p. 42).

[89] H. P. West, Jr. "A Primitive Version of Luke in the Composition of Matthew", *NTS* 14 (1967), pp. 75-95, esp. p. 94.

[90] Ibid.

[91] O. Linton, "The Q-Problem Reconsidered," in *Studies in N.T. and Early Christian Literature. Festschrift to A. P. Wikgren,* ed. by D. E. Aune (Leiden, 1972), pp. 43-59, esp. p. 45.

"sheer guesswork, and for those who retain the hypothesis Q is only what they choose to make it."[92]

Nevertheless, the specific problem of the variety of reconstructions has been met by J. M. Robinson with the remark that "the difficulty of reconstructing a source is not identical with the question of whether the source existed."[93] He has rightly insisted that "if at some place a written source is visible, then the question becomes merely how extensive the source was, and what character it had."[94] For the existence of the Q-Document one of the principle clues is the link between the first and the second units of the alleged document; for if a document does exist, it must show up early at the beginning. In this connection the link between Lk 3.7-9 and 3.16f. (cf. Mt 3.7-12) is indeed striking.[95]

On the other hand, the variety of opinions does not in itself mean that the hypothesis is unsound. However tantalizing and imperfect the results may be, this does not constitute conclusive argument; for even an existing document, such as Mark, has been the subject of a wide variety of opinions.[96] Linton, moreover, has drawn attention to the same variety of opinions among those who from time to time have attacked the hypothesis.[97] In the light of studies as those of Tödt, Davies, Robinson, Hoffmann and others,[98] some form of Q-Hypothesis would appear to be necessary for making sense of the material, and for those who reject the hypothesis it is necessary to produce another which does make sense of the material.

As to the way, finally, the Q-Hypothesis was ridiculed, the answer given by R. McL. Wilson to a similar case provides the best reply to Petrie and the others: "the demolition of a hypothesis by means of the gentle art of ridicule may be quite admirable; but is it scholarship?"[99]

---

[92] "'Q' is Only What you Make it," *NT* 3 (1959), pp. 28-33, esp. p. 33. Petrie went on to suggest that "the whole synoptic problem should be thrown back into the melting pot, and the matter of literary relationships, if any, be faced anew' (ibid.).

[93] "The Johannine Trajectory," p. 242.

[94] Ibid.

[95] Cf. C. E. Carlston - D. Norlin, "Once more- Statistics and Q," *HTR* 64 (1971), pp. 59-78, esp. p. 74.

[96] See R. P. Martin, *Mark: Evangelist and Theologian* (Exeter, 1973); also An N. Vo Thien, "Interpretation of St. Mark's Gospel in the Last Two Decades," *SBT* 2 (1972), pp. 37-62.

[97] "The Q-Problem Reconsidered," p. 43. Farmer, too, noticed that all scholars who do not hold the Q-Hypothesis "in one way or another argue against each other" *(op. cit.,* p.196).

[98] See my dissertation, Ἡ περί τῆς Πηγῆς τῶν Λογίων θεωρία, p. 128ff.

[99] "Farrer and Streeter on the Minor Agreements of Matthew and Luke against Mark", *SE* vol. I, pp. 254-57, esp. p. 255.

## 5. The tendency of the Traditional School to give a more prominent place to Matthew

A further reason for rejecting the Q-Hypothesis, especially amongst traditionalists in Roman Catholic New Testament scholarship, has been a refusal to allow Matthew to be pushed into the background. This Gospel dominated the ecclesiastical tradition for more than eighteen centuries, especially in liturgical usage, and in addition provides the biblical basis for papal primacy (Mt 16.18f.). For this reason it was hardly to be considered secondary to Mark or even to Luke. The resolutions of the Biblical Commission of the Roman Catholic Church in 1911,[100] which required a negative answer to the question of the Two-Source theory, as well as the dismissal from that Church of A. Loisy[101] for (among other reasons) accepting it,[102] has resulted in a more traditional line among her members.[103] This tendency not to undervalue Matthew is nowhere stated better than in X. Léon-Dufour, who after paying tribute to the Two-Document hypothesis, "which served a very useful purpose in its days, but which ought to be consigned to an honourable grave,"[104] he went on to state that "Matthew in particular should not be regarded as a poor relation."[105]

---

[100] *Enchiridium Biblicum* (Rome, 1955), pp. 160ff. An English translation is given in *INT,* pp. 154-58.

[101] Cf. X. Léon-Dufour, "The Synoptic Gospels," in *INT,* pp. 139-324, who writes about Loisy: "among other things he admitted the Two-Source theory, and he drew therefrom ruinous consequences for faith" (p. 148).

[102] See his *Les Evangiles synoptiques* (Paris, 1907); cf. also *The Gospel and the Church* (ET, London, 1908), which is Loisy's proposed "reconciliation of Catholicism with Criticism" (p. v.).

[103] Fitzmyer is of the opinion that "the Commission's earlier opposition to the Tow-Source Theory was basically the reason why an older generation of Roman Catholic scholars sought for solutions to the Synoptic Problem that differed considerably from the Two-Source Theory" *(art. cit.,* pp. 163f. n. 7); cf. also L. Cerfaux, *The Four Gospels* (ET, London, 1960), p. 39.

[104] *The Gospels and the Jesus of History* (ET, London, 1971 ), p.191.

[105] Ibid., p. 192 (italics mine). It is not to be forgotten, however, that J. A. Fitzmyer is a Roman Catholic who has vigorously defended the Q-Hypothesis in recent times *(art. cit.,* pp. 147ff). Among other Roman Catholic studies in favor of the Q-Hypothesis see B. de Solages, *op. cit.* (see n. 29); also idem, "Mathematiques et évangiles. Response au R. P. Benoit," *BLE* 61 (1960), pp. 287-311; *The Jerome Biblical Commentary* (London, 1968); A. Wikenhauser, *Einleitung in das Neue Testament* (Basel, 1953); G. T. Montague, "The Emergence of the Gospels," *BT* 1 (1964), pp. 892-904; P. Hoffmann, *Studien zur Theologie der Logienquelle* (Münster, 1972). Today there is admittedly more freedom among Roman Catholics in scientific research; as Léon-Dufour himself has recently stated, "Catholic criticism is (today) perfectly free to chose the theory which seems most consistent with the demands of science" ("Redaktionsgeschichte of Matthew and Literary Criticism," in *Jesus I,* pp. 9-35, esp. p. 10). For the Eastern Orthodox attitude towards Synoptic criticism see my dissertation, Ἡ περί τῆς Πηγῆς τῶν Λογίων θεωρία , pp. 24ff.

Similar reasons made non-Catholics too, to be quite skeptical to the Q-Hypothesis. This is evident in Farrer, who in accordance with his own line of interpretation wrote: "Once rid of Q, we are...free to let St. Matthew write as he is moved;"[106] and a little earlier in his essay: "The surrender of the Q Hypothesis...will free the interpretation of Matthew from the contradiction into which it has fallen."[107]

## 6. The alleged lack of homogeneity of the Q-material

The Q-Document seems to have consisted of a few narratives, a dozen parables, approximately the same number of groups of sayings, and about thirty single sayings.[108] This mass of material can only be labeled "document," or even an independent source in a fairly fixed form, if it is shown to be homogeneous. One of the arguments against the Q-Hypothesis was indeed its alleged lack of homogeneity. "It is impossible," wrote P. -L. Couchoud, "to find in the source 'Q' that homogeneity which would justify a belief in its existence."[109] Similarly P. Lagrange,[110] J. Chapman,[111] and X. Léon-Dufour,[112] among others drew attention to this in order to establish their theories of an Aramaic Matthew, the priority of Matthew, and the multiple documentation respectively.

In view of Hawkins' findings about the numerous verbal, stylistic and grammatical peculiarities of the three Synoptics (most notably of St. Luke)[113] one would expect the same to have happened with Q. Since, however, we possess the Q-sections only as pieces separated out of their Matthaean and Lucan contexts, it is impossible, or at least unsafe, as Harnack rightly pointed out, "to uphold their homogeneity upon grounds of vocabulary and style."[114] His minute investigation of the vocabulary, grammar and style of Q did not produce convincing proof, apart from the

---

[106] "On Dispensing...," p. 86.

[107] Ibid., p. 85.

[108] Cf. A. Harnack, *The Sayings of Jesus* (ET, London, 1908), p.165. For further discussion on this see my article "The Nature and Extent of the Q-Document," pp. 66ff. [also in this volume].

[109] "Is Marcion's Gospel one of the Synoptics?" *HJ* 34 (1936), pp. 265-77, esp. p. 267. A. Loisy, however, rightly pointed to Couchoud's determination to delay the birth of the Gospel literature because of "his fundamental theory regarding the non-historicity of Jesus" ("Marcion' s Gospel," *HJ* 34, (1936), pp. 378-87, esp. p. 387).

[110] *L' Evangile selon saint Matthieu* (Paris, 1927⁴), p. xliii.

[111] *Matthew, Mark and Luke,* pp. 95ff.

[112] "The Synoptic Gospels," p. 280.

[113] To be sure none of the first three Gospels is distinctly homogeneous.

[114] *Op. cit.,* p. 147. H. J. Cadbury was similarly confident that "the unity of Q can hardly be proved or disproved from its present documents" *(The Making of Luke-Acts,* London, 1958, p. 97).

absence of the prepositions παρά[115] and σύν, and the various constructions of γίνομαι.[116] His provisional conclusion was that "we cannot give a convincing proof of their unity from the results of investigation into their vocabulary and style; and yet...it must be acknowledged that there is in them a certain grammatical and stylistic character and colouring."[117] After having, however, examined the formal characteristics of the subject-matter, Harnack noted—and his note is of great importance—that despite first impressions to the contrary, "as soon as one calls to mind the content of the three gospels and compares Q with it, *then Q appears to be undoubtedly more homogeneous than any of the three.*"[118] J. Hawkins came to a similar conclusion in the second edition of his *Horae Synopticae;* he claimed that his examination "failed to produce any expressions which (he) could definitely label as characteristics of Q."[119] He insisted, however, that this failure does not disprove the use of Q as a source. His explanation was similar to Harnack's: "St. Matthew and St. Luke have so 'worked over' the sources they employed that the Gospels frequently represent to us the substance rather than the words of the original documents."[120]

J. M. C. Crum, in addition, discerned in the saying of Q "the scene and atmosphere in which the life was lived; they recall unconsciously the conditions, and local colouring, the atmosphere of the homely village of Galilee."[121] Although this last remark can hardly be accepted as convincing proof for the authenticity of the Q-sayings, as Crum and others assumed, for such features could equally be due to the conditions under which the community that produced the Q-Document lived, it does point to a distinct peculiarity of Q. Furthermore, P. Parker in a comparison of those passages which Matthew shares only with Luke with those given by St. Matthew alone, was able to show that "since the style of M does not pervade Q and the style of Q does not pervade M, therefore Q and M have different origins."[122] On the other hand, "since Q has not been assimilated to Matthaean types of expressions, and since Q's own distinctive language differs from the rest of the Gospel (of Matthew), therefore Q is really an autonomous source."[123]

---

[115] "In the absence of the proposition παρά we may clearly recognize a distinct characteristic of Q" *(op. cit.,* p.158).

[116] "The various constructions with γίνομαι which are so usual in Luke and are also found in Matthew are likewise entirely absent. This is of importance" (ibid., p.161).

[117] Ibid., pp. 162f.

[118] Ibid., p. 167.

[119] *Horae Synopticae* (London, 1909²), p. 113.

[120] Ibid.

[121] *The Original Jerusalem Gospel* (Cambridge, 1927), p. 52. For references to the nature in Q see also B. Redlich, *op. cit.,* p. 68.

[122] *The Gospel before Mark* (Chicago, 1953), p. 30.

[123] Ibid., pp. 30f.

In the light of the above we may safely say that the Q-material forms a homogeneous entity, or at least as homogeneous as any of the three Synoptics; and therefore the likelihood of its being a document is as high as in the case of Mark, Matthew, and Luke![124]

## 7. The alleged disagreement between Matthew and Luke in the sequence of the Q-material

The common materials of two different documents - even if they are quite homogeneous - can hardly be said to form a single written document, unless they are placed in approximately the same position. On the other hand, if a number of isolated and sometimes independent sayings occur in two documents precisely in the same order, then of course, it is almost certain that either the author of one document drew from the other's

---

[124] More recently K. P. G. Curtis and M. D. Goulder have produced what they claim to be convincing statistical proof in support of, and against, the Q-Hypothesis respectively. The former, ("In Support of Q," *ExpT* 84 (1973), pp. 309f., on examination of the percentage of the passages generally assigned to Q in relation to the peculiar words and phrases of Matthew and Luke listed in Hawkins' *Horae Synopticae* (pp. 1ff.), came to the following conclusion: "Of the 904 instances of Matthaean words or phrases in the whole of Matthew's gospel, 152 occur in Q passages, and, of these, 34 (22.4 %) reappear in Luke. Of the 1.483 instances of Lucan words in the whole of his gospel, 180 occur in Q passages, and, of these, 45 (25%) reappear in Matthew. If one eliminates the words which Hawkins places in brackets as being "less important...," new figures are obtained. The number of Matthean words in Q passages is now reduced to 136 of which 32 (23.5 %) reappear in Luke, and the number of Lucan words in Q passages is reduced to 168, of which 44 (26.2 %) reappear in Matthew. And finally, if one considers only those words which Hawkins marks with an asterisk as being most distinctive of the Evangelists, a third set of figures is produced. 51 instances of words distinctive of Matthew occur in the Q passages, and, of these, 6 (11.8%) reappear in Luke; and 53 instances of words distinctive of Luke occur in Q passages, and, of these, 5 (9.4 %) reappear in Matthew" (ibid.). This consistent similarity, according to Curtis, between the percentage figures for Matthew and Luke could only be accounted for, if the two Synoptists drew from a single written source

Goulder, on the contrary, *(Midrash and Lection in Matthew,* London, 1974), thought that he was able to reverse Curtis' conclusion on similar grounds. Like Curtis, he examined the percentage of characteristic words in the Marcan and Q passages of Matthew both when St. Matthew was copying, and when he was commenting on his source(s) *(midrash).* His conclusion was that the overall percentage in non-Marcan passages is, as in the Marcan ones, around 29%, and that therefore, "the non-Marcan passages are overall St. Matthew's midrash" (pp. 417f.). Thus, the Q-Hypothesis, according to Goulder's calculation, is not necessary.

This sort of isolated statistical calculation, however, is a very unsafe criterion, either for supporting or for questioning a working hypothesis, unless it is undertaken within the context of more general statistical studies covering all the aspects of the synoptic problem.

work,[125] or alternatively they both drew from the same written source.[126] In the case of the double tradition some order seems actually to be present. For if one puts in their Lucan sequence those passages in Luke with more or less close parallel in Matthew in one column, and their Matthaean parallels in another, then with omission of single sayings the sequence appears almost the same; *almost* but not *quite*. For some variations in the order thus established are still visible, and to that extent the argument from the lack of order is still in force. Of course "some exception there certainly must be, if only because the human mind is incapable of absolute regularity".[127] Also some smaller units in Matthew are generally agreed to have been considerably reworked, which as one might expect could cause reasonable confusion in the agreement of order.[128] But even so, the variations of order cannot be removed altogether, and therefore, the entire Q-Hypothesis is in real danger. J. Chapman perhaps went too far when he stated that "there is no agreement at all between Matthew and Luke as to the order of Q."[129] The scholar, however, who most severely questioned the Q-Hypothesis from this angle was C. K. Barrett. In a very stimulating article he pointed out on a close examination of the passages concerned that the hypothesis that the double tradition is derived "from a common document breaks down."[130] For if St. Matthew and St. Luke were both using "the same continuous source we should expect them to show in their use of it some agreement in order which (in general) they show when both are following Mark."[131] Barrett claimed that those sayings in Matthew and Luke which belong to the so-called Double Tradition are in a complete disorder compared with those drawn from Mark.

It was the merit of V. Taylor's two successive articles[132] to have put the question of order back in the position of the most objective and decisive argument for the Q-Hypothesis. These articles have in fact been the turning point in the history of Q research, since they served more than any

---

[125] Cf. e.g. the case of the epistles 2 Peter and Judas.

[126] The improbability of the first alternative with regard to the Q-material will be discussed in detail later in this article (section 9).

[127] B. H. Streeter, "On the Original Order," in *OSSP*, pp. 141-64, esp. p.164.

[128] Cf. the "Sending-Out Discourse" (Mt 9.37-10.18). It has been also suggested by M. Albertz, *Die synoptischen Streitgespräche* (Berlin, 1921), pp. 146ff., and W. L. Knox, *The Sources of the Synoptic Gospels. II: St. Luke and St. Matthew* (Oxford, 1957), pp. 19ff, that in the section about the New Law (Mt 5.17-48) only three antitheses (1, 2 & 4) were original whereas the rest were added by St. Matthew himself.

[129] *Op. cit.*, p. 95.

[130] "Q: A Re-examination," *ExpT* 54 (1943), pp. 320-23, esp. p. 323.

[131] Ibid.

[132] "The Order of Q," *JTS* n.s. 4 (1953), pp. 27-31; and "The Original Order of Q," in *New Testament: Essays in Memory of T. W. Manson*, ed. by A. J. B. Higgins (Manchester, 1959), pp. 246-69.

other else to strengthen confidence in the Q-Hypothesis. Having assigned those passages of the double tradition, in which the linguistic agreement between Matthew and Luke is relatively small, to a source other than Q,[133] Taylor drew attention to the special arrangement of the discourse material in Matthew. He then compared the Lucan order not with that of Matthew as a whole but with that of the five great discourses (Mt 5-7; 9.37-10.42; 13.1-52;18; 23-25) together with any relevant material outside those discourses. The result was that the Lucan sequence of the Q passages could be discerned also in Matthew, for the bulk of smaller units and even for single sayings with negligible exceptions. Taylor's analysis has also shown that St. Matthew used the whole of the material of the Lucan Sermon on the Plain in chs. 5 and 7, and various sayings from Lk 11ff. in ch. 6; this sort of distribution, he said, "has the appearance of a consciously adopted plan."[134] Moreover, in view of St. Matthew's treatment of Mark—in Matthew the Marcan order has been altered eight times[135]—such a complete agreement in order with the Lucan (=Q) original can hardly be considered as a mere accident.

Thanks to Taylor, therefore, the alleged failure of Matthew and Luke to agree between them in placing the Q material in the same position turned out to be the most powerful argument in support of the Q-Hypothesis, *i.e. the argument from order.*[136]

## 8. *The Minor Verbal Agreements of Matthew and Luke against Mark*

"The principle weakness of the Two-Source theory", writes E. P. Sanders in a recent article, "is that it is constructed to explain the synoptic interrelationships on the assumption that there are no agreements between Matthew and Luke against Mark, rather than on the assumption *that there are almost always some, but usually not many* such agreements.[137] Of these, the so-called "Minor Agreements"[138] are more significant than the agreements even of subject matter.[139]

---

[133] These passages were Lk 10.25-28 par; 12.54-56 par; 13.23f. par; 13.25-27 par; 15.4-7,10 par;1 9.12-27 par.

[134] "The Original Order of Q," pp. 249f. n. 4.

[135] Cf: A. Barr, *A Diagram of the Synoptic Relationships* (Edinburgh, 1938).

[136] U. Luz, "Die Wiederentdeckte Logienquelle," *EvT* 33 (1973), pp. 527-33, has recently drawn attention to the order of the pericopes as an argument for a written Q.

[137] "The Overlaps of Mark and Q and the Synoptic Problem," *NTS* 19 (1973), pp. 437-65.

[138] For lists of these minor agreements see E. A. Abbott, *The Corrections of Mark Adopted by Matthew and Luke* (London, 1901), pp. 307-24; J. Hawkins, *op. cit.,* pp. 143-53; and B. de Solages, *op.cit.,* pp. 1052-66.

[139] Cf. N. Turner, "The Minor Verbal Agreements of Mt and Lk against Mk," *SE* vol. I, pp. 223-34, esp. p. 234; also J. A. Fitzmyer, *art. cit.,* p.146.

The importance of this phenomenon was felt very early by all synoptic critics, who, especially in Great Britain, renounced both the Holtzmannian explanation based on the *Ur-Markus* theory and B. Weiss' idea of St. Mark's use of the *Logia*.[140] Scholars from E. A. Abbott, W. Sanday, V. H. Stanton, F. C. Burkitt, and J. Hawkins, and up to C. H. Turner,[141] all realized the significance of this phenomenon, and all attempted to give an answer to the puzzling question: How does it happen that St. Matthew and St. Luke have agreed against Mark, if the one is not supposed to have drawn from the other's work? It can be inferred from what C. H. Turner wrote in 1924[142] that a widely accepted solution had yet to be reached. It was E. W. Lummis who first noticed that there were still agreements between Matthew and Luke against Mark that none of V. H. Stanton's four explanations[143] could account for. Some of these, he insisted, "cannot be explained at all except by an acquaintance of St. Luke with Matthew."[144] With the publication, however, of Streeter's *Four Gospels* the problem was settled and a general consensus was reached. In ch. XI of that book Streeter classified carefully the minor agreements and treated them in the

---

[140] Holtzmann advanced the *Ur-Markus* theory in his earlier work *(Die synoptische Evangelien)*, but renounced it later *(Lehrbuch der hisrorisch-kritischen Einleitung in das N.T.*, Freiburg, 1892³), pp. 351ff, 537) in favor of St. Luke's acquaintance with Matthew, together with Weiszäcker, Wendt, Allen and others. For an account of B. Weiss' views in English see his *Manual of Introduction to the New Testament* (ET, London, 1898), pp. 246ff.

[141] Cf. E. A. Abbott, *op. cit.*, pp. 300ff ; W. Sanday, "A Survey of the Synoptic Problem," *Expositor* 4th s., vol. III (1891), pp. 180ff; also idem, "The Conditions under which the Gospels were written, in their Bearing upon some Difficulties of the Synoptic Problem," *OSSP,* pp. 19ff.; V. H. Stanton, "Some Points in the Synoptic Problem. III: Some Secondary Features," *Expositor* 4th s., vol. VII (1893), pp. 263ff.; also idem, *The Gospels as Historical Documents,* vol. II (Cambridge, 1909), pp. 142ff ; F. C. Burkitt, *The Gospel History and its Transmission* (Edinburgh, 1906), pp. 42ff ; J. Hawkins, *op. cit.,* pp. 172ff ; C. H. Turner, "Historical Introduction of the Textual Criticism", *JTS* 10 (1909), pp. 174ff. For a detailed survey of the debate on the minor agreements prior to Streeter see W. Farmer, *op. cit.,* pp. 94ff.

[142] "So long as it is supposed that there is a residium of agreements between Matthew and Luke against Mark in matter taken from Mark..., so long will research into synoptic question be hampered and final solution be delayed" ("Marcan Usage," *JTS* 25-29 (1924- 28), p. 377).

[143] V. H. Stanton's four explanations were: (i) "Differences between the text of the Marcan document used by the first and third evangelists and our Mark;" (ii) "Undesigned agreements between the first and third evangelists in revising their Marcan document;" (iii) "The influence of parallel accounts in the Logia, or other documents, or of oral tradition, or habits of oral teaching;" and (iv) "Textual assimilation" *(The Gospels..* pp. 142ff.).

[144] *How Luke was Written* (Cambridge, 1915), p. 23; also idem, "'A Case against Q," pp. 757ff. Similarly H. G. Jameson, *The Origin of the Synoptic Gospels: A Revision of the Synoptic Problem* (Oxford, 1922), found the arguments adduced up to his time inadequate to account for the phenomena.

following order: (i) *Irrelevant agreements,* the majority of which "do not require any explanation at all," being rather obvious improvements of the Marcan style;[145] (ii) *Deceptive agreements,* namely those which "are explicable as a result of independent editing;"[146] (iii) Agreements due to the *influence of Q,* which, however, Streeter confined only to those sections where Mark and Q seem to overlap;[147] (iv) Agreements due to *textual corruption* in terms both of an actual corruption of the original text of Mark, and of an assimilation of parallel passages;[148] Streeter's success is to be seen both in bringing together most of the earlier arguments (synthesis), and in treating separately and with undeniable skill most of the cases on their merits (analysis). With Streeter the debate on this crucial issue seemed to have been brought to an end.

Streeter's view remained unchallenged for more than thirty years until Farrer claimed that behind Streeter's argumentation lies a fundamental error of method. "The forces of evidence," he wrote, "are divided by the advocate and defeated in detail."[149] This contention was made even more forcibly by Farmer in whose view Streeter "followed the eclectic method of drawing upon various causes which had been put forward by different scholars to explain these agreements, without entering into critical discussion of these causes."[150] Thus, Streeter "succeeded in bringing order out of chaos;"[151] but his procedure "tends to atomize the phenomena."[152] Farrer did not argue that Streeter's plea was incapable of being sustained; all he insisted for was that it was "a plea against apparent evidence, and that other things being equal, we should accept the evidence and drop the plea."[153] To him the "apparent evidence" was St. Luke's acquaintance with Matthew, which will concern us in the next section. The minor agreements in his view are just what one would expect on the supposition that St. Luke had read Matthew, but decided to work direct upon the more ancient

---

[145] *The Four Gospels,* p. 295.

[146] Ibid., p. 304.

[147] Ibid., pp. 305ff.

[148] Ibid., pp. 306ff. It is to be noted that to the last case Streeter brought a great deal of MS evidence to justify his explanation.

[149] "On Dispensing with Q," p. 62.

[150] *Op. cit.,* p.117.

[151] Ibid.

[152] Ibid., p. 119, quoting (n.2) F. M. Keech, *The Agreements of Matthew and Luke against Mark in the Triple Tradition* (unpublished thesis, Drew University Library, Madison New Jersey, 1962), pp. 38-41. That Streeter did atomize the phenomena is of course true as it is also true that he treated the minor agreements having first established his "Fundamental Solution." In ch. VII, pp. 78-81 he only briefly referred to the problem transferring the final solution to ch. XI, where the priority of Mark could be relied upon. However, it is equally true that Farmer himself used the same method of atomizing the phenomena is his criticism of the Two-Document theory *(passim)*

[153] "On Dispensing....," p. 62.

narrative of Mark for himself. He does his own work of adaptation, but small Matthaean echoes keep appearing because St. Luke is after all acquainted with Matthew."[154] It was these minor agreements along with other points discussed so far that made Farrer decide that "the Q hypothesis is not, of itself, a probable hypothesis."[155]

W. H. Blyth Martin, however, the first who dealt with Farrer's article, pointed out that the minor agreements "have nothing to do with Q. The reason why Streeter explained them away was because they affected the question of the priority of Mark in its present form."[156] This particular problem of Streeter's treatment of the minor agreements with regard to their bearing upon the Q-Hypothesis, and its criticism by Farrer was exclusively dealt with in a paper read by R. McL. Wilson at the First Biblical Congress at Oxford. He, too, pointed out with even more precision that "the purpose of his (Streeter's) argument was not to demonstrate the existence of Q, or to disprove St. Luke's knowledge of Matthew; it was to overthrow the Ur-Markus theory."[157] This becomes most evident it that Streeter's treatment ends with the famous plea: "Renounce once and for all the chase of the phantom Ur-Marcus..."[158] Wilson further pointed out that "Dr. Farrer does not do justice to Streeter's argument from the evidence of the text."[159] Indeed, Streeter's use of the MS evidence to eliminate some of the minor agreements is not by any means arbitrary but highly consistent.[160] We may, therefore, say that Farrer's criticism of Streeter's treatment of the minor agreements in connection with the Q-Hypothesis was quite successfully met by Wilson; but the question as such still remained.

Thus, in a lively paper, read also at the First Biblical Congress at Oxford, N. Turner reopened the discussion on the minor agreements. He doubted Streeter's main solution of the textual assimilation,[161] and noted

---

[154] Ibid., p. 61.

[155] Ibid., p. 62.

[156] "The Indispensibility of Q," *Theology* 59 (1956), pp. 182-88, esp. p. 184. Blyth Martin also claimed that Farrer's entire criticism had its cause in the fact that Q is a hypothesis, "and Farrer does not like hypotheses!" (p.182).

[157] "Farrer and Streeter on the Minor Agreements of Matthew and Luke against Mark," *SE* vol. I, pp. 254-57, esp. p. 256.

[158] *Op. cit.,* p. 331.

[159] "Farrer and Streeter...," p. 256.

[160] Ibid. In fact, in Streeter's treatment there are 3 more cases where Q was brought in, apart from Mk 4.21 par, 4.22, par and 8.21 par; these are Mt 3.5=Lk 3.3; Mt 3.16=Lk 3.21; and Mt 4.1=Lk 4.1 *(op. cit.,* p. 305).

[161] "The Minor Verbal Agreements of Mt and Lk against Mk," *SE* vol. I, pp. 223- 34, esp. p. 224. N. A. Dahl, "Die Passionsgeschichte bei Matthäus," *NTS* 2 (1955), pp. 17-32, also doubted whether the minor agreements, especially in the Passion Narrative, can be attributed to scribal errors. He argued that much of the additional material in Matthew's

that we cannot "very well expand the scope of Q to cover all passages, without making Q a meaningless symbol."[162] In his view "the weightiest of Streeter's explanation is (probably) that of independent improvements of Mark's style."[163] Turner went on to state that in a number of cases St. Luke appears to have drawn from Matthew.[164] After examining Mk 2.23-3.6 par., 4.1-20 par., 6.7-11 par., 8.27-9.1 par., he found the evidence "quite cumulative and not confined to the weight of any single example in itself."[165] In his view "there cannot be any other reason than literary dependence to explain (the facts);... it is reasonable to suppose that either they had a common written source other than Mark (and Q will not answer for all these Marcan sections), or else that one of them is dependent on the other. Because these agreements are so often inconsistent with St. Luke's style elsewhere, it is more likely that Luke depends on Matthew than vice-versa."[166] Turner, however, admitted that the evidence he had adduced of the minor agreements was not "sufficient to discredit the Q-hypothesis."[167] The probability of St. Luke's having seen Matthew "does not mean that it is unlikely that St. Luke used anything else than Matthew and Mark, but it renders it unnecessary to suppose that he used a special source for those passages which correspond with passages in Mt-Q in fact."[168] In short Turner's article, especially in the light of his later treatment of the Q-problem,[169] was not hostile to the Q-Hypothesis, but rather a plea for "some means" to explain away remaining literary questions, if the view that Luke is independent of Matthew is to be retained.[170]

---

Passion Narrative was due to the author's "acquaintance with an independent non-Marcan account," which was preserved more faithfully than the Marcan one (p. 24).

[162] "The Minor Verbal...," p. 224.

[163] Ibid. A. W. Argyle, however, even regarded as doubtful Streeter's argument about independent stylistic alterations ("Agreements between Matthew and Luke," *ExpT* 73, (1961), pp. 19-22); he also dismissed the argument about MSS corruption and he considered the remaining explanation (i.e. the influence of Q) as a *petitio principii* (p. 21), since it presupposes the existence of Q, against which he had earlier put a question mark. R. S. Cherry replying to Argyle ("Agreements between Matthew and Luke," *ExpT* 74 (1962), p. 63), tried to solve the problem by suggesting the acceptance of C. K. Barrett's definition of Q as a stratum of the tradition "but not necessarily derived from a single document" (ibid.).

[164] "The Minor Verbal...," p. 225.

[165] Ibid., p. 223.

[166] Ibid., p. 234.

[167] Ibid.

[168] Ibid., p. 223.

[169] "Q in Recent Thought," *ExpT* 80 (1968), pp. 324-28.

[170] Cf. F. Neirynck, "The Argument from Order and St. Luke's Transpositions," *ETL* 49 (1973), pp. 784-815, who states with reservations: "Minor agreements in Matthew-Luke require an explanation and St. Luke's use of Matthew is a possible (although unnecessary) solution" (p. 804); cf. also idem, "Minor Agreements Matthew-Luke in the

From the discussion so far one point at least seems quite certain, namely that Streeter's argumentation on the minor agreements, though highly ingenious and persuasive, has not been conclusive. Even on the most probable MS evidence such agreements between Matthew and Luke against Mark still stand.[171] Streeter's solution, however, was nothing but a further attempt to build upon those made previously, especially by British scholars who believed in the priority of Mark but not in the various *Ur-Markus* theories. It is not insignificant that Streeter was quite open[172] to Sanday's hypothesis that "these facts were not so much editorial as textual."[173] Sanday himself was later influenced by Abbott and spoke of *"a recension of the text of Mark different from that which all the extant MSS of the Gospel are discended."*[174] Nevertheless, Streeter's attempt to draw attention to "the grouping of MSS and the history of the text"[175] rather than to a "recension" seemed to have blocked Sanday's suggestion for the time being.

However, J. P. Brown redirected attention toward Sanday's solution.[176] After considering 71 readings, he came to the conclusion that *"the text of Mark which eliminates the most agreements between Matthew and Luke is the "Caesarean; particularly fam. 13."*[177] On that basis he conjectured that

---

Transfiguration Story," in *Orientierung an Jesus. Zur Theologie der Synoptiker, Festschrift to J. Schmid*, ed. by P. Hoffmann, N. Brox, W. Resch (Freiburg, 1973), pp. 253-66. Unfortunately I was unable [before finishing my dissertation] to make use of his latest book *The Minor Agreements of Matthew and Luke against Mark* (Gembloux, 1975).

In addition to the studies mentioned so far, see also S. MacLoughlin, "Les accords mineurs Mt-Lk contre Mc et le problème synoptique: Vers la theorie des Deux Sources," in I. de la Potterie S.J. (ed.), *De Jésus aux Evangiles: Tradition et rédaction dans les évangiles synoptiques* (Gembloux, 1967), pp. 17-40.

[171] It is true that most of the attempts to account for these agreements sometimes give the impression of being desperate attempts to iron out the difficulties at any cost (cf. I. H. Marshall, *Luke: Historian and Theologian* (Exeter, 1970), p. 57).

[172] *Op. cit.*, pp. 295ff., 180f.

[173] "A Survey of the Synoptic Problem," p. 191.

[174] "The Conditions under which...," p. 21. This view was also shared by Burkitt and C. H. Turner (cf. Streeter, *The Four Gospels*, p. 295).

[175] *The Four Gospels*, p. 295.

[176] The subject was in fact reopened by T. F. Glasson, who argued that some of the minor agreements are due to "the use by St. Matthew and St. Luke of copies of Mark in which the same corruptions occurred—corruptions which have been transmitted to us in the western MS (D) tradition" ("Did Matthew and Luke Use a Western text of Mark," *ExpT* 55 (1944), pp. 180-84, esp. p. 184). C. S. C. Williams, however, argued in reply quite successfully that D as it stands, though containing early elements, has probably been influenced by Tatian ("Did Matthew and Luke Use the 'Western' Text of Mark," *ExpT* 56 (1944), pp. 41-45). He thus deprived Glasson's hypothesis of its most important evidence (cf. also their further debate in *ExpT* 57 (1945), pp. 53ff.; and *ExpT* 58 (1947), p. 251).

[177] "An Early Revision of the Gospel of Mark", *JBL* 78 (1959), pp. 215-27, esp. p. 226.

"*there existed in the first century a revised version or versions of Mark, which accounts for many textual variants in our MSS of Mark, for many divergences from Mark in Matthew and Luke against Mark; and that to this recension the best witness is the Ceasarean.*"[178] N. Perrin, on the other hand, has rightly pointed out that "the optimism about establishing the original text of the gospels to a degree of high probability... is not as widespread today as it was in the era of Westcott and Hort. This tends to diminish the importance of more purely theological factors."[179]

To sup up: apart from the inconclusiveness of Streeter's argumentation with regard to the minor agreements between Matthew and Luke against Mark, the following two points emerge from the discussion so far: (a) there are quite good reasons for believing that the minor agreements owe their existence to the indecisiveness of Textual Criticism with regard to the original text of the Synoptics; and (b) *that the existence as such of theses agreements does not affect the Q-Hypothesis*. All it can do is that it provides some means for revising the generally accepted view of independence between Matthew and Luke. The entire question, therefore, turns on whether there are good reasons of St. Luke or St. Matthew's having used the other's work instead of both having drawn from a common source.

## 9. The alleged use of Matthew by St. Luke

"The Q-Hypothesis," wrote Farrer, "is not, of itself, a probable hypothesis. It is simply the sole alternative to the supposition that St. Luke had read Matthew. It needs no refutation except the demonstration that its alternative is possible."[180] So far we have seen how untrue the first part of Farrer's statement (i.e. the improbability of the Q-Hypothesis as such) is. It remains to be seen whether the degree of probability of the second part is high enough to discredit Q.[181]

---

[178] Ibid. Glasson, however, still prefers, on the basis of seven additional cases, "Western" to Brown's "Caesarean" as the most adequate available label for the text tradition in which these variants are most fully presented ("An Early Revision of the Gospel of Mark," *JBL* 85 (1966), pp. 231-33. In any case, the existence of such a revised edition of Mark, no matter whether "Western" or "Caesarean" or whatever else, has started gaining more ground today, and has been accepted with reservations even by N. Turner ("Q in Recent...," p. 325). Cf. also O. Linton, "Evidences for a Second-Century Revised Edition of St. Mark's Gospel," *NTS* 13 (1967), pp. 321-55.

[179] *Rediscovering...*, p. 34.

[180] "On Dispensing...," p. 62.

[181] In the past the view that St. Luke drew from Matthew his common matter with him was held among others by H. G. Jameson, *The Origin of the Synoptic Gospels: A Revision of the Synoptic Problem* (Oxford, 1922), *passim*; A. Schlatter, *Der Evangelist Matthäus* (Stuttgart, 1929), p. 51; also idem, *Das Evangelium des Lukas: Aus seinem Quellen erklärt* (Stuttgart, 1960²), pp. 427-561; J. Chapman, *op. cit.*, p. v.—all three

*Did Q Exist?*

Earlier in this century the view of St. Luke's acquaintance with Matthew to account for the material common to both has been regarded as untenable on the following grounds:[182] (i) The divergence in Luke subsequently to the Temptation story from the Matthaean order is extremely wide (Streeter,[183] Hawkins[184]); (ii) the absence from Luke of all Matthaean additions to the Marcan text is remarkable (Hawkins,[185] J. Schmid[186]); (iii) it is not only Matthew but Luke also that can give the original setting (Streeter,[187] Schmid,[188] Vaganay[189]); (iv) the breaking-up in Luke of Matthew's Sermon on the Mount is inexplicable (Kümmel[190]); (v) the complete divergence in the Birth and Infancy chapters, and the differences in the Passion and Resurrection narratives show that Matthew and Luke cannot but be independent works (V. Taylor[191]).

These observations[192] have nevertheless been met with strong counter arguments not only by those who believe in the priority of Matthew, but also by those who accept the Priority of Mark. Even before Streeter's *Four Gospels,* H. G. Jameson pointed out against argument (i) that *"Luke does*

---

accepting with modifications the Augustinian hypothesis of the Matthew-Mark-Luke sequence—E. W. Lummis, *op. cit.;* K. H. Rengstorf, *Das Evangelium nach Lukas* (Göttingen, 1962⁹), pp. 8f; M. S. Enslin, *Christian Beginnings* (New York, 1938), p. 433; and J. H. Ropes, *The Synoptic Gospels* (Massachusetts, 1934). Their views, however, remained unnoticed until B. C. Butler, *The Originality...,* made a scholarly appeal to them. Ropes, in particular, had complained that "the fundamental assumption that Luke and Matthew were independent of each other has been but lightly treated, and often critical significance of this question for the problem does not seem to have been present to the critics' mind" *(op. cit.,* p. 67). And he went on: "There is, however, an alternative, namely that St. Luke drew these sayings (the Q-sayings) from Matthew, and in the present state of the investigation it ought not to be excluded from consideration" (ibid.).

[182] P. Wernle, *Die synoptische Frage* (Freiburg, 1899), had in fact convincingly shown the impossibility of this theory (40-80). Having compared Luke with Matthew with regard to content, sequence, and wording, he concluded that "although not strictly demonstrable, it is nevertheless probable, that Matthew was entirely unknown to Luke" (p.80). His views, however, made very little, if any, impact on British scholarship.

[183] *The Four Gospels,* p. 183.

[184] "Probabilities as to the so-called Double Tradition of St. Matthew and St. Luke," *OSSP,* pp. 91-138, esp. p, 102.

[185] Ibid., pp. 102ff.

[186] "Mt und Lk. Eine Untersuchung des Verhältnisses ihrer Evangelien," *BS* 23 (1930), pp. 25ff.

[187] *The Four Gospels,* p.183.

[188] "Markus und die Aramaische Matthäus," in *Synoptische Studien für A. Wikenhauser* (Leiden, 1959), pp. 148ff, esp. pp. 183ff.

[189] *Le Problème...,* pp. 293ff.

[190] *Introduction...,* p. 50.

[191] *The Gospels: A Short Introduction* (London, 1920), p. 24, n. 2.

[192] For a comprehensive exposition of these arguments see J. A. Fitzmyer, *art. cit.,* pp. 148ff.

not attempt to insert his 'Q' matter into the Marcan context at all, but collects it all into some three or four large sections, which are interimposed between similar large sections of Marcan matter."[193]

Argument (ii), which is related to the special problem of narrative sequence has recently been met by E. P. Sanders who noted that there are clear instances where St. Luke has agreed with St. Matthew to insert the same material at the same place in the Marcan outline (e.g. Lk 13.20f=Mt 13.3; Lk 17.3=Mt 18.10-22).[194] We must therefore, says Sanders, "become more open to the possibility that there was more contact between St. Matthew and St. Luke than their independent employment of the same two sources suggests."[195] And in conclusion, be pointed out that "the simplest explanation is that one knew the other with the possibility being higher in the case of St. Luke's having come across Matthew than the other way round."[196]

Sanders, however, did not discredit Q in this article; what he tried to do in several independent studies was to show that the arguments for the classical view are far less secure than is generally assumed. A pioneer in this method of discrediting the generally accepted solution was undoubtedly B. C. Butler who in the first two chs. of his main critical work[197] dealt exclusively with Q. In ch. II entitled "Arguments for Q,"[198] Butler argued against the two reasons (argument (iii) included) presented by Streeter[199] to rule out the possibility that St. Luke used Matthew. "The advocates of the Two-Document hypothesis", Butler contented, "show no sign, as a rule, of having noticed that the passages where they are forced to suggest that Matthew conflated Mark and Q can be easily explained by the

---

[193] *The Origin...*, p. 16.

[194] Even Hawkins had noted two long sections in Matthew (chs. 8-13) and Luke (9.51-18.14) which largely ignore Marcan arrangement and order ("Three Limitations to St. Luke's Use of St. Mark's Gospel: I. The Disuse of the Marcan Source in St. Luke ix.51-xvii.14," in *OSSP,* pp. 29-59, esp. pp. 29ff.).

[195] "The Argument from Order and the Relationship Between. Matthew and Luke," *NTS* 15 (1969), pp. 249-61, esp. p.161. Sanders also noted that 'the assurance with which it is usually said that Matthew and Luke were independent of each other rests on the assertion that they never agree together in such a way that it cannot be explained by reference to their independent use of Mark and Q" (ibid.).

[196] Ibid. F. Neirynck, in reply to Sanders, rightly points out that the phenomenon of order has been studied (by him) "with an undue limitation of the creative activity of the evangelist (St. Luke)" ("The Argument from Order and St. Luke's Transpositions," *ETL* 49 (1973), pp. 784-815, esp. p. 815).

[197] *The Originality of St. Matthew*, pp. 1ff.

[198] Ibid., pp. 23ff. In ch. I, under the title "The Q Hypothesis Tested" (pp. 1ff), Butler drew attention "to four or five Q passages where direct derivation of Luke from Matthew is a far more satisfactory critical hypothesis than their common derivation from a third document" (pp. 1f.).

[199] *The Four Gospels,* p.133.

*Did Q Exist?* 31

direct dependence of Luke on Matthew."[200] Both these reasons, according to Butler, proved "too insecure to support the hypothesis of a conjectural document."[201] With regard to argument (iii) in particular, Butler, after making an appeal to Harnack's work, argued that it could not be used "in recommendation of that hypothesis without begging the question."[202] Finally, as far as the remaining two arguments (iv & v) are concerned these were most effectively met by Farrer, who for the greater part of his essay[203] undertook to make St. Luke's use of Matthew intelligible. In his view, the Q-Hypothesis "wholly depends on the incredibility of St. Luke's having read St. Matthew's book. That incredibility depends in turn on the supposition that St. Luke was essentially an adapter and compiler."[204] With this observation Farrer entered into the heart of the problem; for if it were ever possible to show convincingly that Luke emerged out of Matthew, then the Q-Hypothesis would collapse. Farrer's own suggestion was that in Luke we can have the ingenious work of an author with an Hexateuchal arrangement in mind, not so clear as Matthew's but still discernible. Thus, he identified Matthew's opening chs. (1-2) with Genesis, the Sermon on the Mount (chs. 5-7) with Exodus, the Mission Charge (ch. 10) with Leviticus, the Parables (ch. 13) with Numbers, the Discourse on Discipleship (ch. 18) with Deuteronomy, and the Eschatological Discourse (chs. 24-25) with Joshua. He then tried to show how St. Luke applied the same method to his own work without, however, keeping the same divisions. Thus, Genesis in Luke, similarly to Matthew is the Infancy narratives (chs. 1-2), but his Exodus is the following chs. (3ff) including the Temptation in the Wilderness, the Rejection at Nazareth, and the Miraculous Fishing. This leads to his Leviticus which is the Sermon on the Plain (6.20ff), but which corresponds to Matthew's Exodus. Accordingly the Lucan Numbers were seen in Matthew's Leviticus (i.e. The Sending Out Discourse Lk 9.1ff), whereas Deuteronomy was said to be the Lucan Central Section (9.51-18.14[205]). Finally, "the triumphant passion and resurrection compose the "Book of Jesus" *par excellence.'*[206] In this way it is conceivable why St. Luke has broken up the Matthaean Sermon on the

---

[200] *The Originality...*, p. 23.

[201] Ibid., p. 36.

[202] Ibid., p. 30. So also Farrer who "would not base any argument on such grounds" ("On Dispensing....," p. 65). On the same argument he wrote that "there is a deceptive simplicity...which evaporates as soon as we try to apply it" (p. 64).

[203] "On Dispensing....," pp. 66-85.

[204] Ibid., p. 56.

[205] On the connection between Deuteronomy and the Lucan Central Section Farrer referred to C. F. Evans, "The Central Section of St. Luke's, Gospel," *SG*, pp. 37-53.

[206] "On Dispensing....," p. 81.

Mount,[207] and completely deviated from the Infancy, Passion, and Resurrection narratives of Matthew.

Replies to this were soon forthcoming. Thus, W. H. Blyth Martin dealt in the following year with Farrer's thesis, and reached unfavorable judgments on his arguments. "If we had to dispense with Q, the reverse thesis, to argue that St. Matthew had read Luke, would be simpler."[208] He insisted that "there is not a single instance in which Dr. Farrer can produce definite knowledge by St. Luke of Matthew."[209] Farrer himself, however, in a letter to the editor of *Theology*[210] replied to Blyth Martin's criticism insisting that his essay was in fact an attack on the old principles of proof. When he (Blyth Martin) argues, he wrote, "that the Lucan phenomena can be more easily worked out from Q than from Matthew, I agree with him."[211] In brief, Farrer's main point was that the alternative view, namely St. Luke's use of Matthew, can be fairly made out."[212] From this reply of

---

[207] Another explanation for the breaking-up of the Sermon on the Mount by St. Luke has been more recently given by the distinguished Jewish scholar Samuel Sandmel in his study The First Christian Century in Judaism and Christianity (New York, 1969). Looking at the problem from the Lucan perspective of the *Heilsgeschichte,* Sandmel, holding like Farrer that St. Luke utilized Matthew (p. 215, n. 39), argues that St. Luke represents Christianity in an unbroken continuity with ancient Judaism, whereas the Sermon on the Mount implies something new. "Accordingly, St. Luke breaks up the unity of the Sermon on the Mount deliberately, and he deliberately scatters the portion of the material which he retains to utilize" (ibid.; cf. also idem, *The Genius of Paul* (New York, 1958) pp. 180-86).

[208] "The Indispensibility of Q," p. 183. However, the challenge to the Q-Hypothesis from the quarter of "Luke-Priorists" has never been strong. Only W. Lockton, "The Origins of the Gospels," CQR 94 (1922), pp. 216-39, favored the Lucan Priority disavowing the existence of Q. More recently H. P. West Jr., "A Primitive Version of Luke in the Composition of Matthew," NTS 14 (1967), pp. 75-95, has suggested that a primitive Luke, used also as a source by Marcion, could be "at least as probable as Q as a source of Matthew and Luke" (p. 95). Another supporter of the Lucan Priority, R. L. Lindsey, ("A Modified Two-Document Theory of the Synoptic Dependence and Interdependence," NT 6 (1963), pp. 239-63; also idem, *A Hebrew Translation of the Gospel* of *Mark Jerusalem,* no date), did not challenge the existence of Q.

[209] "The Indispensibility...," p.186, So also O. E. Evans, "Synoptic Criticism since Streeter," ExpT 72 (1961), pp. 295-99, who referring to Streeter's arguments wrote: "It can hardly be said that Farrer - or Butler either- has adequately answered either of these objections" (p. 298). With regard to Blyth Martin's criticism in particular, R. T. Simpson who, like Farrer argued for St. Luke's acquaintance with Matthew, found it valid but "only against the form of this theory which supposes that St. Luke must have used Matthew as a main source" ("The Major Agreements of Matthew and Luke against Mark," NTS 12 (1966), pp. 273-84, esp. p,183).

[210] *Theology* 59 (1956), pp. 247f.

[211] Ibid., p. 247.

[212] *Theology* 59, p. 247. This applies to A. R. C. Leany too *(A Commentary on the Gospel According to St. Luke,* London, 1958), who dealing with Farrer (pp. 13ff.) found unlikely "had (St. Luke) known Matthew, that he would either have omitted certain portions of Matthew, or used his Matthaean material in the way in which he has used it"

Farrer one point, at least, became clear; his views had to be contested on different and more neutral grounds.

Thus, E. L. Bradby believed that Farrer's theory "can fairly be judged by reference to quite a small number of key passages, in which all three Synoptic Gospels treat the same material."[213] He therefore, set out to examine four passages where all three Synoptics are in parallel but Matthew is fuller than Mark.[214] The outcome of his study, contrary to what would normally be expected, namely that St. Luke would take the later and *fuller* version and in that case Matthew's - or at least would follow sometimes the one and sometimes the other, was in fact that "the later and fuller version (was) consistently spurned in favour of the earlier and shorter."[215] This would seem to stand against Farrer's case, and to make the Q-Hypothesis indispensable. N. Turner, however, has rightly pointed out that even Bradby's approach was largely subjective, "based on what one supposes St. Luke's aims and methods were."[216] Turner was still convinced that "if St. Luke could employ beautiful Septuagint *pastiche* in chapters one and two, he may well have been competent enough to deal in an independent way with Mark and Matthew.[217]

This was also the conclusion to which R. T. Simpson came on examination of the major agreements of Matthew and Luke against

---

(p. 13). "Farrer for his part", writes Leany, "dispenses with Q but does not show it to be more of a hypothesis by choosing another" (p.16). This, however, is exactly what Farrer argued for, namely just for the possibility of St. Luke's acquaintance with Matthew. Leany, nevertheless, made a quite significant point by doubting that Matthew and Luke 'both emanate from the same literary regions" (p.14). This was made more clearly by O. E. Evans who wrote against Farrer: "One cannot escape the feeling that this attempt to press both Gospels into the same hexateuchal pattern is very strained" ("Synoptic Criticism since Streeter," *ExpT* 72 (1961), pp. 295-99, esp. p. 297). For some valuable remarks on the symbolical approach evident in all Farrer's critical studies see Helen Gardner, *The Limits of Literary Criticism* (London, 1956): also by her, *The Business of Criticism* (Oxford, 1959).

[213] "In Defense of Q," *ExpT* 68 (1957), pp. 315-18, esp. p. 315. Passages which are common only to Matthew and Luke, argued Bradby, can be equally used "to support either side of the argument, and cannot be conclusive" (p. 316).

[214] The passages chosen were Mk. 2.23-3.6 par; Mk 4.1-20 par; Mk 6.7-11=Mt 10.1-42=Lk 9.1-5; Mk 8.27-9.1 par (ibid., pp. 316f.).

[215] Ibid., p. 318.

[216] "The Minor Verbal Agreements...," p. 224.

[217] "Q in Recent Thought," p. 325. On quite different grounds, namely the editorial agreements between Matthew and Luke, most evident in the difference of the audience between the opening and closing verses of the Sermon on the Mount/Plain A. W. Argyle, ("Evidence for the View that St. Luke Used St. Matthew's Gospel," *JBL* 83 (1964), p. 390-96) suggested that "the view that St. Luke knew Matthew's gospel is not only a possible one, but is very probably true" (p. 396). His evidence, however, is not conclusive since it can be used for either side.

Mark.[218] "The simplest explanation of this phenomenon", he insisted, "is that either St. Matthew or St. Luke made use of *both* the other synoptics."[219] Taking the priority of Mark for granted, Simpson argued that "the major agreements could have been produced only as a result of St. Luke's use of an edited form of Mark."[220] In his view, therefore, the phenomenon of the major agreements "greatly strengthens the probability that Matthew was one of the sources employed by St. Luke in the composition of his gospel."[221]

This particular issue, however, of the independent use by St. Luke of both Mark and Matthew, shared to some extent by Farrer, Turner, Argyle, Simpon, and Wilkens, raises the question of how it came about that St. Luke was dependent on Matthew *only in a limited area* while at the same time following Mark in the wider area; especially as the distinction between Marcan material and the so-called double tradition could hardly have been so obvious to a first century reader of Matthew (as St. Luke is supposed to have been), as it is to the modern user of a synopsis.[222]

This must have obviously been in F. G. Downing's mind when he tried to rehabilitate Q.[223] For the Q-Hypothesis was still suffering from Farrer's criticism, which despite several counter arguments had stood in its main points almost unchallenged for about ten years. Downing realized that what he had to consider was St. Luke's supposed "use of passages where St. Matthew has apparently conflated a Marcan record of teaching with similar but distinct material of his own from some other source."[224] After a minute statistical analysis of the most appropriate passages, namely the Baptism and Temptation stories, the Beelzebul controversy, the Sending-Out Discourse, and the Synoptic Apocalypse, he found that St. Luke had in all probability used "Matthew's extra material without Matthew's obviously Marcan additions."[225] St. Luke had apparently decided "not to follow Matthew throughout, but to follow Matthew *only where the latter*

---

[218] "The Major Agreements of Matthew and Luke against Mark," *NTS* 12 (1966), pp. 273-84. Simpson examined the following three passages: Mk 1.1-13 par; Mk 3.27-37 par; and Mk 12.28-34 par.

[219] Ibid., p. 273.

[220] Ibid., p. 275.

[221] Ibid., p. 284. W. Wilkens, "Zur Frage der Literarischen Beziehung zwischen Matthäus und Lukas," *NT* 8 (1966), pp. 48-57, came to similar conclusion examining eight passages of the double tradition (Lk 3.7-9; 3.16f.; 6.41f; 10.2; 12.22-31; 13.28-30; 7.1-10; 12.39-46 and their parallels), plus the verbal peculiarities of Matthew, and the Marcan material in Luke. He argued that large portions of the so-called double tradition seem to be St. Luke's copying from Matthew, which, however, does not replace Mark as a source for Luke, but rather supplements it.

[222] Cf. I. H. Marshall, *Luke: Historian and Theologian,* p. 59.

[223] "Towards the Rehabilitation of Q," *NTS* 11 (1965), pp. 170-81.

[224] Ibid., p. 170.

[225] Ibid., p. 175.

*(had) added new material to Mark or (had) largely altered him.*"[226] On these grounds, therefore, Downing suggests that "it is much more reasonable to suppose that St. Luke's apparent ignoring of every clear use by St. Matthew of Mark is due to St. Luke's ignorance of St. Matthew's use of Mark. St. Luke knew Matthew's source (or sources) 'before' it had its parallels with Mark conflated with the latter; and this source (or these sources) is what has come to be known in part as Q."[227] Downing's analysis was an effective blow against Farrer and the criticism of the Q-Hypothesis dependent on him.[228] It was mainly his study that most effectively restored the credibility in Q.

In conclusion, we may say that Farrer and all the others have succeeded, not in abolishing the Q-Hypothesis, but only in questioning Streeter's (and Hawkins' and others') arguments concerning the impossibility of St. Luke's knowledge of Matthew. Their arguments are effective only *ad homines*,[229] and against their methods. It is notable from the discussion so far how consideration of the same passage could lead to widely different and sometime contradictory results.[230] In this situation the use of statistical studies on the whole of the Synoptic Problem cannot be ignored; and Honorés conclusions that "St. Matthew did not use Luke", and "St. Luke did not use Matthew,"[231] is a very promising point to start with, being cogent as results of objective studies.[232]

---

[226] Ibid.

[227] Ibid., p.180. Fitzmyer has pointed, in addition, to "the converse phenomenon in Luke, i.e. his apparent failure to follow Matthew in omitting Marcan passages (e.g. Lk 4.33-37=Mk 1.23-28 (Jesus in the synagogue of Capernaum); Lk 9.49-50=Mk 12.41-44 (the widow's mite)", *(art. cit.,* pp. 167f. n. 63).

[228] Simpson, *art. cit.,* p. 283, n.1, attempted, but without success, to discredit Downing's study by claiming inconsistency in two of his conclusions (!)

[229] Cf. Farrer's review of Butler *(JTS* n.s. 3 [1952], p.102).

[230] Thus, examination of Baptism and Temptation stories made Simpson decide in favor of, and Downing against, St. Luke's acquaintance with Matthew; the evidence from the story about the Beelzebul controversy is found by Butler and Simpson to support the dispensability of Q, and by Downing the indispensability of it; finally, the account of the Sending-Out Discourse according to Butler's analysis provides definite evidence of St. Luke's use of Matthew, and in Bradby and Downing's view proves exactly the opposite!

[231] "A Statistical Study...," p.147.

[232] The only limitation, so far as St. Luke's use of Matthew is concerned, is that both studies which produced that result, namely "Comparison of lengths and Verbal Agreements in Double and Triple Traditions," and "Quantitative use of Sources can be objected to as resting on an *a priori* judgment about St. Luke's behavior as an author (St. Matthew's use of Luke is excluded on the most objective study of the "Triple Link Analysis"). Nevertheless, Downing's statistical study, though covering only a limited area, could well be considered as a valid supplement to Honoré. On the other hand, R. Morgenthaler's *Dreiquellentheorie,* namely the view that Mark and Q were the main sources used by St. Matthew and St. Luke, but that St. Luke had occasionally subsidiary contact with Matthew as a third source *(Statistische Synopse* (Zürich, 1971), p. 301),

In any case, until a new suggestion more reasonable than Farrer's is provided to explain how St. Luke could have worked out his Gospel, either from both the other Synoptics, or even from Matthew alone,[233] the view of St. Luke's ignorance of Matthew remains in the field, and the Q-Hypothesis provides the most satisfactory explanation of the Lucan (and Matthaean) phenomena.[234] The principle weakness, on the other hand, of most attempts that attribute the double tradition to St. Luke's use of Matthew is that they started from alleged weaknesses of the Two-Document Hypothesis and not with positive suggestions.[235]

## 10. The positive arguments for holding the Q-Hypothesis

Having completed the survey of the various criticisms of all kinds with regard to the Q-Hypothesis, we may now proceed to the positive arguments. We have seen so far how all criticisms which have been directed against Q have eventually been refuted by various scholars. This can apply not only to those studies urged by emotion rather than by reason, but also to the well documented objections, either to the Two-Document theory as

---

though not affecting the Q-Hypothesis, it is an unnecessary expansion, which in addition ignores Downing's evidence.

[233] M. D. Goulder, a pupil of Farrer, in his quite recently published study on Matthew *(Midrash and Lection in Matthew,* London, 1974), still holds that "St. Matthew knew Mark, and that St. Luke knew Mark and Matthew" (p. 452; cf. also his joint article with M. L. Sanderson, "St. Luke's Genesis," *JTS* n.s. 8 (1957), pp. 12-30). Matthew, in particular, was in his view the work of a "scribe, who had only Mark before him- no Q, no M, and very little oral tradition - and who expounded Mark in standard Jewish ways" (p. xiii). The reason why St. Matthew had attempted to rewrite Mark was, according to Goulder, the fact that "liturgically Mark was unsatisfactory" (p. 453).

Goulder's enormous attempt, however, to revive an approach to the Gospels via standard Jewish expository techniques *(midrash),* and lectionary schemes, can hardly be justified. W. D. Davies' important remarks on similar cases still stand unshaken (cf. W. D. Davies, "Reflections on a Scandinavian Approach to the Gospel Tradition," in *Neotestamentica et Patristica, Festschrift* to O. Cullmann (Leiden, 1962), pp. 14-34; also idem, "Reflections on Archbishop Carrington's *The Primitive Christian Calendar,"* in *The Background of the N.T. and its Eschatology. Studies in Honour of C. H. Dodd,* ed. by W. D. Davies and D. Daube (Cambridge, 1964), pp. 124-152). Not to mention, of course, that Goulder completely ignores the objective statistical evidence produced by Downing.

[234] It is not incidental that so learned a scholar as C. H. Dodd remarked in his last book, *The Founder of Christianity* (London, 1973): "Attempts which are made to show that Luke is based on Matthew (or alternatively Matthew on Luke) have not, in my judgment, succeeded" (p.179, n. II, 2).

[235] Bishop Cassian's theological approach in his paper "The Interrelation of the Gospels: Matthew-Luke-John," *SE* vol. I, pp. 129ff, seems to neglect all literary grounds on which the Q-Hypothesis has been argued.

*Did Q Exist?* 37

a whole, or to the Q-Hypothesis alone.[236] Two decades ago Farrer was able to write that the Two-Document Hypothesis had suffered from "the lack of an effective opposition."[237] Today, strong opposition by Barrett, Butler, Farrer and others has in fact provided additional arguments which were added to those already existing.[238] On the other hand, the mere fact that the Q-Hypothesis has survived such strong and consistent criticism during the last two decades or so may well be considered as a further positive argument in its favor.

In brief, the positive arguments for the Q-Hypothesis are the following:

(a) The agreement in wording of the common non Marcan material in Matthew and Luke, which in some parts is very extensive (up to 97%),[239] whereas in those cases where it appears less extensive (up to 50%) it is easily explicable. This argument, as H. J. Cadbury rightly points out, "is sufficient evidence of a literary relationship of some kind."[240] And given the improbability of a dependence of Luke on Matthew, or *vice versa*,[241] the only logical conclusion is the use by St. Matthew and Luke of a common source of some kind.

(b) The existence of several doublets in Matthew and Luke;[242] these are single sayings which each of those Synoptics has twice, one shared by all three Synoptics taken up from Mark, and the other shared only by Matthew and Luke presumably from another source.[243]

(c) The existence of double traditions in Luke; these are similar traditions which are found in Luke in two different forms, one taken up from Mark, and the other from elsewhere.[244]

(d) The agreement in order in which the common non-Marcan material was inserted in the first and third Gospels; this can hardly be a coincidence,

---

[236] It can hardly be argued today that the Q-Hypothesis still stands strong only because "the patient work over many years...(cannot) be blithely dismissed in few pages" (so R. H. Fuller, *New Testament in Current Study* (London, 1963), p. 87, n. 4, referring to Farrer's comparatively small essay).

[237] *JTS* n.s. 3 (1953), p.102.

[238] Similarly, others fell into the background depriving thus the opposition from discernible targets.

[239] B. de Solages, *op. cit.*, p.1047; cf. also J. A. Fitzmyer, *art. cit.*, pp. 150f.

[240] *The Making...*, p. 98.

[241] See above (section 9).

[242] It is worth noting that Mark shows only one doublet (Mk 9.35=10. 3f). For a complete list of doublets in the Synoptic tradition see J. Hawkins, *op. cit.*, pp. 80ff.; B. de Solages, *op. cit.*, 928ff.; and T. Stephenson, "Classification of Doublets in the Synoptic Gospels," *JTS* 20 (1919), pp. 1-8.

[243] Both Streeter, *op. cit.*, p. 185, and Koester, *Synoptische Überlieferung...*, passim have challenged the strength of this argument by showing that the doublets may be due to the oral tradition.

[244] In Matthew such traditions are always conflated with those taken up by Mark, and therefore they can hardly be discerned.

especially when in essential points such an order is natural and intelligible.²⁴⁵

(e) The thematical arrangement of the such material,²⁴⁶ which has undoubtedly played quite a part in the arrangement of Matthew (cf. the first, second, and fifth of his five discourses), and to a lesser degree of Luke (cf. the conclusion of his second eschatological discourse, mainly taken from Mk 13, i.e. Lk 21.34-36).²⁴⁷

(f) The sufficient homogeneity of those passages for which there are good reasons to assign to the double tradition.

(g) The statistically evidenced similarity in the treatment by the later Synoptists both of Mark and of the common non-Marcan material.²⁴⁸

Some of the above arguments, e.g. (b), point generally to the use by St. Matthew and St. Luke of other sources beside Mark, but the majority of them, especially the last four combined with the remaining three, would seem to demand the use of a single written document. It is worth noting that the two main arguments, which the Q-Hypothesis has started from, are either no longer valid (i.e. The Papias' testimony), or have ceased to be strong enough to bear the weight of the hypothesis as a written document (i.e. the existence of doublets).²⁴⁹

---

²⁴⁵ Cf. A. Harnack, *op. cit.,* p.178; also P. Wernle, *op. cit.,* pp. 266ff.

²⁴⁶ T. W. Manson, in addition, has drawn attention to the fact that "the document begins and ends with the thought of the coming judgment" *(The Sayings...,* p.16).

²⁴⁷ H. E. Tödt, *The Son of Man in the Synoptic Tradition* (ET, London, 1965), pp. 269f.

²⁴⁸ We have argued elsewhere that "a further reason which confirms the hypothesis that Q was a *single written document* is the way in which the various sections in Q follow one another.... This order in some cases is more intelligible than that of Mark. Moreover, *all sections in Q end in the same formal way,* making the passing from one section to the other natural and smooth" ("The Nature and Extent of the Q-Document," *NT* 20 [1978] 49-73, p. 73).

²⁴⁹ Fitzmyer gives the following three main reasons for postulating a Greek written source: wording, order, and doublets; he includes, however, in the last one the double traditions too *(art. cit.,* p.152).

# 2
# THE NATURE AND EXTENT OF THE Q-DOCUMENT

It is beyond question that the Q-Hypothesis, namely the assumption that both St. Matthew and St. Luke, independently of each other, used besides Mark a second source which is now by general consent referred to as Q, had its climax in the Literary Critical era.[1] Subsequently, the new direction which Form-Criticism gave to Synoptic scholarship, (i.e. the period of oral tradition[2]), as well as some successful studies on the Aramaic background of the individual sayings,[3] diminished interest in Q. However, with the rise of Redaction-Criticism a renewal of the study of Q became inevitable since Redaction-Criticism depends very much upon Source-Criticism. Thus, H. E. Tödt[4] made a significant contribution to the redactional theology of Q, while W. D. Davies[5] some time later began to explore the purpose and theological emphasis of Q from a new angle. In addition, J. M. Robinson[6] showed how important for the study of the primitive Christianity the Q material may be. Even statistical studies on Q[7] and recently some very important and weighty studies on its theology have been published.[8] Elsewhere[9] we consider in some detail all arguments

---

[1] Cf. A. Harnack, *The Sayings of Jesus*, ET, London 1907; and B. H. Streeter, *The Four Gospels. A Study of Origins*, London 1924.

[2] In that particular area, as R. Bultmann pointed out, "the enquiry can be conducted without any special source theory...for it matters little whether this or that editorial process peculiar to the written tradition took place before the Gospels were formed" (*The History of the Synoptic Tradition*, ET, Oxford $1972^2$, p. 321).

[3] Especially by M. Black, An Aramaic Approach to the Gospels and Acts, Oxford $1967^3$, a study which summed up all previous works, especially those by G. Dalman, J. Wellhausen, C. C. Torrey, and C. F. Burney; and J. Jeremias whose studies are now collected in *Abba: Studien zur neutestamentlichen Theologie und Zeitgeschichte*, Göttingen 1966.

[4] *Der Menschensohn in der synoptischen Überlieferung*, Gütersloh, 1959, translated into English under the title *The Son of Man in the Synoptic Tradition*, London 1965. Tödt deals with Q in detail in pp. 232ff.

[5] *The Setting of the Sermon on the Mount*, Cambridge 1964, pp. 366ff.

[6] "ΛΟΓΟΙ ΣΟΦΩΝ: Zur Gattung der Spruchquelle Q,", in *Zeit und Geschichte, Festschrift to R. Bultmann*, ed. by E. Dinkler, Tübingen 1964, pp. 77-96, of which the English translation under the title "LOGOI SOPHON: On the Gattung of Q," in *Trajectories*, pp. 71-113 represents a considerable enlargement. All references hereafter are to this English translation.

[7] Cf. C. E. Carlston-D. Norlin, "Once More-Statistics and Q," *HTR* 64 (1971), pp. 59-78; see in addition, A. M. Honoré, "A Statistical Study of the Synoptic Problem," *NT* 10 (1968), pp. 59-147.

[8] Cf. S. Schulz, *Q: Die Spruchquelle der Evagelisten*, Zürich 1972, 508 pages; P. Hoffmann, *Studien zur Theologie der Logienquelle*, Münster 1972, 365 pages; cf. also D.

against the Q-Hypothesis and we found that a second source, the Q-Document, must have really existed. In this article we propose to examine the nature of that document and its extent. More precisely we shall ask whether Q circulated in oral or written form, in Aramaic or in Greek, and whether it consisted of one or more units at the time of its utilization. We shall also consider the problem of Q's reconstruction. Since earlier writers, perhaps with the exception of Streeter,[10] have not given reasons for choosing one passage and excluding another from Q, we propose to offer seven procedural principles to cover all cases of the non-Marcan tradition, thus attempting our own reconstruction. We regard this procedure as very important, because recent writers who have dealt with the theology of Q have not paid sufficient attention to the selection and final grouping of the Q-material.

## A. THE NATURE OF THE Q-DOCUMENT

### 1. Written or Oral?

In the earliest phase of the Q-Hypothesis it was generally assumed that Q was a written document. The agreement in wording in parallel passages of considerable extent, and the use of unusual expressions made scholars in the literary critical era decide that it was "highly probable that Q was a written source."[11] However, interest in the Aramaic background during the first half of this century[12] led to attempts to link the origin and transmission of the synoptic tradition to the methods of contemporary rabbinic schools.[13] In the light of the strong ability of the ancient world to learn by heart, and memorize large amounts of oral traditions, as well as the poetic character of most of the dominical sayings, a number of scholars explained the common material in Matthew and Luke on the assumption of a common *oral* tradition. Thus, oral tradition was an integral part of L. Vaganay's solution of the Synoptic Problem,[14] and of W. L. Knox's theory of the one-sheet "tracts";[15] the same is true of M. Dibelius,[16] who spoke of

---

Lührmann, *Die Redaktion der Logienquelle,* Neukirchen 1969; R. A. Edwards, *The Sign of Johan in the Theology of the Evangelists and Q,* London 1971.

[9] "Did Q Exist?" Ἐκκλησία καὶ Θεολογία 1 (1980) 287-327.
[10] *The Four Gospels,* pp. 184f., 283ff.
[11] J. Hawkins, *Horae Synopticae,* Oxford 1909², p. 107 (italics mine).
[12] See above n. 3.
[13] For an extreme approach on this point see B. Gerhardsson, *Memory and Manuscript,* Uppsala 1961; also M. D. Goulder, *Midrash and Lection in Matthew,* London 1974.
[14] *Le Problème Synoptique,* Paris 1954.
[15] *The Sources of the Synoptic Gospels: II. St. Luke and St. Matthew,* Oxford 1957.
[16] *From Tradition to Gospel,* ET, London 1934, p. 67.

## The Nature and Extent of the Q-Document

Q as a layer *(schicht)* or stratum of tradition rather than a writing *(schrift)*, or C. K. Barrett,[17] who seems to accept B. W. Bacon's[18] definition of Q as stratum of tradition, S. Petrie,[19] A. W. Argyle,[20] R. H. Fuller,[21] and more recently of D. Hill.[22] However, it was only J. Jeremias,[23] and after him H. T. Wrege,[24] who produced positive evidence and argued in detail for this solution, while support from statistical analysis was given by T. R. Rosché,[25] who assigns the double tradition to carefully memorized oral materials.

Jeremias' thesis was mainly based upon suggestions made earlier by T. Soiron[26] with regard to the catchword connection as a mnemonic aid in the New Testament era. On examination of seventeen cases in which sometimes the linking-word in Luke is different from that found in Matthew, Jeremias concluded that "the hypothesis that the *entire* sayings material common to Matthew and Luke stems from the same *written* source Q (or sources), cannot be held."[27]

Only quite recently Wrege, one of Jeremias' pupils, has expanded his teacher's theory, making special reference to the Sermon on the Mount. He noticed that wherever a word-for-word, or almost word-for-word agreement between Matthew and Luke is to be found, it is in most cases where there is particularly memorable material (metaphors, short parables, etc.), which could have found a fixed form even in oral tradition.[28]

However, both Jeremias and Wrege's arguments would have proved a written Q an unnecessary hypothesis, only if they had been able to cover the entire double tradition; for in the most characteristic and indisputable

---

[17] "Q: A Re-examination," *ExpT* 54 (1943), pp. 320-23, esp. 320.

[18] Cf. e.g. his "The Nature and Design of Q, the Second Synoptic Source," *HJ* 22 (1924), pp. 674-88, where he stated that "much confusion will be avoided if it be remembered that the symbol Q designates not a source...but only coincident material of Matthew and Luke not found in Mark" (p. 674, n.1).

[19] " 'Q' is only what you Make it," *NT* 3 (1959), pp. 28-33.

[20] "Agreements between Matthew and Luke," *ExpT* 73 (1961), pp. 19-22.

[21] *New Testament in Current Study*, London 1963, p. 88.

[22] *The Gospel of Matthew*, London 1972. Hill speaks of Q as a "layer of tradition partly written and partly oral" (p. 30).

[23] "Zur Hypothese einer schriftlichen Logienquelle", *ZNW* 31 (1932), pp. 147-49.

[24] *Die Überlieferungsgeschichte der Bergpredigt*, Tübingen 1968.

[25] "The Words of Jesus and the Future of the 'Q' Hypothesis," *JBL* 79 (1960), pp. 210-20, esp. p. 219f.

[26] *Die Logia Jesu: Eine literarkritische und literargeschichtliche Untersuchung zum synoptischen Problem*, Münster 1916.

[27] "Zur Hypothese...," p. 149. By underlining the word *entire* (gesamte) Jeremias might have directed his criticism only to part of the sayings material common to Matthew and Luke. In his *New Testament Theology, vol. I: The Proclamation of Jesus*, London 1971, however, he made quite clear that his attack was directed against the entire Q-Hypothesis (pp. 38f.).

[28] *Die Überlieferungsgeschichte...* See also J. Jeremias, *New Testament Theology, I*, p. 38.

section of Q, "John's Question and Jesus' Testimony to the Baptist" (Lk 7.18-35=Mt 11.2-19), such an explanation would hold only for Jesus' answer to John's messengers (Lk 7.22bf. par.), the final parable (Lk 7.31-35 par.) —by no means a short parable - or the climax of Jesus' testimony (Lk 7.28 par). To explain the whole chapter verse by verse on these grounds would hardly be possible, not to mention the agreement in order.[29]

Finally, Rosché came to the conclusion that on statistical analysis the verbal agreements between Matthew and Luke in those sayings usually assigned to Q are less than in those taken from Mark.[30] C. E. Carlston-D. Norlin, however, following earlier suggestions by J. M. Robinson[31] have shown that this conclusion of Rosché's is the result of an error in method present throughout his investigation. They rightly pointed out that, to be reliable, statistics on the double tradition should not be based on an unequal examination of the Triple and Double traditions, as with Rosché (i.e. a. Triple Tradition: $Mt^{Mk}Lk$ against b. Double Tradition (Q?): Mt<—> Lk), but on an examination of both equally (i.e. a. Triple Tradition: $Mt^{Mk}Lk$ against b. Double Tradition (Q?): $Mt^{Q}Lk$).[32] Their statistics in turn proved Rosché's conclusion false and have shown that St. Matthew and St. Luke, "as far as the wording is concerned, used Q at least as conservatively as they used Mark."[33] According to their statistics "the use of Q is even more conservative than the use of Mark, possibly something like 27% more conservative. Since Mark was written it is overwhelmingly probable that Q was."[34]

On the important question of the form in which Q circulated before its use by St. Matthew and St. Luke, W. D. Davies suggests that "the distinction between these forms (written and oral) should not in any case be exaggerated in the first century milieu."[35] Similarly G. N. Stanton regards "the distinction between Q as a written document and Q as a layer or oral tradition with fairly fixed order as comparatively unimportant."[36] This is of course true, but some documentary form has still to be assumed,

---

[29] G. Schille, "Literarische Quellen-hypothesen im Licht der Wahrscheinlichkeitsfrage," *TLZ* 97 (1972), pp. 331-40, tried to overthrow the idea of Q as a written document on different grounds. He argued against the Q-Hypothesis from the divergence of theology in various sayings usually attributed to Q. He seems, however, to ignore the legitimacy of considering Q as consisting of various and sometimes not surprisingly contradictory strata. This phenomenon is also evident elsewhere most notably in Mark.

[30] "The Words of Jesus...".

[31] "Basic Shifts in German Theology," *Interpretation* 16 (1962), pp. 76-97, esp. p. 82, n. 28.

[32] "Once More- Statistics and Q," p. 60.

[33] Ibid., p. 75.

[34] Ibid., p. 77.

[35] *The Setting of The Sermon...*, p. 366.

[36] "On the Christology of Q," in *Christ and Spirit, Festschrift to C. F. D. Moule*, ed. by B. Lindars and S. Smalley, Cambridge 1973, pp. 27-42, esp. p. 27, n.2.

## The Nature and Extent of the Q-Document

if only for the simple reason of lack of sophisticated editorial techniques in the early years of Christian history.[37] For it is extremely difficult to explain how a writer in the first century milieu, such as St. Matthew (or even the School of St. Matthew, or he who had already before the composition of Matthew fused M with Q,[38] could have succeeded in producing the detailed redaction of Mark (and Q) he has with his familiar method of conflation, with only the omission of negligible parts of Q-material,[39] if he had used Q by heart only. This would appear even more difficult, if we take into account that St. Matthew has spoiled in many cases the original order of Q. The same can be said about St. Luke, or the compiler of Proto-Luke.[40] Furthermore, the fact that a number of Q sayings both in Matthew and in Luke[41] are found without any close connection with their context is only explicable, if a written source has been drawn upon. A saying from the oral tradition can hardly come up to a writer's mind, unless it is quite relevant to the context.

Nevertheless, we have to allow the influence of oral tradition both in the pre-canonical circulation of the Q-Document, but mainly at the redactional level, i.e. by the Evangelists themselves. As W. A. Beardslee correctly remarks, "in the early years of Christian history, there seems to have been a great deal of freedom to move back and forth between written and oral tradition."[42] In other words, without disputing Q's existence in a fixed written form, we must allow some influence of the oral tradition between the time of its crystallization and its use by the two Synoptics.[43] It is quite natural that the probability of such an influence is higher towards the end of that period.

---

[37] Cf. W. Marxsen, *The Beginnings of Christology: A Study in Its Problems*, ET, Philadelphia 1969, p. 4.

[38] Cf. K. Stendahl, *The School of St. Matthew*, Uppsala 1954; also J. P. Brown, "The Form of Q Used by Matthew," *NTS* 8 (1961), pp. 27-42, who argues for a combination of Q and M sayings (without the parables) as a form of the Q-Document used by St. Matthew.

[39] On the possible omissions see below section B.

[40] Among these who support this hypothesis first advanced by B. H. Streeter, "Fresh Light on the Synoptic Problem," *HJ* 20 (1921), pp. 103-12 (also *idem, The Four Gospels*, pp. 199-222), and embellished by V. Taylor, *Behind the Third Gospel*, Oxford 1926, are J. Jeremias, H. Schürmann and H. Rehkopf. For the history of this theory and the adherent's views see V. Taylor, *The Passion Narrative of St. Luke,* ed. posthumously by O. E. Evans, Cambridge 1972, pp. 3ff.

[41] Cf. e.g. Lk. 6.39=Mt 15.4; Lk 6.43ff.=Mt 12.33ff.; Lk 11.24ff.=Mt. 12.43ff. etc.

[42] *Literary Criticism of the New Testament,* Philadelphia 1970, p. 73.

[43] J. A. Fitzmyer, "The Priority of Mark and the 'Q' Source in Luke", *Jesus and Man's Hope* vol. I, ed. by D. G. Buttrick (Pittsburgh, 1970), pp. 131-70, is "more inclined to admit this for Luke than for Matthew" (p. 162), but this is quite debatable (see below).

## 2. The Original Language of Q

The question of the original language of Q is of interest, because since Schleiermacher's time it has been alleged to have been Aramaic. In the early decades of this century several eminent scholars were so impressed by the Aramaic element of the Gospels that they suggested our extant Gospels were originally composed in Aramaic and later translated into Greek.[44] However, these theories have never gained wide support, and yet they influenced considerably the studies of Q. Thus, T. W. Manson argued that Q was originally composed in Aramaic, but St. Luke drew from a Greek translation of it which was later revised again with reference to the Aramaic and edited in that form by St. Matthew.[45] One of the strongest arguments for a "translation-hypothesis" with regard to the Q-Document was the existence of some obscurities in the language of Jesus in the Q-passages which were said to be due to mistranslation. F. Bussby, following Manson, was ready on these grounds to state that "a semitic source for part of Q at any rate is inescapable."[46]

However, M. Black on examination of the linguistic peculiarities of the Q material was quite certain that "the most Aramaic element can *prove* is an Aramaic origin, not always translation of an Aramaic original; and *it is the Greek literary factor which has the final word with shaping the Q tradition."*[47] F. C. Grant had earlier dismissed the "translation-hypothesis"

---

[44] Cf. C. C. Torrey, *Our Translated Gospels*, London no date; C. F. Burney, *The Aramaic Origin of the Fourth Gospel,* Oxford 1922.

[45] "The Problem of Aramaic Sources in the Gospels", *ExpT* 47 (1935) 7ff., esp. p. 10; cf. also *idem,* "The Life of Jesus: IV. The Gospel According to St. Matthew", *BJRL* 29 (1946), pp. 4ff.

[46] "Is Q an Aramaic Document?" *ExpT* 65 (1954), pp. 272ff., esp. p. 275; cf. also H. F. D. Sparks, "Some Observations on the Semitic Background of the New Testament," *SNTS* Bulletin II (Oxford, 1963²), pp. 33-42, who noted on the same grounds that "Q cannot have been a single Greek source" (p. 40), see H. Von Soden, *Early Christian Literature,* ET, London 1906, pp. 140ff.

[47] *An Aramaic Approach...,* p. 191; so also H. J. Cadbury, in whose view an "Aramaic original is possible for Q... but the language does not require it either when the gospels agree or when they disagree" *(The Making of Luke-Acts,* London 1958, p. 105). A. W. Argyle, "The Accounts of the Temptations of Jesus in Relation to the Q Hypothesis," *ExpT* 64 (1953), pp. 38, on the other hand, came to the same conclusion but on different grounds: "the fact that Matthew and Luke (in the Temptation story) follow the LXX even where this differs from the Hebrew means that we must either deny that the Q material was originally written in Aramaic or refuse to assign the account of the Temptation story to Q" (p. 382). B. M. Metzger, "Scriptural Quotations in Q Material," *ExpT* 65 (1954), p. 125, however, was quite skeptical about Argyle's "either-or" dichotomy on the ground of the Evangelist's familiarity with LXX no matter whether he was reporting Aramaic accounts. Argyle, "Scriptural Quotations in Q Material," *ExpT* 65 (1954), pp. 258f., retorted with the evidence of other passages from Q, like Lk 10.15; 12.53; 13.27; Mt 11.23; 10.35f.; 7.23, where the citations follow the Hebrew text. However, we should not forget that Argyle forcibly attacked the Q-Hypothesis (see previous ch. "Did Q Exist?"). Arguing in a similar case, Argyle stated: "The Q-

on the basis of the results of Form-Criticism: "the Aramaic must have lain some distance behind."[48]

But the strongest arguments against the "translation-hypothesis" were undoubtedly given by N. Turner. He pointed that of Torrey's three principles for testing the possibility of a translation (namely [i] the Semitic sound of certain passages, [ii] the presence of mistranslations, and [iii] the Semitic idioms) only the second is of real force since the remaining "do no more than to indicate that the author was thinking in Semitic forms or writing in a dialect of Greek which was influenced by Semitic idioms.[49] Therefore, "what is required to be effective is evidence of mistranslation, and there is very little of it."[50] Turner found that the characteristically free Greek μέν...δέ construction, and the "genitive absolute" occur relatively often in Q.[51] Finally, by applying to Q four tests of style of a "good" (i.e. non-translational) Greek,[52] namely [i] the use of co-ordinating particles in second place; [ii] the word-order: subject-object-verb; [iii] the relative frequency of καί and δέ to introduce clauses; and [iv] the insertion of other words between a noun and its definite article, he came to the conclusion that the Q language "offers appreciably from the typical translation Greek of which there are abundant examples in the Septuagint."[53] In general, "the Semitic element is not too pronounced in the sections of Matthew and Luke usually ascribed to Q, and no evidence demands a translation hypothesis."[54] We may, therefore, safely say that Q was a Greek document with only pre-literary connection with Aramaic.[55]

## 3. Number of Sources

The problem of the original language of the Q-Document is inevitably associated with the possible duality or even plurality of sources, so far as the double tradition is concerned. This tradition consists of two sorts of

---

Hypothesis in any of its forms, whether Greek or Aramaic, or a combination of both, is rendered completely superfluous" ("The Methods of the Evangelists and the Q hypothesis," *Theology* 67 (1964), pp. 156f.)

[48] *The Earliest Gospel,* New York 1943, p. 124.
[49] *Grammatical Insights into the New Testament,* Edinburgh 1965, p. 175.
[50] "Q in Recent Thought," *ExpT* 80 (1968), pp. 324-28 esp. 326.
[51] Ibid. ; also *Grammatical Insights...*, p. 177.
[52] "Q in Recent Thought," pp. 326ff.
[53] Ibid., p. 326.
[54] Ibid., p. 328.
[55] Since the Q-Document is very often connected with Syria (cf. P. Vassiliadis, "Acts 18:24 -19:7 and the Q-Document. A Reconsideration of the Provenance, Time, and Author of Q", in *Biblical Hermeneutical Studies,* Thessaloniki 1988, pp. 282-296, in Greek), whether eastern, or western, one might think of Q as written in Syriac. But this possibility, too, has to be excluded on the same ground, namely on the lack of evidence which would require a translation hypothesis.

material;[56] those passages showing close agreement in the two major Synoptics, and those showing considerable variation. This variation in the degree of agreements has been from time an argument against derivation from a single written source. Furthermore, scholars have tended, especially in the Literary-Critical era, to give different and sometimes contradictory answers. V. Taylor, therefore, rightly pointed out that no "further progress can be made in working out the Q hypothesis until scholars can come to a more general agreement as to the causes of this perplexing phenomenon."[57] Harnack, after a careful literary analysis resulting in a far more restricted document than that presupposed by previous scholars, decided for a single document, explaining the differences as *editorial modifications*.[58] Others came to the conclusion that St. Matthew and St. Luke used *different recensions* of the same document; thus, C. S. Patton wrote: "Q would always be growing by the aid of oral tradition; and if Q was written before Mark there was ample time, say twenty five years at least before it was used by St. Matthew and St. Luke for the two recensions, circulating in different communities and perhaps originally shaped to suit the needs of different readers, to acquire many dissimilar features."[59] W. Haupt similarly spoke of *successive editions* of Q ($Q^1$, $Q^2$, $Q^3$, etc.).[60] Streeter's suggestion that *parallel versions* better explains away the existing disagreements between Matthew and Luke in the double tradition, was also accepted by T. W. Manson. They both distinguished Q from M (special source of Matthew) and L (special source of Luke).[61]

W. Bussmann,[62] however, arguing from these disagreements thought that he was able to split up Q into two distinct sources, T and R. On his analysis, the former was a Greek document which both Matthew and Luke were dependent upon, whereas the latter was an Aramaic original of which both the evangelists had, or had made, separate Greek versions.[63] By thus making Q a *composite document* and explaining the differences of the Matthaean and Lucan text as "translation variants", Bussmann nearly abandoned the Q-Hypothesis. Of course "the phenomena prove nothing more than ultimate common derivation and do not preclude intermediate

---

[56] A third division where the differences between Matthew and Luke are very great is usually excluded from Q: cf. A. Harnack, *The Sayings,* pp. 118-26; also V. Taylor, "The Order of Q," *JTS* n.s. 4 (1953), p. 27-35 esp. p. 27.

[57] "The Elusive Q," *ExpT* 46 (1934), pp. 68-74, esp. p. 71.

[58] *The Sayings,* pp. 1ff.

[59] *Sources of the Synoptic Gospels,* New York 1915, pp. 126f.

[60] *Worte Jesu und Gemeindeüberlieferung: Eine Untersuchung zur Quellengeschichte der Synopse,* Leipzig 1913; cf. also P. Wernle, who differentiated Q from Q', Q'', etc. on the ground that the original document consisted exclusively of brief logia *(Die Synoptische Frage,* Freiburg 1899, p. 255).

[61] B. H. Streeter, *The Four Gospels,* pp. 238ff.; T. W. Manson, *The Sayings,* p. 21.

[62] *Synoptische Studien: II Zur Redenquelle,* Halle 1929, pp. 110-56.

[63] Cf. also H. von Soden, *Early Christian Literature,* p. 140.

redactorial stages or a plurality of common sources."[64] This view continues to be influential; some scholars still think of "several common sources rather than of one written document".[65] However, as B. S. Easton stated, the hypothesis for a *single* written source, though cannot be vigorously proved, "it is wholly likely, particularly as dividing into two or more documents simply leads to needless complexity."[66] Bussmann's special case of Q as a composite document, was considered by Manson and found to be "not convincing", when tested by the application of the rule Bussmann himself used for the Q-Document to another field.[67] He suggested in turn that the problem of divergences could be better solved "by recognition of the possibility of the overlapping of sources and so transferring passages where verbal agreements between Matthew and Luke is small, from Q to M or L."[68] Unfortunately Manson did not remain consistent with his own principles, since he assigned to Q almost all the passages attributed by Bussmann to his document R. In any case, this is matter of reconstruction with which we shall be concerned below. M. Black, however, dealt with Bussmann's 122 alleged "translation variants", and although he admitted that there was some evidence of an Aramaic origin, he was nevertheless confident that Q, especially in Matthew, "is not just a translation; *it is a Greek literary composition.*"[69]

On the other hand, as H. Koester[70] has shown, a living free tradition of Jesus' sayings was a strong factor in the Church as late as the first half of the second century, and if so, it would not be surprising if St. Matthew, or St. Luke, in some eases preferred versions current in their local churches in place of those found in the Q-Document.

---

[64] H. J. Cadbury, *The Making,* p.104.

[65] I. H. Marshall, *Luke: Historian and Theologian,* Exeter 1970, p. 61; a similar implication was made by F. G. Dowing, "Towards the Rehabilitation of Q," *NTS* 11 (1965), 170-81, esp. p. 180. Among other earlier adherents of a divided Q, see E. de W. Burton, *Principles of Literary Criticism and the Synoptic Problem,* Chicago 1904, who argued that the Q material was derived from two documents; so also W. L. Knox, who stated: "the evidence of a single document Q as a source for all, or most of the material common to Matthew and Luke is by no means conclusive" *(The Sources,* p. 45). For his part, Knox postulated numerous "one-sheet-tracts", as common sources of Matthew and Luke.

[66] *The Gospel according to St. Luke,* Edinburgh 1926, p. xx. Fitzmyer too, regards - with some reservation - the distinction of two written forms of Q as acceptable hypothesis only if it means that "a passage in the written source was from time to time replaced by a better form of the same story or sayings which was derived from oral tradition. So, revised, the Q source might have been used at different times by St. Matthew and St. Luke" ("The Priority...," p. 154).

[67] Manson compared Lk 7.24-28, 31-35 par. of Bussmann's T source with Daniel 7.9-14 where there is a Greek translation by both LXX and Theodotion. The result had shown that T was a translation (!) whereas Bussmann considered it as Greek *(The Sayings,* pp. 20ff.).

[68] Ibid., p. 21.

[69] *An Aramaic Approach,* p. 181.

[70] *Synoptische Überlieferung bei den apostolischen Vätern,* Berlin 1957.

In the statistical field Honoré found "nothing to show that Q was a single document. At best one might think of a collection of source material arranged in no particular order."[71] His conclusion, however, was drawn from part III of his investigation; but Part III deals with "The Sequence of the Sections," to which Taylor had already given the answer.[72] This was realized by Carlston and Norlin who on their analysis, reverse the result to: "Q is not a collection of source material arranged in no particular order...but a single document."[73]

We accept this conclusion not for the entire non-Marcan material of the Synoptic tradition, since it is generally agreed that St. Matthew and St. Luke had access to special traditions too, but for the bulk of the Double tradition. Whether now every passage of this tradition belonged to the Q-Document will be examined in the next section in which we shall attempt our own reconstruction. For if Q *was a single written Greek document* at the stage of its utilization by St. Matthew and St. Luke, we may legitimately ask about its original extent, order, and, as far as possible, wording of the material it contained.

## B. THE RECONSTRUCTION OF THE Q-DOCUMENT

*1. The Present State of the Debate*

If we are to consider Q as a written document, then any attempt to restore it in its original extent, wording and order, must be based mainly on the arguments which have established it as a written document.

Harnack, in fact, sought to restore the original Greek text of Q,[74] but his only guide was the editorial modifications made by the two evangelists.[75] F. C. Burkitt reviewing his book made some valuable comments on the

---

[71] "A Statistical Study of the Synoptic Problem," *NT* 10 (1968), pp. 59-147, esp. p. 134.

[72] See further discussion in my article "Did Q Exist?"

[73] "Once More...," pp. 78, 74-76. Most recently J. C. O'Neill, "The Synoptic Problem," *NTS* 21 (1975) pp. 273-85, has revived the Lessing Hypothesis in a more elaborate form. He advanced the hypothesis that "our Greek Gospels according to Matthew, Mark, and Luke incorporate independent translations from Hebrew or Aramaic of a common document" (p. 273). In his view, the procedure took place in four stages. As a result, O'Neill rejected the view that "Q ever existed as one connected document independently employed by St. Luke; rather they seem to be drawing on a number of different sources with different histories of transmission, and different translators" (p. 284). The main reasons, according to O'Neill, are two: first, that "they almost never set down the paragraphs they share in the same order" (ibid.), and second, that they show signs of translation -Greek. However, as we have seen, both reasons have been effectively refuted by V. Taylor, and M. Black-N. Turner respectively (see above).

[74] *The Sayings*, pp. 127-46.

[75] Ibid., pp. 1ff.

hazards of such a task.[76] Since then the majority of scholars have confined themselves to indicating the sections where Q has been used.[77] However, fully agreed results have not been reached for the simple reason that the attempts were sufficiently governed by clear reliable criteria. It is certainly true that an approximate reconstruction is possible, but it must be attempted before further progress can be made.

Streeter was the first who realized that most of the earlier reconstructions had set out from "false premises."[78] He himself attached particular importance to the following three points: (i) the probability of different versions for some widely divergent sections; (ii) the certainty that some passages have been preserved either in Matthew or in Luke alone; and (iii) the possibility that some short sayings, especially those in a proverbial form, might have been handed down by word of mouth, and therefore may not stem from Q.[79] His further criteria were; (iv) the originality of the Lucan order so far as the Q material is concerned;[80] (v) the arrangement of Luke's central section (9.51ff.) in alternate blocks;[81] (vi) St. Matthew's tendency to conflate Q with his special source (M) and Mark;[82] and of course (vii) the theological ideas of these two evangelists.[83] Finally, Streeter accepted that neither St. Matthew nor St. Luke omitted many Q passages,[84] and thus he produced a reconstruction of the Q-Document, which was more solidly based and more detailed than previous attempts. This comprised 273 verses, with the original form of the various sayings more often preserved in Luke.[85]

With regard to this particular problem, namely which of the two later Synoptic Gospels has preserved the original Q-Document more accurately, the majority of scholars in the first stage of the Q-Hypothesis preferred Matthew either under the influence of Papias' notice, or because of the alleged Aramaisms in it. The first to consider the Lucan version as the more original were A. Wright, J. A. Robinson, and H. von Soden. As to the order of Q it is noteworthy that of the sixteen reconstructions given by J.

---

[76] "The Lost Source of our Lord's Sayings," *JTS* 8 (1907), pp. 454-59. Burkitt put the puzzling question: "What would Mark have been if it had been lost?" (p. 456).

[77] It is worth noting that S. Schulz has recently published the Greek text of Q with a German translation, as they appear in the Synopses of Huck and Wilckens *(Griechisch-Deutsche Synopse de Q-Überlieferungen,* Zürich, 1972.

[78] Streeter drew attention to this in his article "Fresh Light...," but his arguments are more fully presented in *The Four Gospels* (see the following notes).

[79] *The Four Gospels,* pp. 184f.

[80] Ibid., pp. 273ff.

[81] Ibid., pp. 278ff.

[82] Ibid., pp. 281ff.

[83] Ibid., p. 290.

[84] Ibid., p. 289.

[85] Ibid., p. 291. Apart from Streeter, T. W. Manson also produced his own reconstruction, which in essential points was similar to his *(The Sayings,* pp. 21ff.).

Moffatt,[86] only those by von Soden, B. Weiss, O. Holtzmann and Harnack[87] follow the Lucan order. Von Soden, in particular, was the first, so far as I know, to raise the question of the originality of the Lucan order: "if we place together those passages in Luke that have closed parallels in Matthew but are foreign to Mark, we find that we have a collection of sayings systematically arranged according to distinct leading ideas."[88]

The problem seemed to have been settled by Streeter who drew attention to St. Matthew's rearrangement of the Marcan order. "If, therefore, he (St. Matthew) completely disregards the order of a document relating a series of events...he would be more indifferent to the original order of a document which was plainly only a loose collection of sayings."[89] He further pointed to St. Matthew's method of rearranging his material deliberately in discourses according to leading ideas.[90] With the publication of Streeter's influential *Four Gospels*, as well as with the major contributions of W. Bussmann[91] and T. W. Manson,[92] the originality of the Lucan order received strong support, and from that time onwards the formula has usually run as follows: "Prefer Luke for the order of Q, prefer Matthew for its wording."[93]

Since the time of Streeter, however, some progress has been made and in some respects the picture of Q has altered. Thus, there are nowadays useful insights available, which are a better guide for determining the approximate extent and wording of the original document. Quite apart from V. Taylor's suggestions as to how the Q order is to be detected,

---

[86] *An Introduction to the Literature of the New Testament*, Edinburgh 1911, pp. 197ff.

[87] Harnack's reference to the Lucan order in not quite clear; for despite his preference to the Lucan order in the reconstruction *(The Sayings*, pp. 127ff.; cf. also J. Moffatt, *op. cit.*, p. 200), in the text insisted that "St. Matthew has preserved the order of the source more faithfully than St. Luke" *(The Sayings...*, p. 180).

[88] *Early Christian Literature*, p. 129. J. Hawkins found this argument interesting but not convincing; he asked; "if it were so, would the eschatological warnings be found partly in Lk 12.35ff., and partly in Lk 17.24ff?" ("Probabilities as to the So-Called double Tradition of St. Matthew and St. Luke," in *Oxford Studies in the Synoptic Problem*, ed. by W. Sanday, Oxford 1911, hereafter *OSSP*, pp. 91-138, esp. p. 120, n.2).

[89] "The Original Order of Q," in *OSSP*, pp. 141-164, esp. pp. 145f.

[90] Ibid., p. 151. Streeter concluded that "when St. Luke claimed to write καθεξῆς he meant in the chronological order as determined from his original authorities" (p. 164). Matthew has been arranged so far as the sayings material are concerned in five great discourse sections (chs. 5-7; 9.37-10.42; 13.1-52; ch. 18; chs. 23-25), all concluding with the formula καὶ ἐγένετο ὅτε ἐτέλεσεν ὁ Ἰησοῦς. To these one must add ch. 11 which because of its narrative introduction was left out. St. Luke, on the other hand, has arranged his non-Marcan material in the so called "Small" and "Great Insertions" (Lk 6.20-8.3; and 9.51-18.14).

[91] *Synoptischen Studien II.*

[92] *The Sayings of Jesus.*

[93] Cf. F. C. Grant, *The Gospels: Their Origin and their Growth*, London 1957, p. 58. C. K. Barrett had in fact reopened the question, but this was effectively closed by V. Taylor (see previous ch. "Did Q Exist?").

Rosché[94] has pointed out, and C. E. Carlston-D. Norlin have confirmed it statistically,[95] that both St. Luke and St. Matthew have treated more conservatively the sayings material.[96] Carlston and Norlin, in addition, noted that St. Luke "used Q more freely in the earlier than in the later part of his work."[97] Earlier in this century J. M. C. Crum has discerned in those passages generally attributed to Q a frequent reference to the nature and to the use of the language of the countryside in Q.[98]

Any attempt, therefore, to detect the approximate extent of Q, which in view of the originality of the Lucan order will eventually lead to an approximate restoration of the original Q- Document, must be based on certain procedural principles derived from all the above criteria plus the positive arguments that established Q as a written document.[99]

However, the Q-Document is now lost and it can be reconstructed only from the non-Marcan material of Matthew and Luke. But have all sections of Q been preserved in Matthew and Luke? To this Harnack, Streeter and Manson have answered "yes,"[100] but A. Resch "no."[101] The latter view has been recently revived by Honoré, who argued that there was a great deal of Q material which neither St. Matthew nor St. Luke copied.[102] With the remark that the first and third Synoptists "presumably did not regard Q as more important than Mark,"[103] and finding that the net taking by the two Synoptists was roughly 60% of the original document, he concluded that "the remaining 40% some 8,000 words has been lost to us."[104] Therefore,

---

[94] "The Words of Jesus...," pp. 210ff.

[95] "Once More...," p. 68.

[96] This applies not only to the words attributed to Jesus, as R. A. Edwards, *The Saying of John in the Theology of the Evangelists and Q*, London 1971, thinks (p. 37), but to every sayings; in fact the non-Dominical sayings were treated more conservatively because "in some cases the words of Jesus often had to be modified for new situations precisely because they were more important" (Carlston-Norlin, "Once More...," p. 68).

[97] Ibid., p. 78. "The case with Matthew," they point, "is highly uncertain", (ibid.).

[98] *The Original Jerusalem Gospel*, Cambridge 1927, pp. 49ff. H. Schürmann, "Sprachliche Reminiszenzen an abgeänderte oder ausgelassene Bestandteile der Spruchsammlung im Lk. und Mt.," *NTS* 6 (1960), pp. 193ff. has suggested that the methodology for discovering the exact wording and extent of Q should be directed toward what he calls "linguistic reminiscences", a criterion derived from the way in which St. Matthew and St. Luke altered Mark in using it. This criterion, however, is extremely precarious, and Schürmann's final conclusion, that St. Matthew and St. Luke read certain sections of Q but omitted them, may be used only with caution.

[99] See P. Vassiliadis, "Did Q Exist?".

[100] Harnack, *The Sayings*, pp. 187ff.; Streeter, *The Four Gospels*, pp. 289ff.; Manson, *The Sayings*, p. 16; cf. also K. Lake, "The Date of Q," *Exp* 7th ser. I (1909), pp. 494-507, who argues that from St. Matthew and St. Luke's treatment of Mark "we have probably got the greater part of Q in the two Gospels" (p. 498).

[101] *Die Logia Jesu*, Leipzig 1898.

[102] "A Statistical Study...," p. 135.

[103] Ibid., p. 134.

[104] Ibid., p. 135.

the original "Q was between 22,720 and 17,040 words,"[105] or in a rough estimate about 20,000 words, *i.e.* five times as long as it is usually assumed. Carlston-Norlin, however, rightly points out that Honoré's statistics were based on the assumption that St. Matthew and St. Luke "were equally interested in sayings-matter and in narrative material, which we now know not to have been the case."[106] In their view "a more reasonable way of estimating Q's length is by assuming that (roughly speaking) St. Matthew and St. Luke used all available sayings-material (from either Mark of Q) in another."[107] They, thus, reckoned Q to have consisted of 8.000 words, *i.e.* only twice as long as in Manson's reconstruction, but they concede that this must be a very tentative conclusion. Indeed, statistics in this particular case are very precarious, since they cannot but ignore the exact circumstances under which a writing such as Matthew, or Luke has come into existence, not to mention that they take the omissions from Mark as deliberate. Moreover, they are unable to distinguish between Q and other possible sources (M, L, or even oral tradition). O. Linton, on the other hand, has recently argued on examination of a number of relevant passages that the Q-Document "contained only part of the Q material and also Marcan material."[108] His last point, however, is not sufficiently documented.

In any case, if we are to depart from Harnack and Streeter's conclusion that no substantial sections from Q have been omitted by both St. Matthew and St. Luke —this point cannot be held today with the assurance with which it was held in the past, especially in view of the possibility of Q's heretical orientation[109]—all we can say is that only a small amount of Q- sayings has been lost to us. But if the greater part of the Q matter has been preserved in Matthew or in Luke in one or in another way, it is quite likely, as we know from the editing of Mark by St. Matthew and St. Luke, that some parts have been preserved only by one of them. Streeter insisted that "the probability is high that the passages of Luke that we can identify as Q represent that document, not only approximately in its original

---

[105] Ibid., p. 134.

[106] "Once More...," p. 76; cf. also W. Bussmann, *Synoptische Studien II,* pp. 106-109.

[107] "Once More...," p. 76.

[108] "The Q-Problem Reconsidered," in *Studies in N.T. and Early Christian Literature, Festschrift to A. P. Wikgren,* ed. by D. E. Aune, Leiden 1972, pp. 43-59, esp. p. 59. H. T. Fowler, "Paul, Q, and the Jerusalem Church," *JBL* 43 (1924), pp. 9-14, is another scholar who suggested that the Q-Document contained "some Marcan logia", too, (p. 10).

[109] See further discussion in my *The Q-Document Hypothesis;* A. F. J. Klijn, *An Introduction to the New Testament,* Leiden 1967, *e.g.* wonders "whether Q contained more about John the Baptist" (p. 20), and comes to the conclusion that "there is no reason to suppose that both (St. Matthew and St. Luke) included the whole of Q in their writings" (ibid.).

order, but very nearly in its original extent."[110] R. H. Hiers, on the other hand, has recently suggested that St. Luke probably "utilized less Q than did St. Matthew. In that case, one might expect that at least some of the "M" traditions were actually derived from Q."[111] However, this is a matter of reconstruction to the principles of which we now turn.

## 2. Principles for Reconstruction of the Q-Document.

The procedural principles for restoring the Q-Document have to deal with different kinds of Q-material: (A) Those sections of the Double Tradition which occur in Matthew and Luke in almost the same form *(Principle 1)*; (B) Those which show a slight variation between Matthew and Luke, and these are mainly larger units of either narrative or discourse material *(Principles 2,3,4,5)*; (C) Those which show considerable disagreement between Matthew and Luke, and therefore the probability that they stem from Q is less certain *(Principle 6)*; and (D) those which occur only in one of the two gospels, being either completely absent from, or preserved in a different version in, the other; for these are good reasons to have stood in the original Q-Document, despite their conjectural character *(Principle 7)*.[112]

The Q sections detected by principles 1-5 constitute the core of the Q-Document which any critical investigation and conclusion must be bases upon, whereas principles 6 and 7 can provide only extra evidence for secondary characteristics.

PRINCIPLE 1: (a) All extensive or consecutive sayings in Matthew and Luke which show an almost verbatim agreement in wording *quite certainly* belong to Q. (b) Short apophthegms or sayings of a proverbial character, especially those found in a different context in Matthew and Luke should be excluded as possibly due to the oral tradition. (c) Wherever a divergence in order between Matthew and Luke is to be found in the components of these units of closely agreeing material the Lucan order must be preferred.

---

[110] *The Four Gospels*, p. 291. G. D. Castor, "The Relation of Mark to the Source Q," *JBL* 31 (1912), pp. 82-91, was among those who had earlier attributed to Q certain Lucan material not found in Matthew.

[111] "The Problem of the Delay of the Parousia in Luke-Acts," *NTS* 20 (1974), pp. 145-155, esp. p. 147, n. 3.

[112] A. Polag, *Der Umfang der Logienquelle,* Trier 1966, attempted to reconstruct Q from a different angle, namely by indicating in the passages concerned the degree of probability of their stemming from Q. Having no doubt about those passages in Matthew and Luke which agree almost verbatim, Polag considered the following three cases: (i) those verses with small verbal agreement (pp. 14-52); (ii) the special matter of Matthew and Luke (pp. 53-105); and (iii) those verses which Matthew and Luke have in parallel with Mark (pp. 106-122). His main criteria were Schürmann's linguistic reminiscences (see above, n. 98), and the context of Q. Our attempt in what follows, is a further step toward the final solution of this important issue.

PRINCIPLE 2: All large units of the double tradition with no close agreement in their narrative parts, but which agree verbatim or almost verbatim in their sayings matter, *almost certainly* belong to Q.

PRINCIPLE 3: All extensive discourses in Luke with their components found in Matthew in a slightly or even quite modified form, but in the same overall context as in Luke, *almost certainly* belong to Q.

PRINCIPLE 4: Wherever a unit similar to , or double of, an already existing Marcan unit is to be found in only Matthew or Luke alone, this unit *almost certainly* belongs to Q, if components of it are also scattered in the other Gospel in a parallel or conflated form.

PRINCIPLE 5: Wherever both Matthew and Luke agree in diverging from a Marcan section, we have *almost certainly* to do with a Q passage.

PRINCIPLE 6: Those semi-extensive sections of the double tradition although they do not disagree completely nevertheless show considerable variation are *likely* to stem from the Q-Document, if (a) they do not break the original order of Q (as this was examined by Taylor), (b) they can fit in the context of the document when restored by the above principles (1-5), and (c) there are good reasons to account for their variation.

PRINCIPLE 7: In the special material of Luke or Matthew which is either without parallel, or exists in a different version, in the other, only those passages which fulfill some of the following conditions seem *likely* to stem from Q: (a) they have to do with components of either a text assigned to Q by principles 1-6; or a major unit of the document reconstructed so far; (b) they accord with the theological ideas of the Q-Document as reconstructed using principles 1-6; (c) they accord with the country-life language of Q; (d) they do not show any sign of editorial activity; (e) there are good reasons for the other Synoptist to have omitted them; (f) they fall into the Q-blocks of the so-called Great Insertion of Luke (9.51 - 18.14).[113]

---

[113] St. Luke seems to have arranged his Marcan and non-Marcan material apart from the first and last chapters of his work, in alternate blocks: (a) Lk 4.31- 6.19 (Marcan); (b) 6.20- 8.3 (non-Marcan); (c) 8.4-9.50 (Marcan); (d) 9.51-18.14 (non-Marcan); (e) 18.15-43 (Marcan); (f) 19.1-27 (non-Marcan); (g) 19.28-21.19 (Marcan). The same is true for the arrangement of the Q and non-Q material in the so-called "Small Insertion": (a) Lk 6.20- 7.10 (Q); (b) 7.11-17 (non-Q); (c) 7.18-35 (Q); (d) 7.36-8.3 (non-Q). But Q-sections detected by principles 1-5 seem to have been arranged in blocks in the so-called "Great Insertion", too. Cf. Lk 9.56-10.24; 11.9-12.46; 17.22-37, with only the parables of the Mustard Seed and Leaven (13.18-21, and the Lament over Jerusalem (13.34f.), being left out.

This view, however, namely that St. Luke followed in the "Great Insertion" the order of the Q-Document seems to have been challenged among others by C.F. Evans, "The Central Section of St. Luke's Gospel", in *Studies in the Gospels: Essays in Memory of R. H. Lightfoot*, ed. by D. E. Nineham (Oxford, 1955), pp. 37-53, and W. C. Robinson, "The Theological Context for Interpreting Luke's Travel Narrative (ix 51ff.)", *JBL* 79 (1960), pp. 20-30. The former has produced evidence that the Lucan Travel Narrative was

According to the principle (1a) the following verses from the double tradition are assigned to Q: Lk 3.7-9=Mt 3.7-10; Lk 3.16bf.=Mt 3.11f.; Lk 7.31-35=Mt 11.16-19; Lk 9.57-60=Mt 8.19-22; Lk 10.13-15=Mt 11.21-23a; Lk 10.21-24=Mt 11.25-27, 13.16f. (1c); Lk 11.9-13=Mt 7.7-11; Lk 11.29-32=Mt 12.39-42 (1c); Lk 12.39-46=Mt 24.43-51a; Lk 12.22-34=Mt 6.25-31, 19-21 (1c);[114] Lk 13.34f.=Mt 23.37-39.

On the other hand, according to (1b) the following verses must be excluded from Q; Lk 6.39=Mt 5.14; Lk 6.40=Mt 10.24f.; Lk 11.34=Mt 6.22f.; Lk 12.34=Mt 6.21; Lk 12.28a=Mt 8.12b (= 24.51b); Lk 13.30=Mt 20.16 (cf. 29.30=Mk 10.31); Lk 14.11 (=18.14b)=Mt 18.4 (23.12); Lk 16.13=Mt 6.24; (cf. Lk 17.33=Mt 10.39); Lk 19.26= Mt 25.29.

According to principle 2 we may assign to Q the following passages: Lk 4.1-13=Mt 4.1-11;[115] Lk 7.1b-10=Mt 8.5-10.13; Lk 7.18-28=Mt 11.2-11; on the other hand the parable of the Talents/Pounds (Lk 19.11-24=Mt 25.14-30), and the parable of the Great Supper (Lk 14.5-24=Mt 22.1-10) must be excluded - at least on this principle - as evidencing insufficient verbal agreement in their sayings matter.[116]

According to principle 3 the following discourses of the double tradition are to be assigned to Q: The Sermon on the Plain/Mount (Lk 6.20-7.1a par); the Denunciation of the Scribes and Pharisees (Lk 11.39-52 par); and the Exhortation to Fearless Confession (Lk 12.2-13 par).

---

arranged by the author in the pattern of Deuteronomy; this, of course, implies that the guiding factor in the order of the material concerned was not the actual order of St. Luke's sources but the similarity of verbal expressions between Deuteronomy and the material available. The latter argued that this section (Lk. ix 51ff.) "was arranged by the final editor author of Luke-Acts in accord with his view of Heilsgeschichte, which he seems to have conceived as a "way" (p. 20); this view also implies that "the final editor/author" did not take the original order of Q seriously into account.

Nevertheless, in view of the evidence that St. Luke kept throughout his Gospel the original order of Q, as well as the fact that the Marcan and Q material fall generally into distinct blocks, the above criterion still stands strong.

[114] Lk 12.32 is missing from Matthew, and Lk 12.33 differs slightly from its parallel; but the difference is clearly the result of the Matthaean hand.

[115] D. Lührmann, *Die Redaktion der Logienquelle*, Neukirchen 1969, suggests that the Temptation story does not stem from Q but belongs to the evangelist's special material (p. 56). Indeed this story differs widely from the rest of the Q material (cf. the use of LXX, and the title υἱός τοῦ Θεοῦ) but at least on literary grounds it must belong to Q, unless the verbal agreement is a coincidence. Moreover, P. Pokorny defends the story's connection with Q, on the ground of the theological relation between the Temptation and the basic tradition of the Sermon on the Plain Mount ("Die Worte Jesu der Logienquelle im Lichte des zeitgenössischen Judentums" *Kairos* IX (1969), pp. 172-80; also *idem*, "The Temptation Stories and their Intention", *NTS* 20 (1974), pp. 115-27, esp. p. 126, n. 3). A further evidence for the story's connection with Q is also, in his view, the fact that all three dialogues we have in Q, namely the Temptations (Lk 4.1ff. par.), the Centurion's Servant (Lk. vii 1b ff. par.), and the Beelzebul Controversy (Lk 11.14ff. par.), "concern authority over devil spirits and over Devil" ("The Temptation...", p. 122, n. 5).

[116] Cf. also principle 7.

According to principle 4 we may attribute to Q the following sections: The second Sending-Out Discourse in Luke (10.1-12 par), and the second Eschatological Discourse in Luke (17.22-37 par); but on the other hand, we must reject any connection of Q with the following sections; the Baptism story in Lk. 3.21f.;[117] the Rejection at Nazareth in Lk 4.16-30;[118] the Anointing in the House of a Pharisee in Lk 7.36ff.; the Great Commandment in Lk 10.25ff.; and finally various passages from the Passion Narrative.[119]

According to principle 5, quite apart from Lk 3.16f. par, and Lk 4.1ff. par. which have already been assigned to Q, the following sections must also stem from Q: The Beelzebul Controversy (Lk 11.14-26=Mt 12.22-30, 43-45); and the parables of the Mustard Seed and Leaven (Lk 13.18-21=Mt 13.31-33).[120] On the other hand, we must exclude on the same principle the saying on Offenses (Lk 17.1f.=Mt 18.6), and the saying about the Twelve Thrones (Lk 22.28-30=Mt 19.28).[121]

According to principle 6 the only passages from the considerably diverging double tradition which are likely to have stood in Q are: The Divisions in the Households (Lk 12. 49, 51-53=Mt 10.34-36), and the Lord's

---

[117] Since Streeter, *The Four Gospels*, p. 188, many scholars have inclined to derive the Baptism story in Luke from Q (cf. *e.g.* V. Taylor, "The Order of Q", pp. 27ff.), mainly because of the D variant of v. 22 υἱός μου εἶ σύ ἐγώ σήμερον γεγέννηκά σε. H. Conzelmann, *The Theology of St. Luke* , ET. London 1960); rejected the originality of this variant (p. 21, n. 4), and more recently G. D. Kilpatrick has stated that even if the D reading was the original there is nothing to suggest that it was taken from Q ("The Gentiles and the Strata of Luke," in *Verborum Veritas, Festschrift für G. Stählin*, Wuppertal 1970, pp. 83-88, esp. p. 83).

[118] H. Schürmann, "Zur Nazareth-Perikope Lk. 4.16-30," in *Mélanges Bibliques en hommage au R. P. Béda Rigaux*, Gembloux 1970, pp. 185-205, argued that Lk 4.16-30 stems from Q because of the use of Is. lxi, but his argument is not completely convincing (so G. N. Stanton, "On the Christology of Q," pp. 30f.)

[119] F. C. Burkitt, *The Gospel History and its Transmission*, Edinburgh 1906, suggested that "Q contained a story of the passion" (p. 135); cf. also B. W. Bacon, *Studies in Matthew*, New Haven 1930, p. 115; and E. Hirsch, *Frühgeschichte des Evangeliums: II Die Vorlagen des Lukas und das Sondergut des Matthäus*, Tübingen 1941, who suggested without conviction that Lk. 22.48,62,64,69,70; 24.47 stem from Q-Document (pp. 245ff.). In fact, though Matthew and Luke depart from Mark in the Passion story, there is not a single case in which they agree.

[120] It has been suggested, among others by C. F. Burney, *The Poetry of our Lord* (Oxford, 1925), that Mt. x 18-22 stood in Q and that St. Mark transferred it in the eschatological discourse (ch. xiii) - in the Matthaean context the logion fits better (pp. 8f, 118ff.). For an alternative solution to this particular problem see P. Vassiliadis, "Behind Mark: Towards a Written Source," *NTS* 20 (1974), pp. 155-60. Similarly, R. H. Hiers, "The Problem of the Delay of the Parousia in Luke-Acts," *NTS* 20 (1974), pp. 145-55, argues from St. Luke's attitude toward the delay of the Parousia that Mt 23 "could have been in Q... (but) deliberately omitted by St. Luke" (p. 147). In that case, if Mt 10.18-22 really stood in Q, there is no reason why Mt 10.23 should not; which means that Burney's argument looses weight.

[121] Mt 21.44 is due to a textual assimilation with Lk 20.18. On the other hand Mt 16.2f. (=Lk 12.54-56) is not original being absent from our earliest MSS.

Prayer (Lk 11.2-4=Mt 6.9-13). The possibility for the former is higher than for the latter.[122]

Finally, according to principle 7 the following passages from the special material of Luke and Matthew might also have stood in Q: Lk 9.60b-62;[123] Lk 10.9f.; Lk 11.27f.; Lk 12.32-38; Lk 12.54-56; Lk 13.23-30; Lk 21.34-36; Mt 10.16b; Mt 11.12f. (cf. Lk. 16.16).[124]

Having no doubt about the original *order* —Luke is overwhelmingly acknowledged to have preserved it more accurately—the only thing to be determined is the original *wording*. There is no real difficulty for those passages detected by the first principle. The small differences are more or less due to the theological preoccupation of the evangelists themselves, and therefore can easily be eliminated. This is also the case for all the passages detected by principles 2-5. In general Luke seems to give more sayings in the original than Matthew, but Streeter's readiness to generalize the originality of Luke so far as the wording of Q is concerned[125] can hardly be maintained nowadays. He was no doubt so preoccupied with the idea that Proto-Luke could provide a further source for discovering the Historical Jesus, that he had no other option but to decide in favor of the originality of the Lucan tradition. However, this issue is still a matter of discussion.[126] With regard, further, to those passages detected by principle 6, these apparently show an expansion of the original form in Matthew, but this does not rule out the possibility of an editorial hand in the Lucan version. Finally, the original wording for those passages detected by the last principle can only be a matter of conjecture; nevertheless both Luke and Matthew do not seem to depart considerably from the original Q.

## C. CONCLUSIONS

From the investigation so far the following points have emerged:

---

[122] Streeter, *The Four Gospels*, pp. 275ff., suggested that St. Matthew and St. Luke had access to different traditions (M and L).

[123] J. M. Robinson, "Basic Shifts...," suggests that Lk. 3.2b belonged to Q, too (p. 83). K. Stendahl, however, in a private correspondence with M. J. Suggs, *Wisdom, Christology, and Law in Matthew's Gospel*, Massachusetts 1970, p. 12, n. 21, seems to reject his suggestions.

[124] Mt. 11.28-30 is unlikely to stem from Q unless we take wisdom motives to be prominent in the Q-Document (on this see below);

[125] *The Four Gospels*, pp. 199ff.

[126] J. P. Brown, "The Form of Q Used by Matthew", argued that the form of Q used by St. Luke ($Q^{Lk}$) was more original than the form used by St. Matthew and St. Mark; so also J. Lambrecht, "Die Logia-Quellen von Markus 13," *Biblica* 47 (1966), pp. 321-60. On the other hand, C. Michaelis, "Die π-Alliteration der Subjectworte der ersten 4 Seligpreisungen in Mt. v 3-6 und Ihre Bedeutung für den Aufbau der Seligpreisungen bei Mt. -Lk. und in Q," *NT* 10 (1968), pp. 148-61, insists that the preservation in Matthew of both the π-Alliteration and the parting in the first strophe of Beatitudes (v 3-6) suggests that St. Matthew rather than St. Luke kept the form and structure of Q.

1. The Q-Document was at the time of its utilization by St. Matthew and St. Luke in a fixed *written* form. However, some sayings might have undergone slight alterations due to the influence of the oral tradition.

2. The Q-Document was originally written in *Greek*; there is no sufficient evidence to prove that it was translated from Aramaic, or other Syrian language.

3. The Q-Document was a *single* document used by St. Matthew and St. Luke in the same form.

4. The *Sequence* in which the Q sections of the Double Tradition occurred in the original Q-Document is the one found in Luke.

5. With regard to the *wording* of the Q-Document Luke seems to preserve it more accurately in most of the cases, but Matthew, too, has some original words to show. However, today when it is generally accepted that the evangelists did not always copy verbatim their sources but sometimes they expressed in addition their theological ideas altering them where it was needed radically, it would not be surprising if in some cases where St. Matthew and St. Luke diverge considerably none of them has preserved the original form.

6. According to our principles set out above the Q-Document must have consisted originally of the following verses (we give below only the Lucan verses; those passages detected by the last two principles, and therefore less probable, are given in brackets): Lk 3.7-9, 16bf.; 4.1-13; 6.20-23, 27-38, 41-49; 7.1-10, 18-20, 22-28 (Mt 11.12f.), Lk 7. 31-35; 9.57-60a, (60b-62); 10.2-3, (Mt 10.16b), Lk 10.4-16, (19f.), 21-24; 11.(2-4), 9-26, (27f.), 29-32, 39-52; 12.2-12, 22-31, (32-38), 39f., 42-46, (49,51-56); 13.18-21, (23-30), 34f.; 17.23-37; (21.34-36). Unbracketed verses 175; Total verses 211. The above verses certainly form the core of the Q-Document. One possibility, nevertheless, has to be taken seriously into account; namely that some sayings, though not many, might have been totally eliminated by St. Matthew and St. Luke mainly because of the Q-Document's heretical orientation.[127]

7. The verses detected by our principles can be easily classified under the following headings (in each section we give only the first and last Lucan verses of the table including those in brackets): (a) Prologue: John the Baptist and Jesus (Lk 3.7-17); (b) The Confirmation of Jesus' authority: The Temptations (Lk 4.1-13); (c) Jesus' Teaching (Lk 6.20-49); (d) Response to Jesus' Teaching (Lk 7.1-9.62); (e) Jesus and his Disciples (Lk 10.2-11.13); (f) Jesus and his Opponents (Lk 11.14-12.4); (g) The Time of Crisis and Preparation for it (Lk 12.5-13.35); (h) Epilogue: The Eschatological Discourse (Lk 17.23- 21.34). This classification shows how indispensable the Q-Hypothesis is. For *the order of the sections is quite intelligible;*

---

[127] See additional note.

each section shows affinities with both the preceding and the following one.

8. A further reason which confirms the hypothesis that Q was a *single written document* is the way in which the various sections in Q follow one another, and this order in some cases is more intelligible than in Mark. Moreover, *all sections end in the same formal way* making the passing from one section to the other natural and smooth.[128]

*Additional note:* After examining the role John the Baptist plays in Q and Mark ("The Function of John the Baptist in Q and Mark," Θεολογία 46 [1975] pp. 405-13), as well as the alleged anti-Baptist attitude of the 4th Gospel, ("Τὸ Πρόβλημα τοῦ Βαπτιστῆ Ἰωάννη στὸ Δ' Εὐαγγέλιο," ΔΒΜ 4, 1976, pp. 99ff.), we started becoming more and more convinced that the Q-Document contained some version of Jesus' Baptism. However, the structure of the Marcan Version of Jesus' Baptism (see "The Function...," p. 412), as well as the 4th evangelist's opposition to the overestimation of John which was directed, in our view, not against the fictitious Baptist sect but against the Q-community located at Ephesus, makes us believe that the Q version of Jesus' Baptism differed widely from that of the canonical Synoptics; perhaps the role of John in it was somewhat overtoned at the expense of Jesus.

---

[128]*E.g.* the sections on Jesus and his Disciples ends with "The Blessedness of the Disciples"; the section on Jesus and his Opponents ends with the Denunciation of them; and the section on the Preparation of the End with "The Lament over Jerusalem", namely with sayings which sum up the whole section.

# 3
# THE ORIGINAL ORDER OF Q.
# SOME RESIDUAL CASES

To deal in the eighties with the original order of Q may at first glance give the impression of a desperate attempt to turn the clock of Gospel criticism back more than half a century. Since the majority of N.T. scholars from all denominations[1] have come to the significant conclusion that the bulk of the synoptic material stems from two major sources of a discernible theology, insistence on such a minute literary question could well mean an undesirable return to—or at least a leaning towards—the era of literary criticism. Till the dawn of this century, and indeed up to the first World War, scholars attempted to solve all problems concerning the origins of Christianity solely by literary means. With the rise of Form-criticism however, this method was abandoned. R. Bultmann has convincingly argued that it matters little "whether this of that editorial process peculiar to the written tradition took place before the Gospels were formed."[2]

It is not surprising therefore, that N.T. scholars are becoming today more and more reluctant to pay much attention to minor literary questions. The majority of them are quite rightly turning their attention to the more important, and to some extent more fascinating, issues of theology and redaction of the oldest source of our Gospel accounts. Nevertheless, the effects of the various attacks on the Q-hypothesis, and to a lesser degree on the entire Two-document theory,[3] are still being felt. Yet, none of the alternative solutions to the synoptic problem can really

---

[1] For the least known trends among eastern orthodox N.T. scholars see my dissertation, Ἡ περί τῆς Πηγῆς τῶν Λογίων θεωρία, pp. 24-28.

[2] R. Bultmann, *The History of the Synoptic Tradition*, Oxford 1970², p. 321.

[3] Some scholars are still challenging the classical solution to the synoptic problem. A number of them, like E. P. Sanders, A. Fuchs, H. F. D. Sparks, do not appear to give preference to an alternative solution. Others like M. D. Goulder, M. S. Enslin, O. Linton, accept the Marcan priority but reject the Q hypothesis. Still others, like M.-E. Boismard, prefer more complicated documentary solutions. However, the most active group of scholars like W. R. Farmer, D. L. Dungan, B. Orchard, H.-H. Stolt, T. R. W. Longstaff support the Griesbach hypothesis. For an account on the development of this latest group see W. R. Farmer, "Modern Developments of the Griesbach Hypothesis," in *NTS* 23 (1977), 275-295. For criticisms prior to 1974-75 see my article "Did Q Exist?". In general, the argument, first put forward by F. G. Downing, "Towards the Rehabilitation of Q," *NTS* 11 (1964) 169-181 from the evidence of Luke's ignorance of the distinctive Matthaean elements and his clear adherence to the Marcan characteristics in those passages in which Matthew supposedly "conflates" his material, has, to my knowledge, yet to be effectively refuted. Cf. also F. Neirynck, "Recent Developments in the Study of Q," J. Delobel (ed.), *Logia*, Leuven 1982, 29-75, p. 34.

claim, despite some triumphant declarations,[4] to have carried conviction, or so at least it seems to me. None of them have proved to have been adequately applied to the theological issues, at least not to the same extent as the Two-document theory.[5] They have, however, directed our attention to the true nature of our classical solution to the synoptic problem. Far from being the "assured" result of past biblical criticism, the Two-document theory is nothing but a successful—in fact the only successful—"working hypothesis".[6]

Another justification for this reappraisal of purely literary questions is the recent developments in modern linguistics and structuralism,[7] which can make the literary critical analysis of our oldest sources of the synoptic tradition more effective, thus enabling us to solve many hitherto unsolved - or at least not convincingly solved - problems.

The main argument for a written Q document is undoubtedly the argument from order. Although there were previously some very cautious comments heard on this issue,[8] since V. Taylor's ingenious treatment of the matter,[9] it has been overwhelmingly acknowledged that Matthew and Luke generally agree in placing in the same order those passages of the double tradition that most probably stem from the Q document.[10] Furthermore, if we are to reconstruct the actual document we must certainly follow the Lucan order.[11]

---

[4] Cf. E. C. Hobbs, "A Quarter-Century without Q," *PJ* 33 (1980) pp. 10-19.

[5] Although one must recognize some ingenious efforts, especially on the part of W. R. Farmer and M. D. Goulder, the application of their arguments to theological issues cannot be compared with the soundness of the theological consequences of the Two-document theory.

[6] Cf. R. H. Fuller, "Die neuere Diskussion über das synoptische Problem," *TZ* 34 (1978), 129-148.

[7] For a brief account of the recent developments in literary criticism see the relevant articles in the Suppl. Vol. of *IDB*.

[8] Cf. "Did Q Exist?" pp. 308f.

[9] V. Taylor, "The Order of Q," *JTS* n.s. 4 (1953) pp. 27-31; and "The Original Order of Q," A. J. B. Higgins (ed.), *New Testament Essays in Memory of T. W. Manson* (1959) pp. 246-269. Taylor compared the Lucan order of the Q material with their Matthaean parallels by printing them in seven columns instead of two. He, therefore, compared the Lucan order not with Matthew as a whole, but with its five major discourses plus the rest of the Q material outside those discourses.

[10] Even the most objective analysis in recent years by J. B. Tyson, "Sequential Parallelism in the Synoptic Gospels," in *NTS* 22 (1976), 276-308, has shown that, even if we take "Q" the whole of the double tradition, we can still speak of a "relative agreement in order" (p. 297). Apart from possible objections with regard to the over-divided synoptic sections in K. Aland's *Synopsis,* which he chose to use as a basis, one can also argue that his final conclusions (p. 297) do not seem to correspond with his previous scenarios. There, the Two-document theory is found to present less difficulties than either the Griesbach or the Augustinian hypotheses.

[11] Cf. A. Polag, *Fragmenta Q. Texthefte zur Logienquelle,* 1979, *passim;* also his *Die Christologie der Logienquelle,* 1968, pp. 2ff.

*The Original Order of Q* 63

In this short paper we shall not deal with the whole problem. We shall confine ourselves simply to some residual cases. Firstly, we propose to give some brief explanations as to why a number of groups of "saying" material have been replaced by Matthew; secondly, we are going to concentrate on those sayings, or whole sections of sayings, which appear in an inverted order in Matthew and Luke.

For the sake of the argument let us take the Two-document[12] theory as our working hypothesis. We have elsewhere[13] argued that Matthew and Luke have not drawn all their non-Marcan common material from Q. We confine the Q document only to those sayings that are common between the first and third Synoptists and for which there exist good reasons to believe that they have belonged to this hypothetical source, though adding a few more that only one of them has preserved. We believe with all redaction-critics that Matthew and Luke have handled their sources with considerable freedom, sometimes subjecting them to their overall theological plan.

I

What follows is not meant to stand in contradiction to V. Taylor's main argument with regard to the original order of Q. However, we now recognize that the evangelists were far more than mere collectors/compilers, a conviction that was not so widespread at the time Taylor first put forward his arguments. We can, therefore, deal with the problem from a different perspective. After all, Taylor's main concern was to show an objective standpoint, "that the common order is much more impressive than it appears to be, and is, in fact a very strong argument indeed."[14]

From the appended table[15] we realize that as far as the larger sections of Q are concerned Matthew's deviations from the (Lucan) original

---

[12] We stress the documentary aspect of the classical theory, since we can no longer speak loosely of Q either as a "source" or as a "community" with a specific theology without presupposing its existence at some stage in a *written* form. As soon as one tries to reconstruct Q in its entirety, one will certainly recognize this fact. After all Q's very credibility, questioned so severely in the past decades, has been basically restored on literary grounds. It is not an exaggeration to state that, if we are to retain the Q hypothesis at all, this can be done on the basis of its having existed as a *document* rather than as a *layer* of oral tradition. Cf. the objections by O. Linton, "Coordinated Sayings and Parables in the Synoptic Gospels: Analysis versus Theories," *NTS* 26 (1980) 139-163, esp. 159ff.; also J. W. Wenham, "Synoptic Independence and the Origin of Luke's Travel Narrative," *NTS* 27 (1981) 507-515.

[13] Cf. "The Nature and Extent of the Q-Document," pp. 66ff. Cf. also C. J. A. A. Hickling, "The Plurality of Q," J. Delobel (ed.), *Logia*, pp. 425-429.

[14] "The Order of Q," p. 28.

[15] See the Appendix, below.

sequence of the Q material may be satisfactorily explained, if we take into account the evangelist's overall arrangement of the material he used.

a. The "Jesus and John the Baptist" section (Mt 11.2–19) must probably have been taken out of its original setting by Matthew because it did not fit in his Miracle section (Mt 8.1–9.35); he added it, however, as a first pericope in the second narrative section (Mt 11–12), immediately after he had finished with his second ("Sending - out") discourse (Mt 9.36–10.42).

b. The pericope on the "Blessedness of the disciples" (Lk 10.23–24) must have similarly been transferred by Matthew to his third ("Parable") discourse (Mt 13) to serve as a midrash to the Isaiah prophecy of the parable of the Sower (Mt 13.1ff.) and to contrast Jesus' disciples with those outside.

c. The "Lord's prayer" (Lk 11.2–4) had already been transferred by Matthew to his first ("Sermon on the Mount") discourse (Mt 5–7) in what seems to be a different and evidently more elaborate form (Mt 6.9–13).

d. To the same setting the "Answer to prayer" discourse (Lk 11.9–13) had inevitably to be added (Mt 7.7–11).[16]

e. The only real discrepancy between Matthew and Luke with regard to the sequence of the Q material occurs in block VI of our table. A parallel order resumes only with the concluding section of this block, namely the "Lament over Jerusalem" pericope (Lk 13.34–45=Mt 23.37–39) and continues to the supposed end of the document. However, in the original document this whole block of parables and sayings was evidently placed in an eschatological setting which, despite some obvious Lucan redactions, is still discernible in the third gospel. It is hardly a conjecture to argue that the bulk of the material in this block was meant to prepare the Q community for the imminent End. It is for this very reason, we believe, that Matthew decided to scatter almost all sections of this block amongst his other major discourses.[17]

## II

---

[16] The inversion of the pericopae on the "Sign on Jonah" (Mt 12.38–42) and on the "Return of the evil spirit" (Mt 12.43–45) will be discussed below.

[17] Matthew has placed the pericopae on "Earthly things" and on the "Condemnation of Israel and the exclusion from the Kingdom" in the Sermon on the Mount (vv. 6.25–30); 7.13–14, 22–23; cf. 8.11–12); the sections on "Fearless confession" and on "Division in the households" in his sending-out discourse (vv. 10.26–33, 34–36); and the parables of the mustard seed/leaven on the relevant discourse (vv. 13.31–33). Only the discourse on "Watchfulness and Faithfulness" was set in an eschatological setting (vv. 24.43–51). The textual evidence of the only pericope outside the major discourses of Matthew, namely on the "Signs of the times" (16.2–3) is very uncertain, to say the least. One can notice, as Taylor has shown (see note 9 above), that Matthew in each of his major discourses follows the original order.

The most puzzling problem, nevertheless, in regard to a hypothesis of a written Q document which follows more or less the Lucan order is the inversion in a number of cases of phrases or even whole sections. The most obvious cases, to be found are: (a) the difference between Matthew and Luke in the sequence of the second and third temptation (Mt 4.5–7=Lk 4.9–12 and Mt 4.8–10=Lk 4.5–8); (b) the inversion between the discourses of the "Return of the evil spirit" (Mt 12.43–45=Lk 11.24–26) and the "Sign of Jonah" (Mt 12.38–42=Lk 11.29–32); and (c) the inversion in the latter pericope between the logia of "Men of Niniveh" (Mt 12.41=Lk 11.32) and the "Queen of the South" (Mt 12.42=Lk 11.31). In all cases the Matthaean order seems more natural.[18]

I propose to show that the compiler/collector of the Q document, in forming a number of phrases or whole "saying" sections, employed the *cyclical concentric structure.* According to this structure, which can be more graphically described as an *a b...x...b´a´ pattern,* the climax, or the conclusion, or the thrust of the argument, or the heading etc. is always found not at the end (i.e. in the *b´a´* part of a given section) or at the beginning in the case of a heading (i.e. in the *a b* part), but right in the middle (i.e. in the *x* part).

In the past two centuries biblical research has been carried out, consciously or unconsciously, from a historical and/or theological perspective. Very little, if any, attention has been paid during this period to the aesthetic element which was so important for the ancient Semitic world, especially during the early stages of the transmission from the oral to the written period of a given literature. Without going so far as to align with the other extreme, and to consider the biblical texts primarily and exclusively as aesthetic objects deprived of any historical or theological significance and value, we believe that this dimension, especially with the aid of modern linguistics and structuralism, can greatly help us to analyze more effectively, and consequently to understand more accurately, some of the oldest strata of the synoptic material.

In the last two decades or so there has been a tendency to move away from the classical source/form/historical critical approach, without questioning its validity as a starting point.[19] At the same time the

---

[18] In the case of the inverted temptations E. Klostermann's explanation ("durfte dies Akte wie in Mt in Klimatischer Ordnung geboten haben" cf. *Das Matthäusevangelium* (HNT, 4) Tübingen, 1927², p. 26) is quite characteristic.

[19] Cf. E. Güttgemann's, *Offene Fragen zur Formgeschichte des Evangeliums,* München 1971; hopefully the translation into English will give this book the wider recognition it deserves *(Candid Questions concerning Gospel Form Criticism,* Pittsburgh, 1979); also A. N. Wilder, *Early Christian Rhetoric,* Cambridge (Mass.) 1971²; and to some extent G. Theissen, *Urchistlichen Wundergeschichten. Ein Beitrag zur formgeschichtlichen Erforschung der synoptischen Evangelien,* (SNT, 8), Gütersloh 1974

recognition that the chiastic pattern played an important part in the formation of the O.T.—but also of some N.T.—poetic material,[20] was followed by a number of attempts to analyze certain N.T. writings with the aid of what we described above as a cyclical concentric structure.[21]

According to our hypothesis, in all three of the Q-pericopae we mentioned above, which Luke reproduced in the original form, Matthew appears to have grasped the intention of the author of Q and to have tried to decipher the more or less Semitic *a b ... x... b´ a´* pattern by restructuring the passages in the Aristotelian manner.

Thus, Matthew transferred the second, and evidently most important, temptation to the end to serve as a climax of the entire series of temptations (Lk 4.1–2[a], 3–4[b], 5–8[x], 9–12[b´], 13[a´]=Mt 4.1–2[a]; 3–4[b]; 8–10[x]; 5–7[b´], 11[a´]).

Similarly, the "Return of the evil spirit" (Lk 11.24–26=Mt 12.43–45), which was originally meant as a conclusion (x), but placed in the middle between the two closely connected pericopae on the "Beelzebul controversy" (Lk 11.14–23=Mt 12.22–30 [a] and the "Sign of Jonah" (Lk 11.29–32=Mt 12.38–42 [a'],[22] was transferred by Matthew to the end.

Accordingly, the "Queen of the South" logion (Lk 11.31=Mt 12.42[x], originally placed before the "Men of Niniveh" logion (Lk 11.32=Mt 12.41[a']; cf. Lk 11.30=Mt 12.40[a]), was transferred by Matthew to what appears to be its natural position, namely at the end of the passage.

The three passages we examined briefly above are not the only places where we can find signs of a cyclical concentric structure in Q. They merely represent the clearest cases of an inversion in the sequence of the Q material occasioned by Matthew's decision to make the argument of the text he was copying more easily understood by restructuring the Semitic pattern in a Hellenistic manner. There are however, cases in which Matthew acted differently, and yet the cyclical concentric pattern is still visible, though we have no inversion. The following sayings deserve closer consideration:

a. The "Sending-Out" discourse in Matthew (9.36–10.16) is obviously a conflation mainly from the Q (cf. Lk 10.2–12) and the Marcan (Mk 6.6b–13; cf. Lk 9.1–6) accounts. The Q accounts begins with a kind of

---

[20] Cf. N. Lund, "The Presence of Chiasmus in the NT," in *JR* 10 (1930) 74-93.

[21] Cf. A. Vanhoye, *La structure litteraire de l'Epitre aux Hebreux*, Paris 1963; J. Lambrecht, *Die Redaktion der Markus-Apokalypse. Literarische Analyse und Structuruntersuchung* (AB, 28), Rome 1967, esp. p. 299. Id., *Marcus interpretator*, Brugge-Utrecht, 1969, esp. p. 121; cf. also J. Dupont, "Les paroles de Jesus sur la lampe et la mesure dans la tradition synoptique: Mc 4.21-25 parr.," J. Delobel (ed.), *Logia*, esp. p. 206, n. 12.

[22] This is strongly suggested by Lk 11.16 which in the original (Lucan) text is placed in the context of the Beelzebul controversy and which Matthew transferred to introduce his next Q pericope namely on the "Sign of Jonah" (Mt 12.38).

introduction (Lk 10.2–4) which also forms the opening verses of the Matthaean version (cf. Mt 9,37 f.) and proceeds with three smaller sections (Lk 10.5–7=Mt 10.12f. [a]; Lk 10.8f.=Mt 10.7f. [x]; Lk 10.10–12=Mt 10.14–15 [a']), the middle one being transferred by Matthew to the beginning probably because it was taken to serve as a heading or as the crucial point of the entire discourse. Matthew, of course, in his major discourses always makes some rearrangements, but in this case the transposition may not be incidental.

b. The Lucan version on "Loving our enemies" (Lk 6.27–36) consists of three smaller sections: the first of them corresponds to Matthew's fifth antithesis on retaliation (Lk 6.27–30=Mt 538–42[a]) while the third one has been developed by Matthew to form his sixth antithesis (Lk 6.32–36=Mt 5.43–48[a']). The central section (Lk 6.31[x]) was most probably considered by the first evangelist to be the main thrust of the original argument and therefore was moved out to form his "Golden Rule" (Mt 7.12).

c. The saying «τί δέ με καλεῖτε κύριε κύριε καί οὐ ποιεῖτε ἃ λέγω» (Lk 6.46=Mt 7.21[x]), being the link and the central point between the parables of the "Test of Goodness" (Lk 6.43–45=Mt 7.16–20[a]) and the "House on the Rock" (Lk 6.47–49 =Mt 7.24–27[a']) was treated by both the later Synoptists in the same way.

d. Most synoptic critics, who believe in the Q hypothesis, argue[23] that the discourse on "Following Jesus" (which begins with the logion Lk 9.57–58=Mt 8.19–20[a]) most probably contained in the original Q document all three sayings which Luke has preserved. Quite obviously the most important of all, at least in the Lucan version, is the second one (Lk 9.59–60=Mt 8.21–22[x]).[24] If so we can conjecture that Matthew might have decided to close the discourse at this point and omit the third saying (Lk 9.61–62[a']), once he had reached what he considered the crucial point.[25]

Through the above examination we have shown that there is some clear evidence in the double tradition (Q) of what we called cyclical concentric structure, which in Matthew's gospel was repeatedly transformed into a more logical Hellenistic structure. Since Matthew's treatment of his material elsewhere in his gospel (i.e. in the triple/Marcan tradition) does not reveal a similar trend,[26] we can safely argue not only that the

---

[23] Cf. A. Polag, *Fragmenta Q*, p. 42f.

[24] I am grateful to Prof. Jan de Waard, who in a private conversation shared with me his views on this point.

[25] Cf. also Mt 7.1–2=Lk 6.37–38; the central part in the (original?) Lucan version (vv. 37b–38a) might have been dropped by Matthew as an unnecessary expansion.

[26] In fact Matthew does reveal a similar trend in dealing with at least one Marcan pericope i.e. Mk 7.1–15=Mt 15.1–11. But this is a further evidence which favors our hypothesis. For if the entire pericope is structurally analyzed (Introduction: Mk 7.1=Mt

originality of the Lucan order of the Q material is confirmed, but also that a further argument for the existence of the Q document is produced. In fact Q's existence is confirmed in its written form, since we can hardly imagine Matthew's restructuring to have occurred in the orally transmitted material.[27]

---

15,1[a]—Mk 7.2–4 is omitted by Matthew as unnecessary additional information; The Pharisees and Scribes' Question: Mk 7.4=Mt 15.2[b]; Jesus' Accusation: Mk 7.6–7=Mt 15.7–9[x]; Jesus' Counter-Question: Mk 7.8–13=Mt 15.3–6[b´]; General Conclusion: Mk 7.14–15=Mt 15.10–11[a´]), it will appear that Matthew has inverted the b´ with the x of the story so that the latter be brought more closely to its logical continuation (a´).

[27] If our argument is at all sound and Q's author did use the cyclical concentric structure, then the meaning of some Q pericopae may appear in an altogether new light. For instance in the opening pericopae (Lk 3.7–9.16b–17=Mt 3.7–12) the emphasis may be on the messianic statement of John the Baptist (Lk 3.16b=Mt 3.11[x]) and not in the eschatological preaching which both precedes (Lk 3.7–9=Mt 3.7–10[a]) and follows (Lk 3.17=Mt 3.12[a']). Furthermore, the Lord's prayer (Lk 11.2–4) may be revealed in an altogether new setting; namely not as an example given to his disciples on the form of prayer, but as prayer of Jesus himself (a'); cf. Lk 10.21–22 par. (a) and Lk 10.23–24(x).

## APPENDIX

| Q blocks | Luke | Matthew | |
|---|---|---|---|
| | | *Introduction* | |
| I | 3.7–9,16b–17<br>4.1–13 | 3.7–12<br>4.1–11 | John the Baptist's preaching<br>Jesus' temptations |
| | | *Jesus' teaching* | |
| II | 6.20–23<br>6.27–36<br>6.37–38, 41–42<br>6.43–46<br>6.47–49<br>7.21a | 5.3–12<br>5.39–48<br>7.1–5<br>7.16–21<br>7.24–27<br>7.28 | Beatitudes<br>On loving our enemies<br>On judging<br>Test of goodness<br>The house on the rock<br>The ending of Jesus' teaching |
| | | *Response to Jesus' teaching* | |
| III | 7.1b–10<br>7.18–35<br>9.57–62 | 8.5–13<br>11.2–19*<br>8.19–22 | The centurion's servant<br>Jesus and John the Baptist<br>On following Jesus |
| | | *Jesus and his followers* | |
| IV | 10.2–12<br>10.13–16<br>10.21–22<br>10.23–24<br>11.2–4<br>11.9–13 | 9.37–38; 10,7–16<br>11.21–23<br>11.25–27<br>13.16–17*<br>6.9–13*<br>7.7–11 | The sending-out discourse<br>Woes on Galilean cities<br>Jesus' thanksgiving to the Father<br>The blessedness of the disciples<br>Lord's prayer<br>Answer to prayer |
| | | *Jesus and his opponents* | |
| V | 11.14–23<br>11.24–26<br>11.29–32<br>11.39–52 | 12.23–30<br>12.43–45<br>12.36–42*<br>23.4–36* | The Beelzebul controversy<br>The return of the evil spirit<br>The sign of Jonah<br>Woes to the Pharisees |
| | | *Preparation for the imminent End* | |
| VI* | 12.2–12<br>12.22–34<br>12.35–46<br>12.49–53<br>12.54–56 | 10.26–33<br>6.25–34, 19-21<br>24.43–51<br>10.34–36<br>16.2–3 | Exhortation to fearless confession<br>On earthly things<br>On watchfulness and faithfulness<br>Divisions on households<br>The signs of the time |

|     |          |                |                               |
|-----|----------|----------------|-------------------------------|
|     | 13.18–21 | 13.31–33       | The parables of the mustard seed/leaven |
| VI* | 13.23–30 | 7.13–14, 22–23 (cf. 8.11–12) | Condemnation of Israel and exclusion from the Kingdom |
|     | 13.34–35 | 23.37–39       | Lament over Jerusalem         |

*Epilogue: The eschatological discourse*

|          |                   |                           |
|----------|-------------------|---------------------------|
| 17.23–37 | 24.26–28, 37–42   | The coming of the Son of Man |

N.B. The above table does not cover the entire Q-Document. It only consists of those self-contained Q sections in Luke with parallel versions in Matthew. Those sections of Matthew which deviate from the original (Lucan) order are marked with an asterisk (*).

# 4
# PROLEGOMENA TO A DISCUSSION ON THE RELATIONSHIP BETWEEN MARK AND THE Q-DOCUMENT

The revival of the Q-studies in recent years[1] reopened, among others, the question about the relationship between Mark, our earliest extant gospel, and the Q-Document, our earliest known Gospel source. After a long break caused mainly by Form criticism, which had directed N.T. scholarship behind the written documents and their relationships, and towards the separate units of material (pericopae) circulated in the period of oral tradition, scholars motivated by the requirements of Redaction criticism started considering again the possibility of interrelationship between these two sources.[2]

The problem as such is posed by a number of similar statements to be found in these two documents. Some of these are only similarities of content without any considerable verbal agreement;[3] others show extensive verbal agreements.[4] The origin of the problem can be traced to the attitude of N.T. research in the last century and its attempts to determine with the best possible precision the image of the Historical Jesus.

J. Wellhausen wrote about this relation in 1905:[5] "The problem of the literary relationship must at least be propounded and needs thorough investigation. It is indeed most extraordinary, to use only a mild expression, that such an investigation has never been set on foot." Wellhausen's statement is not surprising, for despite his decisive contribution to the establishment of the form-critical approach to the Synoptics,[6] he was still heavily influenced by Literary criticism—the word *literary* in his statement is of particular importance. In fact, although the problem was not thoroughly examined, it nevertheless haunted biblical

---

[1] Cf. my ‘Η περί τῆς Πηγῆς τῶν Λογίων θεωρία, Athens 1977.

[2] Cf. J. Lambrecht, *Die Redaktion der Markus-Apocalypse*, Rome 1967; also E. Schweizer, *The Good News According to Mark*, ET, Richmond 1970; R. G. Hamerton-Kelly, *Pre-existence, Wisdom, and the Son of Man*, Cambridge 1973. D. Wenham, "The Meaning of Mark III, 21," *NTS* 21 (1975), pp. 295-300, has also suggested that St. Mark knew and revised Q (pp. 299f).

[3] Cf. The Beelzebul controversy (Mk 3.20–30=Q [Mt 12.22–32=Lk 11.14–23]); The Denunciation of the Scribes and Pharisees (Mk 12.37b–40=Q [Mt 23.4–36=Lk 11.39–52]) etc.

[4] Cf. Mk 1.7f and Mt 3.11=Lk 3.16 (Q) etc.

[5] *Einleitung in die drei ersten Evangelien*, Berlin 1905, p. 73.

[6] Cf. N. Perrin, *What is Redaction Criticism?* London 1970, pp. 13f.

studies from the establishment of the Two Document Hypothesis onwards. It developed along with the so-called Marcan Hypothesis, aiming like that at the discovery of the Historical Jesus.

To solve the problem all three possible solutions have been in fact suggested in the past: (i) the dependence of Q on Mark; (ii) the dependence of Mark on Q; and (iii) the mutual independence of Q and Mark.

\*\*\*

1. The first solution, i.e. the view that *the Q-Document was dependent on Mark*, was suggested by Wellhausen and adopted by A. Jülicher, who nevertheless made considerable modifications in it. Wellhausen dealt with this problem in all his commentaries, but he summarized his results *in extenso* in a paragraph of his *Einleitung in die drei ersten Evangelien* under the title *Markus verglichen mit Q*.[7] From the beginning of his discussion of the relationship of Q to Mark he ruled out the third solution by stating that "mutual independence is not to be thought of."[8] He thus set out to examine the question of priority by means of a comparison of the overlapping passages,[9] and came to the conclusion, on the basis of the content and form of the two documents as well as because the sayings in Q betray a religious point of view that is almost later than that in Mark, that it was Mark which came first, and that therefore the Q-Document was dependent on it. He put the date of the composition of Q long after AD. 67-68 misled by the words «υἱοῦ Βαραχίου» (Mt 23.35).[10]

A. Jülicher,[11] the only scholar who felt compelled to make some important concessions to Wellhausen, was also convinced that the edition of the Q-Document used by St. Matthew and St. Luke was very probably posterior in time to Mark. He adduced in support the Christology of the temptation story, the recording of a healing at a distance in the story of the Centurion's servant, as well as other individual sayings, but he categorically denied any literary dependence of Q on Mark. As a result of this modification to Wellhausen's claim about the posteriority of the Q-Document, Jülicher conjectured that Q was developed in successive stages, and that at a distinct moment in the course of this development it was influenced by the plan of Mark. Accordingly Q was both older and younger than Mark.

So far as I know, the above scholars were the only supporters of the theory according to which the Q-Document was in a way dependent on

---

[7] Pp. 73-89.

[8] *Op. cit.*, p. 73.

[9] Ibid., pp. 73ff.

[10] Wellhausen took these words to refer not to 2 Chr 24.20f., but to Josephus, *De Bell.Jud.* iv 5.4. For further details and a concise refutation of his view see W. G. Kümmel, *Introduction to the N. T.*, ET, London $1970^2$, pp. 55f.

[11] *Einleitung in das N.T.*, $1906^5$, pp. 320ff.

Mark.[12] As a whole the hypothesis depends on an erroneous consideration of what the relationship between the Q-Document and its users was, without taking into account their redactional attitude, which in recent studies (redaction criticism) is taken almost as established. In fact, Wellhausen's views did not survive a single year; after they had been stated in detail in 1905, Harnack's more thorough investigation of the material concerned gave them their quietus. Before passing to Harnack, however, we shall consider the second solution, which is not only the earlier of all, but which Harnack also criticized.

\*\*\*

2. The view that *Mark was dependent on the Q-Document* goes back as early as the time of B. Weiss. He was the first, so far as I know, who consistently[13] supported this view, not only in Germany but even in the English-speaking world, too. Weiss was accustomed to call "Oldest Source"[14] the Q-Document, because he believed it consisted not only of discourses and sayings but of some narratives too, from which St. Mark derived some of his narrative material. St. Mark, however, used this "Apostolic Source"[15] (another name B. Weiss used for the Q-Document) not faithfully but freely, because his purpose was to set the deeds rather than the teachings of Jesus. However, the *raison d' être* of Weiss' preference of the second solution was not theological but literary-critical; for by favoring the dependence of Mark on Q, Weiss thought that he was able to account for the puzzling question of the minor verbal agreements of the first three Gospels.

In France the second solution was held at the beginning of this century by two of the most prominent scholars there, A. Loisy and M. Goguel. The former[16] argued from the authority lying behind both Q and Mark, namely St. Peter, the place of composition (Jerusalem), and the language (Aramaic) of both documents, as well as their date and spirit. For Loisy Mark was dependent on Q in the following passages: 1.4,7,8; 2.17,19–20, 23–28; 3.1–6, 22–30; 4.1–34; 7.15; 8.12,15,35; 9.33–50; 10.1–12; 10.42–45; 12.38–40;13.1–37. In general Q was controlled by the faith of the earliest Christian community, whereas Mark was influenced by St. Paul's theology.

---

[12] E. Meyer, *Ursprung und Anfänge des Christentums I*, Berlin 1923, pp. 234ff., supports the priority of Mark, following Wellhausen's view that Mt 23.35 is derived from Josephus' report, but he rejects a direct dependence of Q on Mark. E. G. Kraeling, *The Glorified N. T.: vol. I. The Four Gospels,* London 1964 also suggests that Wellhausen' s "position on this point seems to be more nearly correct"(p.15).

[13] B. Weiss, *Manual of Introduction to the N. T.,* ET, London 1898, pp. 246ff. For other literature see V. H. Stanton, *The Gospels as Historical Documents,* Cambridge 1909, p. 49, n. 3.

[14] *Op. cit.,* p. 221.

[15] Ibid., p. 248.

[16] A. Loisy, *Les Evangiles synoptiques,* Paris 1907, p. 114.

M. Goguel[17] held similar views but derived different Marcan passages from Q.

In Great Britain too, a number of scholars supported Mark's dependence on Q. The significant volume *Oxford Studies on the Synoptic Problem* seems to have been oriented towards the view that St. Mark used the Q-Document when composing his Gospel.[18] W. Sanday wrote in the opening article of that volume: "We may believe that the writer (St. Mark) knew of the existence of a previous document (Q), and allowed his work to be in some degree shaped by this knowledge."[19] The word "may" in this case expresses nothing but a "possibility", but Sanday went on to give the reasons for it: "This seems to be the best way of explaining the comparatively summary character of the opening paragraphs, and it would also account for the preponderance of narrative over discourses—if the earlier document consisted mainly of discourses, the later writer would naturally wish to supplement its contents rather than to repeat them."[20]

Finally in America two prominent scholars B. W. Bacon and F. C. Grant also held the view that St. Mark had used the Q-Document when writing his Gospel. Bacon who, as we have seen, defined Q as a layer of oral tradition rather than as a written document,[21] could hardly think of St. Mark's being ignorant of those important elements of the teaching of Jesus which "he frequently refers to, but does not give *in extenso.*"[22] Following Weiss he offered the explanation that St. Mark conceived the "Gospel" in terms of "things done" rather than "things spoken".[23] "Our evangelist has used the ancient common source of Matthew and Luke (Q) to embellish and supplement an earlier narrative."[24] He also noticed that certain passages in Mark "show affinities to the Lucan text of Q."[25] Grant, on the other hand, tried to explain the origin of our earliest Gospel along the lines of his "Multiple Documentation" theory. He asserts that "70 verses, out of a total of 661 (Nestle's text), or just over 18.5 per cent of the

---

[17] M. Goguel, *Introduction au Nouveau Testament, I,* Paris 1923, pp. 250ff. 328ff.

[18] Cf. W. Sanday, "The Conditions under which the Gospels were Written, in their Bearing upon Some Difficulties of the Synoptic Problem", pp. 3-26; B. H. Streeter, "St. Mark's Knowledge and Use of Q," pp. 165-183; also "The Literary Evolution of the Gospels," pp. 209-27; J. V. Bartlet, "The Sources of St. Luke's Gospel," pp. 315-83. Bartlet argued that Q was oral and had a passion narrative. For Streeter see below.

[19] *Op. cit.,* p. 12.

[20] Ibid., pp. 12f.

[21] "The Nature and Design of Q, the Second Synoptic Source," *HJ* 22 (1924), pp. 1f. n. 1.

[22] *The Gospel of Mark: Its Origin and Date,* New Haven 1925, p.138. Bacon, however, has gone too far when declaring that St. Mark's use of Q "is susceptible of critical demonstration"'*(The Beginnings of the Gospel Story,* New Haven 1909, p. xx)

[23] *The Gospel of Mark...,* p. 138.

[24] *The Beginnings...,* p. xxi.

[25] Ibid.

Gospel,"[26] were derived from Q. The reasons which led Grant to this conclusion were:[27] (i) the existence of doublets; (ii) the opening verses about John the Baptist which seem to be "echoing or abridging Q;"[28] and (iii) the Q-like style evidenced in the introductory formula «ἀμὴν λέγω ὑμῖν» used several times in Mark.[29]

In sum, the arguments for this solution are: (i) St. Mark made so scanty a use of Q because his main interest was to record Jesus' deeds rather than his teaching; (Weiss, Bacon); (ii) The opening verses of Mark look like an abridgment of Q's report (Sanday, Bacon, Grant); (iii) Q theology reflects early traditions, whereas Mark seems influenced by a much later Pauline thought (Loisy); (iv) The doublets, quite apart from other synoptic implications, also point to the use by St. Mark of Q (Grant); (v) The expression «ἀμὴν λέγω ὑμῖν» is a take over by St. Mark from Q (Grant).

However, apart from the general impression that the defenders of this solution clearly presupposed a literary growth of the Synoptic Gospels by approaching the problem of the Q-Marcan relationships via source-criticism,[30] the first four arguments can be better accounted for by the assumption of different and independent traditions.[31] As to the last one, this was successfully met by B. H. Throckmorton, Jr., who has convincingly shown that it was due to a methodological error: "If this phrase «ἀμὴν λέγω ὑμῖν» is characteristic of Q and appears thirteen times in Mark, one would expect it to occur many more times in Luke, where there is certainly much more Q; but it occurs in Luke only six times, and adds the writer (Grant), 'three of these are derived from Mark'. . . I should then conclude that the phrase is not characteristic of Q."[32] All these, however, are of less

---

[26] F. C. Grant, *The Gospels: Their Origin and their Growth,* London 1957, p.109. Also idem, *The Growth of the Gospels,* New York 1933, pp. 129-31; Id. *The Earliest Gospel,* New York 1943, pp. 63, 71.

[27] *The Gospels...,* p. 109.

[28] Cf. B. W. Bacon, "The Prologue of Mark," *JBL* 26 (1908) pp. 84-106. H. G. Wood, *Jesus in the Twentieth Century,* London 1960, referring to Grant's point of view writes: "I am not suggesting that Mark had no written sources, but I doubt whether Q was among them" (p. 39). He has not, however, disregarded the view that St. Mark might have been familiar with Q and made some slight use of it (p. 22).

[29] Cf. also F. C. Grant, "The Mission of the Disciples," *JBL* 35 (1916), pp. 293ff, where it is argued that the tradition concerning the Mission Charge in Mark was drawn from Q.

[30] Characteristic is the remark of J. Moffatt, *Introduction to the Literature of the N.T.,* Edinburgh 1911, p. 204 n. 1, that some of those who rejected the various Ur-Markus theories have eventually turned to the conclusion that St. Mark employed Q (cf. B. Weiss, *Die Quellen des Lukasevangeliums,* Stuttgart 1907, pp. 134f. 190).

[31] So H. J. Cadbury who made a very interesting observation: "The literary dependence of Mark upon Q rests...on very much slighter verbal evidence than do the two main hypotheses of literary relationship in the Synoptic problem. The verbal likeness between Mark and Q is never greater than would be likely for two independent streams of oral traditions" *(The Making of Luke-Acts,* London, 1958, p. 107).

[32] "Did Mark Know Q?" *JBL* 65 (1948) pp. 319-29, esp. pp. 320f.

interest compared with the positive argumentation offered especially by Harnack and Streeter who expressly favored the third solution.

\*\*\*

*3. Mutual Independence of Mark and Q.* A. Harnack, whose analysis of the Q material was stimulated by Wellhausen's statement on the relationship between Mark and Q,[33] convincingly refuted all his arguments both by comparison of Mark and Q, and by a more thorough examination of the subject matter of Q. He came to the conclusion that in no case is Q to be regarded as dependent on Mark,[34] but he did not reverse the case. "The dependence of Mark upon Q—for if there exists a relationship of direct dependence between the two this would be the only possible hypothesis—is also difficult to establish; for the assumption is nowhere demanded, and the attitude of St. Mark towards Q would in this case be almost unintelligible".[35] As to Jülicher's modification, Harnack wrote: "I consider it unnecessary to assume that St. Mark influenced Q at a definite moment in its development.[36] The publication of Harnack's book, as well as its translation into English, made a tremendous impact on Q studies that some prominent scholars[37] changed their minds and accepted the mutual independence of Mark and Q.[38]

Harnack's painstaking effort was followed a few years later by J. Moffatt's important argumentation. Moffatt categorically rejected any dependence of Mark on Q on these grounds : (i) "the theory assumes that Q had a monopoly of such sayings;" (ii) "no satisfactory explanation is offered why St. Mark made such scanty use of Q;" and (iii) "in no instance is it absolutely necessary, either on the score of substance or of style, to assume that St. Mark borrowed from Q."[39]

But the most influential case was that of B. H. Streeter, who had previously maintained that St. Mark knew and used Q.[40] He had examined all the cases where Mark and Q overlap and concluded that "the cumulative effect of these instances is irresistible, and must establish

---

[33] A. Harnack, *The Sayings of Jesus* ET, London, 1908), p. v.

[34] Ibid., p.226.

[35] Ibid.

[36] Ibid., p. 226 n. 1.

[37] Cf. C. G. Montefiore, who in the first edition of his *The Synoptic Gospels I* (London, 1909) maintained Mark's dependence on Q (pp. xxxvif), whereas in the second edition (1927) he favored "after Harnack" their independence (p. 1).

[38] For other scholars (up to 1911) who followed B. Weiss, even with considerable modifications see J. Moffatt, *op. cit.,* pp. 204f. He named the following scholars as adherents of the second solution: B. Weiss, van Rhijn, Titius, Resch, Badhaven, Jolley, Bousset, Barth, J. Weiss, O. Holtzmann, Loisy, von Soden, Bacon, Nicolardot, Montefiore.

[39] J. Moffatt, *op. cit.,* p. 205.

[40] B. H. Streeter, "St. Mark's Knowledge and Use of Q," in *OSSP,* pp. 165-183. Streeter completely ignored Harnack's suggestions in this particular article although he did use them in his other articles in the same volume.

beyond reasonable doubt that St. Mark was familiar with Q."[41] As to the crucial question why he did not derive therefrom more than some 16 passages (according to his counting), Streeter gave the answer that this was due to St. Mark's reproducing Q "very freely and often in a much abbreviated form,"[42] and to his "quoting Q from memory."[43] Furthermore, Mark was written "to supplement not to supersede Q."[44] But later in *The Four Gospels* he examined afresh the bulk of the overlapping passages and concluded that "the evidence is decidedly against the view that St. Mark used Q." In that case the general, though not invariable, superiority of the Q version remains to be accounted for. This can only be done if we suppose that "Q was a document of very early date and represents a peculiarly authentic tradition."[45] Streeter's turnabout eventually had the result that this solution was adopted by the majority of scholars, despite the fact that a scholar has claimed that his earlier view was better founded.[46] Even if this was not the case, one can hardly deny that Streeter's change of view was in some way influenced by the concept of the multiple attestation of Jesus' message, since the intention throughout his entire work was "to broaden the basis of evidence for the authentic teaching of Christ."[47]

The same view appeared also in the work of J. M. C. Crum, who was confident that "where Mark and Q give...the same saying of Jesus, the reason for their both giving it is not that St. Mark copied it from Q or that Q borrowed it from Mark. The reason for their giving it is, that the Lord himself said those words."[48] His final remark makes this more clear: Mark and Q represent two traditions, "differing because they are independent; and agreeing because they are trustworthy."[49]

---

[41] Ibid., p. 167.

[42] Ibid., p. 178

[43] Idem, "The Literary Evolution of the Gospels," p. 219.

[44] Ibid., p. 220.

[45] Id., *The Four Gospels,* London 1924, p. 191.

[46] Cf. E. P. Sanders, "The Overlaps of Mark and Q and the Synoptic Problem," *NTS* 19 (1973), pp. 453-65, who noted that Streeter's final solution, i.e. that Mark independently overlapped Q "rests on a systematic avoidance of the evidence which he had assembled, and is methodologically unsound since the definition of what constitutes an overlap of independent traditions does not fit all passages which he chose, while it does fit others ignored by him" (pp. 463f.). So W. R. Farmer, *The Synoptic Problem: A Critical Analysis,* New York 1964, p. 126. For further discussion of this see B. C. Butler, *The Originality of St. Matthew,* Cambridge 1951, pp. 107 ff.

[47] *The Four Gospels,* p. 270. E. P. Sanders, gave a similar explanation for Streeter's change of view, namely that his "first solution weakens the very basis of the (Two-Document) hypothesis" *(op. cit.,* p. 463).

[48] J. M. C. Crum, *The Original Jerusalem Gospel,* Cambridge 1927, p. 167.

[49] Ibid., p. 190.

Finally B. H. Throckmorton Jr.,[50] having first refuted some of the alleged evidence for St. Mark's use of Q,[51] made a significant point by sharply distinguishing between the bulk of the sayings material circulating in the period of the oral tradition and Q as a fixed document. If we define Q as a written document, and if we do not give the same name to the oral tradition, then on the basis of the overlapping passages the conclusion must certainly be that "both Mark and Q drew from a common oral source."[52]

This last solution, namely that Mark and Q are mutually independent of each other was the view that generally came to prevail in Synoptic scholarship.[53] The reasons that made scholars accept it readily are the following:

(i) the immense influence of Harnack and especially Streeter's work;[54] (ii) the fact that conservative scholarship seemed satisfied because the content of Jesus' teaching was thus attested in two major sources; and (iii) form critics were also satisfied because any theory implying dependence between Mark and Q might have implied a revival of the source-critical approach to the Gospels as the only legitimate method in Synoptic scholarship.

All three solutions reflected a current insistence on the importance of literary analysis. Even J. Wellhausen, the admitted pioneer of Form Criticism worked under that burden. "Attempts have been made, he wrote, to lessen the importance of literary scrutiny by the contention that oral tradition is older than its written sediment, and that the former must have contained more than the latter. This consideration is in itself justified... But it must not be overlooked that in the course of time the primary

---

[50] "Did Mark Know Q?" *JBL* 65 (1948), pp. 319-29.

[51] Throckmorton dealt with the following alleged evidences: (i) The existence of Doublets, (ii) The Q-like style in the «ἀμὴν λέγω ὑμῖν» formula (see above), (iii) The agreements of Matthew and Luke against Mark in Marcan contexts, and (iv) The existence of sayings in Mark.

[52] Ibid., p. 328.

[53] Other scholars who expressly favored the view that Mark and Q represent independent overlapping traditions are: H. H. Wendt, *Die Lehre Jesu,* Theil 1886; P. Wernle, *Die Synoptische Frage,* Freiburg 1899, pp. 61ff.. 80ff, 178ff, 244ff.; W. Bousset (cited by Harnack, *op. cit.,* pp. 227 n.1); F. C. Burkitt, *The Gospel History and its Transmission,* Edinburgh 1906, pp. 62ff., 147ff.; V. H. Stanton, *The Gospels as Historical Documents II* (Oxford, 1909), pp. 109ff.; G. D. Castor, "The Relation of Mark to the Source Q," *JBL* 31 (1912), pp. 82-91; C. S. Patton "Did Mark Use Q? Or Did Q Use Mark," *AJT* 16 (1912), pp. 634-642; E. J. Goodspeed, *An Introduction to the New Testament,* Chicago 1937, p. 148; W. G. Kümmel, *op. cit.* p. 55, etc. Similarly C. A. Briggs, "The Use of the Logia of Matthew in the Gospel of Mark," *JBL* 23 (1904), pp. 191-210, suggested that "the original Mark did not use (the Q-traditions), but that these found in Mark were additions from later hands" (p. 191).

[54] Harnack seems to have departed from his original view when stating in a review in *TLZ* (1908) pp. 463f, that "at least St. Mark knew the circle in which Q, or large portions of it, existed orally, before it was committed to writing, and existed substantially in the same form".

tradition decreased and the secondary tradition increased....There is no reason to believe that St. Mark deliberately omitted from his Gospel many sayings and words of Jesus which nevertheless were known to him."[55] With R. Bultmann[56] the scenery was completely changed. "There is no definable boundary, he declared, between the oral and written tradition, and similarly the process of the editing of the material of the tradition was beginning already before it had been fixed in a written form;" therefore, he concluded "the inquiry can be conducted without any special source theory."[57]

\*\*\*

*4. Attempts to compromise the above solutions.* Despite Bultmann's categorical statement, which in fact seemed to suggest the abandonment of all attempts to determine the Q-Marcan relationship by means of literary criticism, some scholars insisted that the existing gap between the above solutions could be bridged by compromise suggestions. With the first solution (i.e. Q's dependence on Mark) being refuted once and for all, scholars directed their efforts towards a mean position between the second and third solutions.

Thus, A. Meyer in an article dealing with the Marcan sources[58] came to the conclusion that St. Mark used q which is related to Q. He, nevertheless, was in full agreement with Bultmann when making his final remark that "one must not start with Q or q or Mark, but with the groups of sayings, or rather with their elements."[59]

A similar view, namely that St. Mark used a source related to, but not identical with, the Q-Document, had already been advanced by A. E. J. Rawlinson, who suggested that St. Mark used Q[R], a collection of sayings akin to but not identical with it, "a version of 'Q' which may be assumed to have been current in Rome."[60]

T. E. F. Honey tried to substantiate Rawlinson's view by analyzing the overlapping passages. "The resemblances between Mark and Q, he pointed out, might indicate that St. Mark knew Q. But we have noted divergences which, in the absence of existing evidence, seriously underline this assumption."[61] To tackle then all objections to that view Honey stated that "we must assume that St. Mark's Roman source differed in some

---

[55] *Op. cit.,* pp. 86f.

[56] M. Dibelius was still under Wellhausen's influence when stating that "it is even not altogether out of the question that those special features of the source Q came into being under the influence of the Gospel of Mark" (*From Tradition to Gospels*, ET, London, 1934, p. 246).

[57] R. Bultmann, *The History of the Synoptic Tradition*, ET, Oxford 1970$^2$, p. 321.

[58] "Die Entstehung des Markus-Evangeliums", in *Festgabe für A. Jülicher zum 70*, Tübingen 1927, pp. 35-60.

[59] Ibid., p. 60.

[60] *The Gospel according to St. Mark,* London 1925, p. xl.

[61] "Did Mark Use Q?" *JBL* 62 (1943), pp. 319-31, esp. pp. 328f.

respects from the tradition of the Eastern Churches which is represented by Q."[62]

However, even this mediating view can be easily refuted. Throckmorton's suggestion of a sharp distinction between sayings from the period of the oral tradition on the one hand, and Q as a written document on the other, makes it automatically fall to the ground. On the other hand, if q, or $Q^R$, or similar sources, are to be considered as written documents not dependent on Q proper, they fall out of our immediate concern.

Another more specific weakness of all the attempts mentioned above is that they were almost all based, in terms of scientific substantiation, on the so-called overlaps of Mark and Q. This is the case with Wellhausen, Harnack, Streeter, Honey, and others. E. P. Sanders, however, who argued in criticism of Streeter that the relations between the Gospels are more complex than it is generally supposed, has shown that overlapping of Mark and Q constitutes a real difficulty for the Two Document Hypothesis itself as well as "for any rigid and simple solution of the Synoptic Problem."[63]

It would seem to follow, therefore, that the relationship between Mark and Q cannot be determined on literary grounds. W. G. Kümmel has rightly pointed out that "the hypothesis of a literary dependence (between Mark and Q) ... is rather the consequence of the erroneous presupposition that parallels between the materials of the tradition can be explained only by literary dependence."[64] Harnack himself had earlier categorically stated that "no one will be able to prove" that St. Mark made use of Q,[65] although he also asserted that "there exists a relationship between Q and Mark, even a literary relationship,[66] which, however, he called indirect.[67] Nevertheless, some striking similarities, linguistic and others, still await a satisfactory explanation, if we are not to abandon the Two-Document Hypothesis, as Sanders seems to suggest. In consequence, it would seem that we have, if not to abandon, at least not to rely solely on literary analysis, especially on a source-critical approach.

***

*5. Other suggestions.* Some scholars, in fact, have drawn attention in the past fifty years to other means, and have tried to solve the problem of the Q-Marcan agreements by using other methods along with, or separately from, literary criticism. So C. F. Burney has argued on the basis of the Aramaic evidence which underlies the Synoptic Gospels; P. Carrington has applied his calendarical hypothesis to the question why St. Mark made only scanty use of Q; J. R. Brown has produced textual evidence to prove that St. Mark did use Q; and finally a more theological explanation is

---

[62] Ibid. p. 329.
[63] "The Overlaps...," p. 65.
[64] *Op. cit.,* p. 55.
[65] *Op. cit.,* p. 226.
[66] Ibid.
[67] See also n. 54.

found in A. M. McNeile-C. S. C. Williams, *Introduction to the New Testament.*

C. F. Burney's suggestions were made as early as 1925. He thought that the evidence adduced in his study on the Aramaic background of the Gospels[68] "should go far to prove that this (i.e. that St. Mark knew and used Q) was the case,"[69] the evidence being that in Mark the antithetical parallelism is very often broken, whereas in Q it remains unbroken. The *logion* in Mk 8.35=Mt 10.25=Lk 9.24 "is an indication that St. Mark knew and used Q and in this case has glossed it to the detriment of the parallelistic form of the antithesis."[70] Burney also countered the plausible suggestion that Mark had been revised with the observation that this was highly improbable on the ground of the use of Mk 13.9–13 by St. Matthew in a different and more appropriate context (vv. 10.17–22).[71]

P. Carrington's suggestions were obviously the result of his calendarical approach to Mark. The abbreviated form in which St. Mark gives the bulk of his sayings material in comparison with their much more extensive form in the Q-Document, was in fact "a signal to his lector that these sayings of Jesus, in some familiar form, might then be read or delivered by memory.[72] This obviously implies that St. Mark was well acquainted with Q, on which he had based his lectionaries.

J. B. Brown approached the problem from a different angle. He insisted that the textual evidence was a challenge to the familiar tendency to answer *a priori* the question whether St. Mark used/knew the Q-Document or not, "on the basis, as he put it, of our general opinion (of) how the sayings of Jesus circulated."[73] Brown produced, indeed, some striking evidence (even if it was insufficient for proof) for the view that *"the Q tradition was fixed early enough for an edited form of it ($Q^{rev}$) to have lain before Mark."*[74] This $Q^{rev}$ is supposed to have been the revised form of the Q-Document which St. Matthew and St. Mark drew upon, and which can explain the frequent agreements of Matthew and Mark in *secondary* features against Luke.[75] From the historical point of view this $Q^{rev}$ is "an ecclesiastically supplemented, altered, and rearranged version of the original Q to which Luke (alone) witnesses."[76]

Finally, in the revised by C. S. C. Williams edition of A. M. McNeile, *An Introduction to the Study of the New Testament*, Oxford 1953², we find a

---

[68] *The Poetry of our Lord,* Oxford 1925.
[69] Ibid., p. 8.
[70] Ibid., p. 74, n. 4.
[71] Ibid., p. 8f.
[72] P. Carrington, *According to Mark: A Running Commentary on the Oldest Gospel*, Cambridge 1960, p. 165.
[73] "Mark as Witness to an Edited Form of Q," *JBL* 80 (1961), pp. 29-44, esp. p. 29.
[74] Ibid., p. 31.
[75] Ibid.
[76] Ibid., p. 44.

more theological approach. Although Mark's independence of Q is the solution eventually arrived at,[77] it is stated that the theory of St. Mark's acquaintance with Q could equally be held. "That St. Mark lays emphasis on the authoritative power of our Lord's teaching and yet records so little of it, is best explained if he knew that his readers were already in position of a collection of sayings, and needed only a narrative to supplement them."[78]

With the analysis, however, of the Q material since H. E. Tödt such explanations become unnecessary. If the theology of Q is to be regarded as either belonging to a peculiar circle with christological traditions altogether different from Mark (as Tödt believes), or circulating on the borders of Primitive Orthodoxy (as J. M. Robinson and H. Koester imply[79]), then the hypothesis of the supplementation of Q by Mark becomes untenable.

There still remain a number of scholars who, in the course of dealing with other subjects, have clearly favored a development of Mark via Q, and have arrived at this result without employing literary critical methods. E. Schweizer e.g. considers it not unlikely that St. Mark "was acquainted with this collection (Q), but deliberately made no use of it."[80] In fact, the author of the second Gospel was trying to combine in his work three elements of the tradition which were separately emphasized in his time: (i) Jesus' words (Q); (ii) Jesus' cross (Pauline churches); (iii) A «θεῖος ἀνήρ» Christology (Syriac Hellenistic churches).[81] In the specific case of Jesus' teaching, of which the Q-Document almost entirely consists, St. Mark has skillfully transferred the center of gravity from a mere recording of Jesus' actual teaching to God's intervention in Jesus' person (cf. Mk 1.22, 27 etc.).[82]

S. Schulz had also in an earlier article[83] expressed similar views and had pointed out that St. Mark's achievement is to be seen as having united Jesus' tradition with St. Paul's kerygma,[84] and as having reinterpreted Q through a Hellenistic epiphany Christology.[85]

---

[77] Ibid., p. 84.

[78] Ibid., p. 83.

[79] See my dissertation (n. 1).

[80] E. Schweizer, *The Good News according to Mark,* ET, Richmond 1970, p.12. However, Schweizer in an earlier article of his ("Mark's Contribution to the Quest of the Historical Jesus," *NTS* 10 (1964), pp. 421-32, appeared to suggest not that St. Mark knew a written source Q, but that Q still shows more or less what the original (oral?) tradition looked like" (p. 415, n.3).

[81] *The Good News...,* p. 380.

[82] "Mark's Contribution...," p. 422.

[83] "Die Bedeutung des Markus für die Theologiegeschichte des Urchristentums," in *Studia Evangelica* vol. II, ed. by F. L. Cross (Berlin 1964), pp. 134-145.

[84] The question of the *relationship between Paul and the Q-material* is somewhat relevant to the problem of the relationship of Q to Mark, but it has almost always been examined from a wider angle, namely that of the relationship between Jesus and Paul, and therefore, outside the Q-Hypothesis proper.

The scholar, however, who more than any other else in the '70s supported the view that St. Mark used Q is undoubtedly J. Lambrecht. He argued that St. Mark worked with sufficient freedom creating new materials as well as modifying already existing ones. For the composition

---

Thus, A. Resch, *Der Paulinismus und die Logia Jesu in ihrem gegenseitigen Verhältnis untersucht*, Leipzig 1904, relying upon a much wider Q-source than is generally now accepted, suggested that all Luke-Paul agreements in vocabulary must have formed the original text of Q whereas all Matthew-Paul agreements in matter must have alluded the original content of Q. Resch claimed to have discovered in Paul nearly a thousand allusions to Jesus' teaching(!). A. Schweitzer, and H. J. Fowler, however, rejected any dependence of Paul on the Q-material; Schweitzer without entering the Q-Hypothesis in any of its forms *(The Mysticism of Paul the Apostle*, ET, London 1953, pp. 172ff. 389ff.), and Fowler accepting it. Fowler argued from the fact that Q came from the Jerusalem church, whereas Paul's writings from the Hellenistic ("Paul, Q, and the Jerusalem Church," *JBL* 43 (1924), pp. 9ff). A. W. Argyle, does not support the Q-Hypothesis in its classical form, but he believes that Paul was acquainted with the Q-material, or at least with Lk. 6.27–49 par., and Lk 10.1–22 par. ("Parallels between the Pauline Epistles and Q," *ExpT* 60 (1949), pp. 318ff). R. Bultmann, on the other hand, accepts the Q-Hypothesis, but is quite categorical that in Paul "the teaching of the historical Jesus plays no role or practical none" *(Theology of the New Testament,* vol. I., ET, London 1952, p. 35; cf. also pp. 187ff). St. Paul's acquaintance with the Q-material, however, is still being defended by a number of scholars such as W. D. Davies, D. M. Stanley and D. L. Dungan. Davies stated that "it was the words of Jesus Himself that formed Paul's primary source" *(Paul and Rabbinic Judaism,* London 1962, p. 136), and gave examples of both literary dependence on, and allusions to the teaching of Jesus as it is recorded in the Synoptic tradition. So also Stanley, who came to the conclusion that "Paul was familiar with the materials in the oral evangelical tradition". ("Pauline Allusions to the Sayings of Jesu," *CBQ* 23 [1961], pp. 26ff., esp. p. 39). More recently Dungan, who disavows Q, has come to similar conclusion, namely that Paul stood "squarely within the tradition that led to the Synoptic Gospels and that he depended indirectly and allusively upon Jesus' sayings" *(The Sayings of Jesus in the Churches of Paul,* Oxford 1971, pp. 139). More about this crucial debate in Jesus-Paul relations see in V. P. Furnish, "The Jesus-Paul Debate: From Baur to Bultmann," *BJRL* 57 (1965), pp. 342-81; also in D. L. Dungan, *op. cit. pp.* 1 ff. An even more specific contribution, however, on this question was made by J. P. Brown in his article "Synoptic Parallels in the Epistles and Form-History," *NTS* 10 (1963), pp. 27-47. Having earlier suggested that the Q-materials came to St. Luke in substantially their original form while St. Matthew and St. Mark drew upon a revision, Brown carried further his views by claiming to have produced sufficient evidence that the "epistolary parallels to Q-materials must be due to the Apostle's having echoed Q-materials, consciously or not" (p. 28). In his view, *"epistolary parallels to Q agree with Luke's form of Q in original matter only; whereas...epistolary parallels to Q frequently agree with Matthew and Mark in secondary matter"* (ibid.).

In any case, as M. Brückener pointed out "the discovery of parallels does not necessarily mean that one has thereby proved the dependence of one source upon the other" ("Zur Thema Jesus und Paulus," *ZNW* 7 (1906), pp. 112ff.). In our view, it seems quite certain that whereas Paul knew some sayings of Jesus, there is insufficient evidence either to prove or to disprove that he has access to the Q-Document itself (cf. G. N. Stanton, *Jesus of Nazareth in N.T. Preaching,* Cambridge, 1975).

85 "Die Bedeutung....," p. 144.

of Mk 13,[86] and Mk 3.20–35,[87] in particular, there is sufficient evidence that the second evangelist knew and used the Q-Document.

Finally, R. C. Hamerton-Kelly has recently suggested that St. Mark "has taken up and interpreted some of the same traditions as occur in Q;"[88] more precisely, "the identification of Jesus in Q as Wisdom's eschatological envoy and the rejected Son of Man is adopted by St. Mark so as to make Q's point more explicit".[89]

\*\*\*

*6. Conclusions:* From the discussion so far two points, at least, seem quite clear: Firstly, the Q-Document cannot have depended on Mark; and secondly the relationship between Mark and Q has to be determined on grounds others than literary. The whole problem, therefore, would seem to reduce itself to the following questions: (i) Did St. Mark have any knowledge of Q-traditions? (ii) If he did, is there any explicit evidence that he was acquainted with the Q-Document itself? (iii) If he was, did he derive any material therefrom? and finally (iv) if so, was his attitude to the Q-materials receptive or critical?[90]

---

[86] *Die Redaction des Markus-Apokalypse,* Rome 1967.

[87] "Ware verwantschap en eenwige ronde Ontstaan en structuur van Mc 3.20–35," *Bijdragen* 29 (1968), pp. 114-50, 234-58, 369-93.

[88] *Pre-Existence, Wisdom, and the Son of Man,* Cambridge 1973, p. 67.

[89] Ibid.

[90] I had finished this essay when I came across V. Devisch's interesting paper "La relation entre l' évangile de Marc at le document Q," read in a conference on Mark held at Louvain, and published in M. Sabbe (ed.), *L'Evangile selon Marc: Tradition et rédaction,* Gembloux 1974, pp. 59-91. Devisch proceeds along similar lines and concludes, among others, that Mark and Q are independent of each other (p. 91).

# 5
# THE Q TEXT.
## A BASIC RECONSTRUCTION OF THE Q-DOCUMENT

The text which follows is a *basic,* i.e. not detailed, reconstruction of the Q-Document at its final stage, when it was actually utilized by the later Synoptists. It is basically based on the preceding literary studies, corresponding with very few exceptions to proposed reconstruction of the second study, which was based on our 7 procedural principles. At the end of the document, however, we include other possible sayings, which are usually attributed to the Q-Document by other scholars.

We decided to avoid the detailed and minute selection of the wording, in order to give a clear overall picture to the student of Q. In the footnote, however, we always give the alternative or variant reading of the other Synoptic, by citing either the entire pericope—in cases of extended divergence—or the alternative phrase or word—in cases of close or verbatim agreement.

The only abbreviations and *sigla* we use are the following:

    add.=*addit/addunt*   (Matthaean/Lucan additions)
    om.=*omittit/omittunt*  (Matthaean/Lucan omissions)
    var.=*varit*  (Matthaean/Lucan variant)
    <   = the following saying/pericope is to be placed *after* the numbered section of the main text
    >   = the following saying/pericope is to be placed *before* the numbered section of the main text

## I. INTRODUCTION

### 1. The Preaching of John the Baptist
(Lk 3:7-9; 16f = Mt 3:7-12)

...Ἔλεγεν (Ἰωάννης) ...[1] Γεννήματα ἐχιδνῶν, τίς ὑπέδειξεν ὑμῖν φυγεῖν ἀπὸ τῆς μελλούσης ὀργῆς; ποιήσατε οὖν καρποὺς ἀξίους τῆς μετανοίας· καὶ μὴ ἄρξησθε λέγειν ἐν ἑαυτοῖς, Πατέρα ἔχομεν τὸν Ἀβραάμ, λέγω γὰρ ὑμῖν ὅτι δύναται ὁ θεὸς ἐκ τῶν λίθων τούτων ἐγεῖραι τέκνα τῷ Ἀβραάμ. ἤδη δὲ καὶ ἡ ἀξίνη πρὸς τὴν ῥίζαν τῶν δένδρων κεῖται· πᾶν οὖν δένδρον μὴ ποιοῦν καρπὸν καλὸν ἐκκόπτεται καὶ εἰς πῦρ βάλλεται. ...

Ἐγὼ μὲν ὕδατι βαπτίζω ὑμᾶς,[2] ἔρχεται δὲ ὁ ἰσχυρότερός μου,[3] οὗ οὐκ εἰμὶ ἱκανὸς λῦσαι τὸν ἱμάντα τῶν ὑποδημάτων αὐτοῦ· αὐτὸς ὑμᾶς βαπτίσει ἐν πνεύματι ...[4] καὶ πυρί· οὗ τὸ πτύον ἐν τῇ χειρὶ αὐτοῦ διακαθᾶραι τὴν ἅλωνα αὐτοῦ καὶ συναγαγεῖν τὸν σῖτον εἰς τὴν ἀποθήκην αὐτοῦ, τὸ δὲ ἄχυρον κατακαύσει πυρὶ ἀσβέστῳ.[5]

### 2. The Temptations of Jesus
(Lk 4:1-13 = Mt 4:1-11)

[Ἰησοῦς δὲ][6] ἤγετο ἐν τῷ πνεύματι ἐν τῇ ἐρήμῳ ἡμέρας τεσσεράκοντα πειραζόμενος ὑπὸ τοῦ διαβόλου. καὶ οὐκ ἔφαγεν οὐδὲν ἐν ταῖς ἡμέραις ἐκείναις, καὶ συντελεσθεισῶν αὐτῶν ἐπείνασεν.

Εἶπεν δὲ αὐτῷ ὁ διάβολος, Εἰ υἱὸς εἶ τοῦ θεοῦ, εἰπὲ τῷ λίθῳ τούτῳ ἵνα γένηται ἄρτος. καὶ ἀπεκρίθη πρὸς αὐτὸν ὁ Ἰησοῦς, Γέγραπται ὅτι Οὐκ ἐπ' ἄρτῳ μόνῳ ζήσεται ὁ ἄνθρωπος.

---

[1] Mt add. Ἰδὼν δὲ πολλοὺς τῶν Φαρισαίων καὶ Σαδδουκαίων ἐρχομένους ἐπὶ τὸ βάπτισμα αὐτοῦ εἶπεν αὐτοῖς. Lk add. Ἔλεγεν οὖν τοῖς ἐκπορευομένοις ὄχλοις βαπτισθῆναι ὑπ' αὐτοῦ.

[2] Mt add. εἰς μετάνοιαν

[3] Mt var. ὁ δὲ ὀπίσω μου ἐρχόμενος ἰσχυρότερός μού ἐστιν

[4] Mt & Lk add. ἁγίῳ.

[5] Some kind of a Baptism story may have possibly existed in Q.

[6] Mt add. Τότε ὁ Ἰησοῦς ἀνήχθη εἰς τὴν ἔρημον. Lk add. πλήρης πνεύματος ἁγίου ὑπέστρεψεν ἀπὸ τοῦ Ἰορδάνου.

Καὶ ἀναγαγὼν αὐτὸν ἔδειξεν αὐτῷ πάσας τὰς βασιλείας τῆς οἰκουμένης ἐν στιγμῇ χρόνου· καὶ εἶπεν αὐτῷ ὁ διάβολος, Σοὶ δώσω τὴν ἐξουσίαν ταύτην ἅπασαν καὶ τὴν δόξαν αὐτῶν, ὅτι ἐμοὶ παραδέδοται καὶ ᾧ ἐὰν θέλω δίδωμι αὐτήν· σὺ οὖν ἐὰν προσκυνήσῃς ἐνώπιον ἐμοῦ, ἔσται σοῦ πᾶσα. καὶ ἀποκριθεὶς ὁ Ἰησοῦς εἶπεν αὐτῷ, Γέγραπται, Κύριον τὸν θεόν σου προσκυνήσεις καὶ αὐτῷ μόνῳ λατρεύσεις.[7]

Ἤγαγεν δὲ αὐτὸν εἰς Ἰερουσαλὴμ καὶ ἔστησεν ἐπὶ τὸ πτερύγιον τοῦ ἱεροῦ, καὶ εἶπεν αὐτῷ, Εἰ υἱὸς εἶ τοῦ θεοῦ, βάλε σεαυτὸν ἐντεῦθεν κάτω· γέγραπται γὰρ ὅτι Τοῖς ἀγγέλοις αὐτοῦ ἐντελεῖται περὶ σοῦ τοῦ διαφυλάξαι σε, καὶ ὅτι Ἐπὶ χειρῶν ἀροῦσίν σε μήποτε προσκόψῃς πρὸς λίθον τὸν πόδα σου. καὶ ἀποκριθεὶς εἶπεν αὐτῷ ὁ Ἰησοῦς ὅτι Εἴρηται, Οὐκ ἐκπειράσεις κύριον τὸν θεόν σου.

Καὶ συντελέσας πάντα πειρασμὸν ὁ διάβολος ἀπέστη ἀπ' αὐτοῦ.[8]

## II. THE TEACHING OF JESUS[9]

### 3. The Beatitudes
(Lk 6:20-23 = Mt 5:3-12)

Καὶ (Ἰησοῦς) ἐπάρας τοὺς ὀφθαλμοὺς αὐτοῦ εἰς τοὺς μαθητὰς αὐτοῦ ἔλεγεν,
    Μακάριοι οἱ πτωχοί,[10]
        ὅτι ὑμετέρα ἐστὶν ἡ βασιλεία τοῦ θεοῦ.[11]
    μακάριοι οἱ πεινῶντες[12] νῦν,
        ὅτι χορτασθήσεσθε.
    μακάριοι οἱ κλαίοντες[13] νῦν,
        ὅτι γελάσετε.

---

[7]Mt has placed the 2nd temptation 3rd.

[8]Mt var. Τότε ἀφίησιν αὐτὸν ὁ διάβολος. Lk add. ἄχρι καιροῦ.

[9]Note the difference in the setting as well as in the audience. Mt has Ἰδὼν δὲ τοὺς ὄχλους ἀνέβη εἰς τὸ ὄρος· καὶ καθίσαντος αὐτοῦ προσῆλθαν αὐτῷ οἱ μαθηταὶ αὐτοῦ· καὶ ἀνοίξας τὸ στόμα αὐτοῦ ἐδίδασκεν αὐτοὺς λέγων (5:1-2); Lk has Καὶ καταβὰς μετ' αὐτῶν ἔστη ἐπὶ τόπου πεδινοῦ, καὶ ὄχλος πολὺς μαθητῶν αὐτοῦ, καὶ πλῆθος πολὺ τοῦ λαου' (6:17).

[10]Mt add. τῷ πνεύματι

[11]Mt var. βασιλεία τῶν οὐρανῶν.

[12]Mt add. καὶ διψῶντες τὴν δικαιοσύνην.

[13]Mt var. πενθοῦντες.

μακάριοί έστε όταν μισήσωσιν ύμας οι άνθρωποι, και όταν αφορίσωσιν ύμας και ονειδίσωσιν και έκβάλωσιν τὸ ὄνομα ύμων ώς πονηρὸν ένεκα τοῦ υἱοῦ τοῦ ἀνθρώπου·[14] χάρητε ἐν ἐκείνῃ τῇ ἡμέρᾳ καὶ σκιρτήσατε, ἰδοὺ γὰρ ὁ μισθὸς ὑμῶν πολὺς ἐν τῷ οὐρανῷ· κατὰ τὰ αὐτὰ γὰρ ἐποίουν τοῖς προφήταις οἱ πατέρες αὐτῶν.[15]

## 4. The Golden Rule
(Lk 6:27-36=Mt 5:39-48)[16]

Ἀλλὰ ὑμῖν λέγω τοῖς ἀκούουσιν,
   ἀγαπᾶτε τοὺς ἐχθροὺς ὑμῶν,
      καλῶς ποιεῖτε τοῖς μισοῦσιν ὑμᾶς,
         εὐλογεῖτε τοὺς καταρωμένους ὑμᾶς,
            προσεύχεσθε περὶ τῶν ἐπηρεαζόντων ὑμᾶς.[17]
   τῷ τύπτοντί σε ἐπὶ τὴν σιαγόνα
      πάρεχε καὶ τὴν ἄλλην,[18]
   καὶ ἀπὸ τοῦ αἴροντός σου τὸ ἱμάτιον
      καὶ τὸν χιτῶνα μὴ κωλύσῃς.[19]
   παντὶ αἰτοῦντί σε δίδου,
      καὶ ἀπὸ τοῦ αἴροντος τὰ σὰ μὴ ἀπαίτει.[20]
καὶ καθὼς θέλετε ἵνα ποιῶσιν ὑμῖν οἱ ἄνθρωποι,
   ποιεῖτε αὐτοῖς ὁμοίως.[21]
καὶ εἰ ἀγαπᾶτε τοὺς ἀγαπῶντας ὑμᾶς,
   ποία ὑμῖν χάρις ἐστίν;
      καὶ γὰρ οἱ ἁμαρτωλοὶ τοὺς ἀγαπῶντας αὐτοὺς ἀγαπῶσιν.[22]
καὶ [γὰρ] ἐὰν ἀγαθοποιῆτε τοὺς ἀγαθοποιοῦντας ὑμᾶς,
   ποία ὑμῖν χάρις ἐστίν;

---

[14]Mt var. ἕνεκεν ἐμοῦ.

[15]Mt var. οὕτως γὰρ ἐδίωξαν τοὺς προφήτας τοὺς πρὸ ὑμῶν.

[16]Mt has placed this pericope within his antitheses.

[17]Mt var. ἀγαπᾶτε τοὺς ἐχθροὺς ὑμῶν καὶ προσεύχεσθε ὑπὲρ τῶν διωκόντων ὑμᾶς

[18]Mt var. ἀλλ' ὅστις σε ῥαπίζει εἰς τὴν δεξιὰν σιαγόνα [σου], στρέψον αὐτῷ καὶ τὴν ἄλλην·

[19]Mt var. καὶ τῷ θέλοντί σοι κριθῆναι καὶ τὸν χιτῶνά σου λαβεῖν, ἄφες αὐτῷ καὶ τὸ ἱμάτιον. Mt add. καὶ ὅστις σε ἀγγαρεύσει μίλιον ἕν, ὕπαγε μετ' αὐτοῦ δύο.

[20]Mt var. τῷ αἰτοῦντί σε δός, καὶ τὸν θέλοντα ἀπὸ σοῦ δανίσασθαι μὴ ἀποστραφῇς.

[21]Mt om.

[22]Mt var. ἐὰν γὰρ ἀγαπήσητε τοὺς ἀγαπῶντας ὑμᾶς, τίνα μισθὸν ἔχετε; οὐχὶ καὶ οἱ τελῶναι τὸ αὐτὸ ποιοῦσιν;

καὶ οἱ ἁμαρτωλοὶ τὸ αὐτὸ ποιοῦσιν.²³
καὶ ἐὰν δανίσητε παρ' ὧν ἐλπίζετε λαβεῖν,
ποία ὑμῖν χάρις [ἐστίν];
καὶ ἁμαρτωλοὶ ἁμαρτωλοῖς δανίζουσιν
ἵνα ἀπολάβωσιν τὰ ἴσα.
πλὴν ἀγαπᾶτε τοὺς ἐχθροὺς ὑμῶν
καὶ ἀγαθοποιεῖτε καὶ δανίζετε μηδὲν ἀπελπίζοντες·
καὶ ἔσται ὁ μισθὸς ὑμῶν πολύς, καὶ ἔσεσθε υἱοὶ ὑψίστου,
ὅτι αὐτὸς χρηστός ἐστιν ἐπὶ τοὺς ἀχαρίστους καὶ
πονηρούς.²⁴ Γίνεσθε οἰκτίρμονες καθὼς [καὶ] ὁ πατὴρ ὑμῶν
οἰκτίρμων ἐστίν.²⁵

### 5. On judging
(Lk 6:37f =Mt 7:1f)

Καὶ μὴ κρίνετε, καὶ οὐ μὴ κριθῆτε·
καὶ μὴ καταδικάζετε, καὶ οὐ μὴ καταδικασθῆτε.
ἀπολύετε, καὶ ἀπολυθήσεσθε·
δίδοτε, καὶ δοθήσεται ὑμῖν·
μέτρον καλὸν πεπιεσμένον σεσαλευμένον ὑπερεκχυννόμενον
δώσουσιν εἰς τὸν κόλπον ὑμῶν· ᾧ γὰρ μέτρῳ μετρεῖτε
ἀντιμετρηθήσεται ὑμῖν.²⁶

### 6. On hypocricy
(Lk 6:41f = Mt 7:3-5)

Τί δὲ βλέπεις τὸ κάρφος τὸ ἐν τῷ ὀφθαλμῷ τοῦ ἀδελφοῦ
σου, τὴν δὲ δοκὸν τὴν ἐν τῷ ἰδίῳ ὀφθαλμῷ²⁷ οὐ κατανοεῖς;
πῶς δύνασαι λέγειν²⁸ τῷ ἀδελφῷ σου,

---

²³Mt var. καὶ ἐὰν ἀσπάσησθε τοὺς ἀδελφοὺς ὑμῶν μόνον, τί περισσὸν ποιεῖτε; οὐχὶ καὶ οἱ ἐθνικοὶ τὸ αὐτὸ ποιοῦσιν;

²⁴Mt var. ὅπως γένησθε υἱοὶ τοῦ πατρὸς ὑμῶν τοῦ ἐν οὐρανοῖς, ὅτι τὸν ἥλιον αὐτοῦ ἀνατέλλει ἐπὶ πονηροὺς καὶ ἀγαθοὺς καὶ βρέχει ἐπὶ δικαίους καὶ ἀδίκους.

²⁵Mt var. ἔσεσθε οὖν ὑμεῖς τέλειοι ὡς ὁ πατὴρ ὑμῶν ὁ οὐράνιος τέλειός ἐστιν.

²⁶Mt var. Μὴ κρίνετε, ἵνα μὴ κριθῆτε· ἐν ᾧ γὰρ κρίματι κρίνετε κριθήσεσθε, καὶ ἐν ᾧ μέτρῳ μετρεῖτε μετρηθήσεται ὑμῖν.

²⁷Mt var. τὴν δὲ ἐν τῷ σῷ ὀφθαλμῷ δοκὸν

²⁸Mt var. ἢ πῶς ἐρεῖς

'Αδελφέ,[29] ἄφες ἐκβάλω τὸ κάρφος τὸ ἐν τῷ ὀφθαλμῷ σου,[30] αὐτὸς τὴν ἐν τῷ ὀφθαλμῷ σοῦ δοκὸν οὐ βλέπων;[31] ὑποκριτά, ἔκβαλε πρῶτον τὴν δοκὸν ἐκ τοῦ ὀφθαλμοῦ σου, καὶ τότε διαβλέψεις τὸ κάρφος τὸ ἐν τῷ ὀφθαλμῷ τοῦ ἀδελφοῦ σου ἐκβαλεῖν.[32]

## 7. On good and bad fruit
(Lk 6:43-45 = Mt 7:16-20)

Οὐ γάρ ἐστιν δένδρον καλὸν ποιοῦν καρπὸν σαπρόν,
οὐδὲ πάλιν δένδρον σαπρὸν ποιοῦν καρπὸν καλόν.
ἕκαστον γὰρ δένδρον ἐκ τοῦ ἰδίου καρποῦ γινώσκεται·
οὐ γὰρ ἐξ ἀκανθῶν συλλέγουσιν σῦκα,
οὐδὲ ἐκ βάτου σταφυλὴν τρυγῶσιν.
ὁ ἀγαθὸς ἄνθρωπος ἐκ τοῦ ἀγαθοῦ θησαυροῦ τῆς καρδίας προφέρει τὸ ἀγαθόν, καὶ ὁ πονηρὸς ἐκ τοῦ πονηροῦ προφέρει τὸ πονηρόν· ἐκ γὰρ περισσεύματος καρδίας λαλεῖ τὸ στόμα αὐτοῦ.[33]

## 8. Building on the rock
(Lk 6:46b-49 = Mt 7:21. 24-27)

Τί δέ με καλεῖτε, Κύριε κύριε, καὶ οὐ ποιεῖτε ἃ λέγω;[34] πᾶς ὁ ἐρχόμενος πρός με καὶ ἀκούων μου τῶν λόγων καὶ ποιῶν αὐτούς, ὑποδείξω ὑμῖν τίνι ἐστὶν ὅμοιος· ὅμοιός ἐστιν ἀνθρώπῳ οἰκοδομοῦντι οἰκίαν ὃς ἔσκαψεν καὶ ἐβάθυνεν καὶ ἔθηκεν θεμέλιον ἐπὶ τὴν πέτραν· πλημμύρης δὲ γενομένης προσέρηξεν ὁ ποταμὸς τῇ οἰκίᾳ ἐκείνῃ, καὶ οὐκ ἴσχυσεν σαλεῦσαι αὐτὴν διὰ τὸ καλῶς οἰκοδομῆσθαι αὐτήν. ὁ δὲ ἀκούσας καὶ μὴ ποιήσας ὅμοιός ἐστιν ἀνθρώπῳ

---

[29] Mt om.

[30] Mt var. ἐκ τοῦ ὀφθαλμοῦ σου

[31] Mt var. καὶ ἰδοὺ ἡ δοκὸς ἐν τῷ ὀφθαλμῷ σοῦ;

[32] Mt var. καὶ τότε διαβλέψεις ἐκβαλεῖν τὸ κάρφος ἐκ τοῦ ὀφθαλμοῦ τοῦ ἀδελφοῦ σου.

[33] Mt var. ἀπὸ τῶν καρπῶν αὐτῶν ἐπιγνώσεσθε αὐτούς· μήτι συλλέγουσιν ἀπὸ ἀκανθῶν σταφυλὰς ἢ ἀπὸ τριβόλων σῦκα; οὕτως πᾶν δένδρον ἀγαθὸν καρποὺς καλοὺς ποιεῖ, τὸ δὲ σαπρὸν δένδρον καρποὺς πονηροὺς ποιεῖ· οὐ δύναται δένδρον ἀγαθὸν καρποὺς πονηροὺς ποιεῖν, οὐδὲ δένδρον σαπρὸν καρποὺς καλοὺς ποιεῖν. πᾶν δένδρον μὴ ποιοῦν καρπὸν καλὸν ἐκκόπτεται καὶ εἰς πῦρ βάλλεται. ἄρα γε ἀπὸ τῶν καρπῶν αὐτῶν ἐπιγνώσεσθε αὐτούς.

[34] Mt var. Οὐ πᾶς ὁ λέγων μοι, Κύριε κύριε, εἰσελεύσεται εἰς τὴν βασιλείαν τῶν οὐρανῶν, ἀλλ' ὁ ποιῶν τὸ θέλημα τοῦ πατρός μου τοῦ ἐν τοῖς οὐρανοῖς.

οἰκοδομήσαντι οἰκίαν ἐπὶ τὴν γῆν χωρὶς θεμελίου, ᾗ προσέρηξεν ὁ ποταμός, καὶ εὐθὺς συνέπεσεν, καὶ ἐγένετο τὸ ῥῆγμα τῆς οἰκίας ἐκείνης μέγα.³⁵

## III. RESPONSE TO JESUS' TEACHING

### 9. The Centurion's servant (son)
(Lk 7:1-10 = Mt 8:5-13)

Ἐπειδὴ ἐπλήρωσεν πάντα τὰ ῥήματα αὐτοῦ εἰς τὰς ἀκοὰς τοῦ λαοῦ,³⁶ εἰσῆλθεν εἰς Καφαρναούμ. Ἑκατοντάρχου δέ τινος δοῦλος³⁷ κακῶς ἔχων ἤμελλεν τελευτᾶν, ὃς ἦν αὐτῷ ἔντιμος. ἀκούσας δὲ περὶ τοῦ Ἰησοῦ ἀπέστειλεν πρὸς αὐτὸν πρεσβυτέρους τῶν Ἰουδαίων, ἐρωτῶν αὐτὸν ὅπως ἐλθὼν διασώσῃ τὸν δοῦλον αὐτοῦ. οἱ δὲ παραγενόμενοι πρὸς τὸν Ἰησοῦν παρεκάλουν αὐτὸν σπουδαίως, λέγοντες ὅτι Ἄξιός ἐστιν ᾧ παρέξῃ τοῦτο, ἀγαπᾷ γὰρ τὸ ἔθνος ἡμῶν καὶ τὴν συναγωγὴν αὐτὸς ᾠκοδόμησεν ἡμῖν. ὁ δὲ Ἰησοῦς ἐπορεύετο σὺν αὐτοῖς. ἤδη δὲ αὐτοῦ οὐ μακρὰν ἀπέχοντος ἀπὸ τῆς οἰκίας ἔπεμψεν φίλους ὁ ἑκατοντάρχης λέγων αὐτῷ, Κύριε, μὴ σκύλλου, οὐ γὰρ ἱκανός εἰμι ἵνα ὑπὸ τὴν στέγην μου εἰσέλθῃς· διὸ οὐδὲ ἐμαυτὸν ἠξίωσα πρὸς σὲ ἐλθεῖν· ἀλλὰ εἰπὲ λόγῳ, καὶ ἰαθήτω ὁ παῖς μου. καὶ γὰρ ἐγὼ ἄνθρωπός εἰμι ὑπὸ ἐξουσίαν τασσόμενος, ἔχων ὑπ' ἐμαυτὸν στρατιώτας, καὶ λέγω τούτῳ, Πορεύθητι, καὶ πορεύεται, καὶ ἄλλῳ, Ἔρχου, καὶ ἔρχεται, καὶ τῷ δούλῳ μου, Ποίησον τοῦτο, καὶ ποιεῖ. ἀκούσας δὲ ταῦτα ὁ Ἰησοῦς ἐθαύμασεν αὐτόν, καὶ στραφεὶς τῷ ἀκολουθοῦντι αὐτῷ ὄχλῳ εἶπεν, Λέγω ὑμῖν, οὐδὲ ἐν τῷ Ἰσραὴλ τοσαύτην πίστιν εὗρον. καὶ

---

³⁵Mt var. Πᾶς οὖν ὅστις ἀκούει μου τοὺς λόγους τούτους καὶ ποιεῖ αὐτοὺς ὁμοιωθήσεται ἀνδρὶ φρονίμῳ, ὅστις ᾠκοδόμησεν αὐτοῦ τὴν οἰκίαν ἐπὶ τὴν πέτραν. καὶ κατέβη ἡ βροχὴ καὶ ἦλθον οἱ ποταμοὶ καὶ ἔπνευσαν οἱ ἄνεμοι καὶ προσέπεσαν τῇ οἰκίᾳ ἐκείνῃ, καὶ οὐκ ἔπεσεν, τεθεμελίωτο γὰρ ἐπὶ τὴν πέτραν. καὶ πᾶς ὁ ἀκούων μου τοὺς λόγους τούτους καὶ μὴ ποιῶν αὐτοὺς ὁμοιωθήσεται ἀνδρὶ μωρῷ, ὅστις ᾠκοδόμησεν αὐτοῦ τὴν οἰκίαν ἐπὶ τὴν ἄμμον. καὶ κατέβη ἡ βροχὴ καὶ ἦλθον οἱ ποταμοὶ καὶ ἔπνευσαν οἱ ἄνεμοι καὶ προσέκοψαν τῇ οἰκίᾳ ἐκείνῃ, καὶ ἔπεσεν, καὶ ἦν ἡ πτῶσις αὐτῆς μεγάλη.

³⁶Cf. Mt's concluding statement on Jesus' sermon on the mount (7:28): Καὶ ἐγένετο ὅτε ἐτέλεσεν ὁ Ἰησοῦς τοὺς λόγους τούτους ἐξεπλήσσοντο οἱ ὄχλοι ἐπὶ τῇ διδαχῇ αὐτοῦ·

³⁷Mt var. παῖς.

ὑποστρέψαντες εἰς τὸν οἶκον οἱ πεμφθέντες εὗρον τὸν δοῦλον ὑγιαίνοντα.[38]

## 10. Jesus and John the Baptist
(Lk 7:18-35 = Mt 11:2-19)[39]

Καὶ προσκαλεσάμενος δύο τινὰς[40] τῶν μαθητῶν αὐτοῦ ὁ Ἰωάννης ἔπεμψεν πρὸς τὸν κύριον λέγων,[41] Σὺ εἶ ὁ ἐρχόμενος ἢ ἄλλον[42] προσδοκῶμεν; ...[43] καὶ ἀποκριθεὶς [ὁ Ἰησοῦς] εἶπεν αὐτοῖς, Πορευθέντες ἀπαγγείλατε Ἰωάννῃ ἃ καὶ ἀκούετε καὶ βλέπετε·[44] τυφλοὶ ἀναβλέπουσιν, χωλοὶ περιπατοῦσιν, λεπροὶ καθαρίζονται καὶ κωφοὶ ἀκούουσιν, νεκροὶ ἐγείρονται,[45] πτωχοὶ εὐαγγελίζονται· καὶ μακάριός ἐστιν ὃς ἐὰν μὴ σκανδαλισθῇ ἐν ἐμοί.

---

[38]The complete Matthaean version is: Εἰσελθόντος δὲ αὐτοῦ εἰς Καφαρναοὺμ προσῆλθεν αὐτῷ ἑκατόνταρχος παρακαλῶν αὐτὸν καὶ λέγων, Κύριε, ὁ παῖς μου βέβληται ἐν τῇ οἰκίᾳ παραλυτικός, δεινῶς βασανιζόμενος. καὶ λέγει αὐτῷ, Ἐγὼ ἐλθὼν θεραπεύσω αὐτόν. καὶ ἀποκριθεὶς ὁ ἑκατόνταρχος ἔφη, Κύριε, οὐκ εἰμὶ ἱκανὸς ἵνα μου ὑπὸ τὴν στέγην εἰσέλθῃς· ἀλλὰ μόνον εἰπὲ λόγῳ, καὶ ἰαθήσεται ὁ παῖς μου. καὶ γὰρ ἐγὼ ἄνθρωπός εἰμι ὑπὸ ἐξουσίαν, ἔχων ὑπ' ἐμαυτὸν στρατιώτας, καὶ λέγω τούτῳ, Πορεύθητι, καὶ πορεύεται, καὶ ἄλλῳ, Ἔρχου, καὶ ἔρχεται, καὶ τῷ δούλῳ μου, Ποίησον τοῦτο, καὶ ποιεῖ. ἀκούσας δὲ ὁ Ἰησοῦς ἐθαύμασεν καὶ εἶπεν τοῖς ἀκολουθοῦσιν, Ἀμὴν λέγω ὑμῖν, παρ' οὐδενὶ τοσαύτην πίστιν ἐν τῷ Ἰσραὴλ εὗρον. λέγω δὲ ὑμῖν ὅτι πολλοὶ ἀπὸ ἀνατολῶν καὶ δυσμῶν ἥξουσιν καὶ ἀνακλιθήσονται μετὰ Ἀβραὰμ καὶ Ἰσαὰκ καὶ Ἰακὼβ ἐν τῇ βασιλείᾳ τῶν οὐρανῶν· οἱ δὲ υἱοὶ τῆς βασιλείας ἐκβληθήσονται εἰς τὸ σκότος τὸ ἐξώτερον· ἐκεῖ ἔσται ὁ κλαυθμὸς καὶ ὁ βρυγμὸς τῶν ὀδόντων. καὶ εἶπεν ὁ Ἰησοῦς τῷ ἑκατοντάρχῃ, Ὕπαγε, ὡς ἐπίστευσας γενηθήτω σοι. καὶ ἰάθη ὁ παῖς [αὐτοῦ] ἐν τῇ ὥρᾳ ἐκείνῃ.

[39]Lk introduces the pericope with καὶ ἀπήγγειλαν Ἰωάννῃ οἱ μαθηταὶ αὐτοῦ περὶ πάντων τούτων; Mt with ὁ δὲ Ἰωάννης ἀκούσας ἐν τῷ δεσμωτηρίῳ τὰ ἔργα τοῦ Χριστοῦ

[40]Mt var. διὰ

[41]Mt var. εἶπεν αὐτῷ

[42]Mt var. ἕτερον

[43]Lk add. παραγενόμενοι δὲ πρὸς αὐτὸν οἱ ἄνδρες εἶπαν, Ἰωάννης ὁ βαπτιστὴς ἀπέστειλεν ἡμᾶς πρὸς σὲ λέγων, Σὺ εἶ ὁ ἐρχόμενος ἢ ἄλλον προσδοκῶμεν;

[44]Lk var. εἴδετε καὶ ἠκούσατε

[45]Mt add. καὶ

Ἀπελθόντων δὲ τῶν ἀγγέλων Ἰωάννου⁴⁶ ἤρξατο⁴⁷ λέγειν πρὸς τοὺς ὄχλους⁴⁸ περὶ Ἰωάννου, Τί ἐξήλθατε εἰς τὴν ἔρημον θεάσασθαι; κάλαμον ὑπὸ ἀνέμου σαλευόμενον; ἀλλὰ τί ἐξήλθατε ἰδεῖν; ἄνθρωπον ἐν μαλακοῖς ἱματίοις⁴⁹ ἠμφιεσμένον; ἰδοὺ οἱ ἐν ἱματισμῷ ἐνδόξῳ καὶ τρυφῇ ὑπάρχοντες ἐν τοῖς βασιλείοις εἰσίν.⁵⁰ ἀλλὰ τί ἐξήλθατε ἰδεῖν; προφήτην; ναί, λέγω ὑμῖν, καὶ περισσότερον προφήτου. οὗτός ἐστιν περὶ οὗ γέγραπται,
Ἰδοὺ ⁵¹ἀποστέλλω τὸν ἄγγελόν μου πρὸ προσώπου σου,
ὃς κατασκευάσει τὴν ὁδόν σου ἔμπροσθέν σου.
⁵²λέγω ὑμῖν, μείζων ἐν γεννητοῖς γυναικῶν Ἰωάννου οὐδείς ἐστιν.⁵³ ὁ δὲ μικρότερος ἐν τῇ βασιλείᾳ τοῦ θεοῦ μείζων αὐτοῦ ἐστιν.....

[ἀπὸ δὲ τῶν ἡμερῶν Ἰωάννου τοῦ βαπτιστοῦ ἕως ἄρτι ἡ βασιλεία τῶν οὐρανῶν βιάζεται, καὶ βιασταὶ ἁρπάζουσιν αὐτήν. πάντες γὰρ οἱ προφῆται καὶ ὁ νόμος ἕως Ἰωάννου ἐπροφήτευσαν (Mt 11:11f.)⁵⁴]

Τίνι οὖν⁵⁵ ὁμοιώσω τοὺς ἀνθρώπους τῆς γενεᾶς ταύτης,⁵⁶ καὶ τίνι εἰσὶν ὅμοιοι;⁵⁷ ὅμοιοί εἰσιν⁵⁸ παιδίοις τοῖς ἐν ἀγορᾷ καθημένοις⁵⁹ καὶ προσφωνοῦσιν ἀλλήλοις,⁶⁰ ἃ λέγει,⁶¹

---

⁴⁶Mt var. Τούτων δὲ πορευομένων
⁴⁷Mt add. ὁ Ἰησοῦς
⁴⁸Mt var. τοῖς ὄχλοις
⁴⁹Mt om.
⁵⁰Mt var. ἰδοὺ οἱ τὰ μαλακὰ φοροῦντες ἐν τοῖς οἴκοις τῶν βασιλέων εἰσίν.
⁵¹Mt add. ἐγὼ
⁵²Mt add. ἀμὴν
⁵³Mt var. οὐκ ἐγήγερται ἐν γεννητοῖς γυναικῶν μείζων Ἰωάννου τοῦ βαπτιστοῦ·
⁵⁴Lk var. Ὁ νόμος καὶ οἱ προφῆται μέχρι Ἰωάννου· ἀπὸ τότε ἡ βασιλεία τοῦ θεοῦ εὐαγγελίζεται καὶ πᾶς εἰς αὐτὴν βιάζεται. (Lk 16:16)
⁵⁵Mt var. δὲ
⁵⁶Mt var. τὴν γενεὰν ταύτην
⁵⁷Mt om.
⁵⁸Mt var. ὁμοία ἐστὶν
⁵⁹Mt var. καθημένοις ἐν ταῖς ἀγοραῖς
⁶⁰Mt var. ἃ προσφωνοῦντα τοῖς ἑτέροις
⁶¹Mt var. λέγουσιν,

Ηὐλήσαμεν ὑμῖν καὶ οὐκ ὠρχήσασθε·
ἐθρηνήσαμεν καὶ οὐκ ἐκλαύσατε.⁶²
ἐλήλυθεν⁶³ γὰρ Ἰωάννης⁶⁴ μὴ⁶⁵ ἐσθίων⁶⁶ μήτε πίνων,⁶⁷ καὶ λέγετε,⁶⁸ Δαιμόνιον ἔχει· ἐλήλυθεν⁵⁶ ὁ υἱὸς τοῦ ἀνθρώπου ἐσθίων καὶ πίνων, καὶ λέγετε,⁶¹ Ἰδοὺ ἄνθρωπος φάγος καὶ οἰνοπότης, φίλος τελωνῶν⁶⁹ καὶ ἁμαρτωλῶν. καὶ ἐδικαιώθη ἡ σοφία ἀπὸ πάντων τῶν τέκνων⁷⁰ αὐτῆς.

## 11. Followers of Jesus
(Lk 9:57-62=Mt 8:19-22)

Καὶ ...⁷¹ εἶπέν τις πρὸς αὐτόν, ἀκολουθήσω σοι ὅπου ἐὰν ἀπέρχῃ. καὶ εἶπεν⁷² αὐτῷ ὁ Ἰησοῦς, αἱ ἀλώπεκες φωλεοὺς ἔχουσιν καὶ τὰ πετεινὰ τοῦ οὐρανοῦ κατασκηνώσεις, ὁ δὲ υἱὸς τοῦ ἀνθρώπου οὐκ ἔχει ποῦ τὴν κεφαλὴν κλίνῃ.⁷³

ἕτερος δε⁷⁴ εἶπεν αὐτῷ, ἐπίτρεψόν μοι πρῶτον ἀπελθεῖν⁷⁵ καὶ θάψαι τὸν πατέρα μου. εἶπεν δὲ αὐτῷ,⁷⁶ Ἄφες τοὺς νεκροὺς θάψαι τοὺς ἑαυτῶν νεκρούς, [σὺ δὲ ἀπελθὼν διάγγελλε τὴν βασιλείαν τοῦ θεοῦ. (Lk 9:60b)]⁷⁷

[Εἶπεν δὲ καὶ ἕτερος, Ἀκολουθήσω σοι, κύριε· πρῶτον δὲ ἐπίτρεψόν μοι ἀποτάξασθαι τοῖς εἰς τὸν οἶκόν μου. εἶπεν δὲ [πρὸς αὐτὸν] ὁ Ἰησοῦς, Οὐδεὶς ἐπιβαλὼν τὴν χεῖρα ἐπ'

---

⁶²Mt var. ἐκόψασθε.
⁶³Mt var. ἦλθεν
⁶⁴Lk add. ὁ βαπτιστὴς
⁶⁵Mt var. μήτε
⁶⁶Lk add. ἄρτον
⁶⁷Lk add. οἶνον
⁶⁸Mt var. λέγουσιν
⁶⁹Mt var. τελωνῶν φίλος
⁷⁰Mt textual var. ἀπὸ τῶν ἔργων
⁷¹Note the difference in the setting: Lk introduces the logion with πορευομένων αὐτῶν ἐν τῇ ὁδῷ; and Mt with καὶ προσελθὼν εἷς γραμματεὺς εἶπεν αὐτῷ, Διδάσκαλε,
⁷²Mt var. λέγει
⁷³Lk add. εἶπεν δὲ πρὸς ἕτερον, ἀκολούθει μοι. ὁ δὲ εἶπεν, Κύριε
⁷⁴Mt add. τῶν μαθητῶν αὐτοῦ
⁷⁵Lk var. ἀπελθόντι πρῶτον
⁷⁶Mt var. ὁ δὲ Ἰησοῦς λέγει αὐτῷ, ἀκολούθει μοι
⁷⁷Mt omm.

ἄροτρον καὶ βλέπων εἰς τὰ ὀπίσω εὔθετός ἐστιν τῇ βασιλείᾳ τοῦ θεοῦ. (Lk 9:61f.)][78]

## IV. JESUS AND HIS DISCIPLES

### 12. The mission charge
(Lk 10:2-12=Mt 9:37-10:15)

ἔλεγεν δὲ πρὸς αὐτούς,[79] Ὁ μὲν θερισμὸς πολύς, οἱ δὲ ἐργάται ὀλίγοι· δεήθητε οὖν τοῦ κυρίου τοῦ θερισμοῦ ὅπως ἐργάτας ἐκβάλῃ[80] εἰς τὸν θερισμὸν αὐτοῦ. ὑπάγετε·[81] ἰδοὺ[82] ἀποστέλλω ὑμᾶς ὡς ἄρνας[83] ἐν μέσῳ λύκων [γίνεσθε οὖν φρόνιμοι ὡς οἱ ὄφεις καὶ ἀκέραιοι ὡς αἱ περιστεραί (Mt 10:16b)][84] μὴ βαστάζετε βαλλάντιον,[85] μὴ πήραν,[86] μὴ[87] ὑποδήματα,[88] καὶ μηδένα κατὰ τὴν ὁδὸν ἀσπάσησθε.[89] εἰς ἣν δ' ἂν εἰσέλθητε οἰκίαν,[90] πρῶτον λέγετε, Εἰρήνη τῷ οἴκῳ τούτῳ.[91] καὶ ἐὰν ἐκεῖ ᾖ υἱὸς εἰρήνης, ἐπαναπαήσεται ἐπ' αὐτὸν ἡ εἰρήνη ὑμῶν·[92] εἰ δὲ μή γε, ἐφ' ὑμᾶς ἀνακάμψει.[93]

---

[78] Mt om.
[79] Note the difference in the Matthaean setting: τότε λέγει τοῖς μαθηταῖς αὐτοῦ. Lk on the other hand introduces with μετὰ δὲ ταῦτα ἀνέδειξεν ὁ κύριος ἑτέρους ἑβδομήκοντα [δύο], καὶ ἀπέστειλεν αὐτοὺς ἀνὰ δύο [δύο] πρὸ προσώπου αὐτοῦ εἰς πᾶσαν πόλιν καὶ τόπον οὗ ἤμελλεν αὐτὸς ἔρχεσθαι.
[80] Lk var. ἐκβάλῃ ἐργάτας
[81] Mt om.
[82] Mt add. ἐγὼ
[83] Mt var. πρόβατα
[84] Lk om.
[85] Mt var. Μὴ κτήσησθε χρυσὸν μηδὲ ἄργυρον μηδὲ χαλκὸν εἰς τὰς ζώνας ὑμῶν
[86] Mt add. εἰς ὁδὸν
[87] Mt add. μηδὲ δύο χιτῶνας
[88] Mt add. μηδὲ ῥάβδον. ἄξιος γὰρ ὁ ἐργάτης τῆς τροφῆς αὐτοῦ.
[89] Mt om.
[90] Mt var. πόλιν ἢ κώμην εἰσέλθητε,
[91] Mt var. ἐξετάσατε τίς ἐν αὐτῇ ἄξιός ἐστιν· κἀκεῖ μείνατε ἕως ἂν ἐξέλθητε. εἰσερχόμενοι δὲ εἰς τὴν οἰκίαν ἀσπάσασθε αὐτήν·
[92] Mt var. καὶ ἐὰν μὲν ᾖ ἡ οἰκία ἀξία, ἐλθάτω ἡ εἰρήνη ὑμῶν ἐπ' αὐτήν·
[93] Mt var. ἐὰν δὲ μὴ ᾖ ἀξία, ἡ εἰρήνη ὑμῶν πρὸς ὑμᾶς ἐπιστραφήτω.

ἐν αὐτῇ δὲ τῇ οἰκίᾳ μένετε, ἐσθίοντες καὶ πίνοντες τὰ παρ' αὐτῶν,⁹⁴ ἄξιος γὰρ ὁ ἐργάτης τοῦ μισθοῦ αὐτοῦ. μὴ μεταβαίνετε ἐξ οἰκίας εἰς οἰκίαν.⁹⁵ [καὶ εἰς ἣν ἂν πόλιν εἰσέρχησθε καὶ δέχωνται ὑμᾶς, ἐσθίετε τὰ παρατιθέμενα ὑμῖν,]⁹⁶ καὶ θεραπεύετε τοὺς ἐν αὐτῇ ἀσθενεῖς,⁹⁷ καὶ λέγετε αὐτοῖς, Ἤγγικεν ἐφ' ὑμᾶς⁹⁸ ἡ βασιλεία τοῦ θεοῦ.⁹⁹ εἰς ἣν δ' ἂν πόλιν εἰσέλθητε καὶ μὴ δέχωνται ὑμᾶς, ἐξελθόντες εἰς τὰς πλατείας αὐτῆς εἴπατε, καὶ τὸν κονιορτὸν τὸν κολληθέντα ἡμῖν ἐκ τῆς πόλεως ὑμῶν εἰς τοὺς πόδας ἀπομασσόμεθα ὑμῖν·¹⁰⁰ πλὴν τοῦτο γινώσκετε ὅτι ἤγγικεν ἡ βασιλεία τοῦ θεοῦ.¹⁰¹ λέγω ὑμῖν ὅτι Σοδόμοις ἐν τῇ ἡμέρᾳ ἐκείνῃ ἀνεκτότερον ἔσται ἢ τῇ πόλει ἐκείνῃ.¹⁰²

## 13. Woes against the cities of Galillee
(Lk 10:13-16=Mt 11:21-23)

Οὐαί σοι, Χοραζίν· οὐαί σοι, Βηθσαϊδά· ὅτι εἰ ἐν Τύρῳ καὶ Σιδῶνι ἐγενήθησαν¹⁰³ αἱ δυνάμεις αἱ γενόμεναι ἐν ὑμῖν, πάλαι ἂν ἐν σάκκῳ καὶ σποδῷ καθήμενοι¹⁰⁴ μετενόησαν. πλὴν¹⁰⁵ Τύρῳ καὶ Σιδῶνι ἀνεκτότερον ἔσται ἐν τῇ κρίσει¹⁰⁶ ἢ ὑμῖν. καὶ σύ, Καφαρναούμ,
    μὴ ἕως οὐρανοῦ ὑψωθήσῃ;
        ἕως τοῦ ᾅδου καταβήσῃ.¹⁰⁷

---

[94] Mt om.
[95] Mt om.
[96] Mt om. repetition
[97] Mt var. ἀσθενοῦντας θεραπεύετε,
[98] Mt om.
[99] Mt var. τῶν οὐρανῶν.
[100] Mt var. καὶ ὃς ἂν μὴ δέξηται ὑμᾶς μηδὲ ἀκούσῃ τοὺς λόγους ὑμῶν, ἐξερχόμενοι ἔξω τῆς οἰκίας ἢ τῆς πόλεως ἐκείνης ἐκτινάξατε τὸν κονιορτὸν τῶν ποδῶν ὑμῶν.
[101] Mt var. τῶν οὐρανῶν
[102] Mt var. ἀμὴν λέγω ὑμῖν, ἀνεκτότερον ἔσται γῇ Σοδόμων καὶ Γομόρρων ἐν ἡμέρᾳ κρίσεως ἢ τῇ πόλει ἐκείνῃ.
[103] Mt var. ἐγένοντο
[104] Mt om.
[105] Mt add. λέγω ὑμῖν
[106] Mt var. ἡμέρᾳ κρίσεως
[107] Mt add. ὅτι εἰ ἐν Τύρῳ καὶ Σιδῶνι αἱ δυνάμεις αἱ γενόμεναι ἐν ὑμῖν, πάλαι ὅτι εἰ ἐν Σοδόμοις ἐγενήθησαν αἱ δυνάμεις αἱ γενόμεναι ἐν σοί, ἔμεινεν ἂν μέχρι τῆς σήμερον.

Ὁ ἀκούων ὑμῶν ἐμοῦ ἀκούει, καὶ ὁ ἀθετῶν ὑμᾶς ἐμὲ ἀθετεῖ· ὁ δὲ ἐμὲ ἀθετῶν ἀθετεῖ τὸν ἀποστείλαντά με.[108]
(εἶπεν δὲ αὐτοῖς, Ἐθεώρουν τὸν Σατανᾶν ὡς ἀστραπὴν ἐκ τοῦ οὐρανοῦ πεσόντα. ἰδοὺ δέδωκα ὑμῖν τὴν ἐξουσίαν τοῦ πατεῖν ἐπάνω ὄφεων καὶ σκορπίων, καὶ ἐπὶ πᾶσαν τὴν δύναμιν τοῦ ἐχθροῦ, καὶ οὐδὲν ὑμᾶς οὐ μὴ ἀδικήσῃ. Lk 10:18-19)

## 14. Jesus' Thanksgiving
(Lk 10:21-22=Mt 11:25-27)

Ἐν αὐτῇ τῇ ὥρᾳ[109] ἠγαλλιάσατο (ὁ Ἰησοῦς)[110]...καὶ εἶπεν:
Ἐξομολογοῦμαί σοι, πάτερ, κύριε τοῦ οὐρανοῦ καὶ τῆς γῆς, ὅτι ἀπέκρυψας[111] ταῦτα ἀπὸ σοφῶν καὶ συνετῶν, καὶ ἀπεκάλυψας αὐτὰ νηπίοις·
ναί, ὁ πατήρ,
ὅτι οὕτως εὐδοκία ἐγένετο ἔμπροσθέν σου.
Πάντα μοι παρεδόθη ὑπὸ τοῦ πατρός μου,
καὶ οὐδεὶς γινώσκει[112] τίς ἐστιν ὁ υἱὸς εἰ μὴ ὁ πατήρ,
καὶ τίς ἐστιν ὁ πατὴρ[113] εἰ μὴ ὁ υἱὸς
καὶ ᾧ ἐὰν βούληται ὁ υἱὸς ἀποκαλύψαι.

## 15. The blessedness of the disciples
(Lk 10:23-24=Mt 13:16-17)

[114]Μακάριοι οἱ ὀφθαλμοὶ οἱ βλέποντες ἃ βλέπετε.[115] λέγω γὰρ[116] ὑμῖν ὅτι πολλοὶ προφῆται καὶ βασιλεῖς[117] ἠθέλη-

---

[108]Mt var. Ὁ δεχόμενος ὑμᾶς ἐμὲ δέχεται, καὶ ὁ ἐμὲ δεχόμενος δέχεται τὸν ἀποστείλαντά με.

[109]Mt var. ’εν ἐκείνῳ τῷ καιρῷ

[110]Mt var. ἀποκριθεὶς ὁ Ἰησοῦς. Lk add. [ἐν] τῷ πνεύματι τῷ ἁγίῳ

[111]Mt var. ἔκρυψας

[112]Mt var. ἐπιγινώσκει

[113]Mt var. οὐδὲ τὸν πατέρα τις ἐπιγινώσκει

[114]Lk introduces the pericope with καὶ στραφεὶς πρὸς τοὺς μαθητὰς κατ' ἰδίαν εἶπεν; Mt. add. ὑμῶν δὲ

[115]Mt var. ὅτι βλέπουσιν, καὶ τὰ ὦτα ὑμῶν ὅτι ἀκούουσιν.

[116]Mt var. ἀμὴν γὰρ λέγω

[117]Mt var. δίκαιοι

σαν¹¹⁸ ἰδεῖν ἃ ὑμεῖς¹¹⁹ βλέπετε καὶ οὐκ εἶδαν, καὶ ἀκοῦσαι ἃ ἀκούετε καὶ οὐκ ἤκουσαν.

## 16. Jesus' Prayer (The Lord's prayer)
(Lk 11:2-4=Mt 6:9-13)¹²⁰

Πάτερ,¹²¹
   ἁγιασθήτω τὸ ὄνομά σου·
      ἐλθέτω ἡ βασιλεία σου·¹²²
   τὸν ἄρτον ἡμῶν τὸν ἐπιούσιον
      δίδου ἡμῖν τὸ καθ' ἡμέραν·¹²³
   καὶ ἄφες ἡμῖν τὰς ἁμαρτίας¹²⁴ ἡμῶν,
      καὶ γὰρ αὐτοὶ ἀφίομεν παντὶ ὀφείλοντι ἡμῖν·¹²⁵
   καὶ μὴ εἰσενέγκῃς ἡμᾶς εἰς πειρασμόν.¹²⁶

## 17. Response to prayer
(Lk 11:9-13=Mt 7:7-11)

[κἀγὼ ὑμῖν λέγω,] αἰτεῖτε, καὶ δοθήσεται ὑμῖν· ζητεῖτε, καὶ εὑρήσετε· κρούετε, καὶ ἀνοιγήσεται ὑμῖν. πᾶς γὰρ ὁ αἰτῶν λαμβάνει, καὶ ὁ ζητῶν εὑρίσκει, καὶ τῷ κρούοντι ἀνοιγήσεται. τίνα δὲ ἐξ ὑμῶν τὸν πατέρα αἰτήσει ὁ υἱὸς ἰχθύν, καὶ ἀντὶ ἰχθύος ὄφιν αὐτῷ ἐπιδώσει; ἢ καὶ αἰτήσει ᾠόν, ἐπιδώσει αὐτῷ σκορπίον;¹²⁷ εἰ οὖν ὑμεῖς πονηροὶ ὑπάρχοντες¹²⁸ οἴδατε δόματα ἀγαθὰ διδόναι τοῖς τέκνοις

---

[118] Mt var. ἐπεθύμησαν
[119] Mt om.
[120] Lk introduces the pericope with εἶπεν δὲ αὐτοῖς, Ὅταν προσεύχησθε, λέγετε; Mt introduces the pericope with οὕτως οὖν προσεύχεσθε ὑμεῖς·
[121] Mt add. ἡμῶν ὁ ἐν τοῖς οὐρανοῖς,
[122] Mt add. γενηθήτω τὸ θέλημά σου, ὡς ἐν οὐρανῷ καὶ ἐπὶ γῆς
[123] Mt var. δὸς ἡμῖν σήμερον
[124] Mt var. τὰ ὀφειλήματα
[125] Mt var. ὡς καὶ ἡμεῖς ἀφήκαμεν τοῖς ὀφειλέταις ἡμῶν
[126] Mt add. ἀλλὰ ῥῦσαι ἡμᾶς ἀπὸ τοῦ πονηροῦ
[127] Mt var. ἢ τίς ἐστιν ἐξ ὑμῶν ἄνθρωπος, ὃν αἰτήσει ὁ υἱὸς αὐτοῦ ἄρτον μὴ λίθον ἐπιδώσει αὐτῷ; ἢ καὶ ἰχθὺν αἰτήσει μὴ ὄφιν ἐπιδώσει αὐτῷ;
[128] Mt var. ὄντες

ὑμῶν, πόσῳ μᾶλλον ὁ πατὴρ ὁ ἐξ οὐρανοῦ[129] δώσει ἀγαθὰ[130] τοῖς αἰτοῦσιν αὐτόν.

## V. JESUS AND HIS ADVERSARIES

### 18. The Beelzebul Controversy
(Lk 11:14-23=Mt 12:22-30)

Καὶ ἦν ἐκβάλλων δαιμόνιον, καὶ αὐτὸ ἦν κωφόν· ἐγένετο δὲ τοῦ δαιμονίου ἐξελθόντος ἐλάλησεν ὁ κωφός. καὶ ἐθαύμασαν οἱ ὄχλοι·[131] τινὲς δὲ ἐξ αὐτῶν εἶπον, ἐν Βεελζεβοὺλ τῷ ἄρχοντι τῶν δαιμονίων ἐκβάλλει τὰ δαιμόνια·[132] ἕτεροι δὲ πειράζοντες σημεῖον ἐξ οὐρανοῦ ἐζήτουν παρ' αὐτοῦ.[133] αὐτὸς δὲ εἰδὼς αὐτῶν τὰ διανοήματα[134] εἶπεν αὐτοῖς, Πᾶσα βασιλεία ἐφ' ἑαυτὴν διαμερισθεῖσα[135] ἐρημοῦται, καὶ οἶκος ἐπὶ οἶκον πίπτει.[136] εἰ δὲ καὶ ὁ Σατανᾶς ἐφ' ἑαυτὸν διεμερίσθη,[137] πῶς[138] σταθήσεται ἡ βασιλεία αὐτοῦ; ὅτι λέγετε ἐν Βεελζεβοὺλ ἐκβάλλειν με τὰ δαιμόνια.[139] εἰ δὲ ἐγὼ ἐν Βεελζεβοὺλ ἐκβάλλω τὰ δαιμόνια, οἱ υἱοὶ ὑμῶν ἐν τίνι ἐκβάλλουσιν; διὰ τοῦτο αὐτοὶ ὑμῶν κριταὶ ἔσονται.[140] εἰ δὲ ἐν δακτύλῳ[141] θεοῦ [ἐγὼ] ἐκβάλλω τὰ δαιμόνια, ἄρα ἔφθασεν ἐφ' ὑμᾶς ἡ βασιλεία τοῦ θεοῦ. ὅταν ὁ ἰσχυρὸς καθωπλισμένος φυλάσσῃ τὴν ἑαυτοῦ αὐλήν, ἐν εἰρήνῃ ἐστὶν τὰ ὑπάρχοντα αὐτοῦ· ἐπὰν δὲ ἰσχυρότερος αὐτοῦ ἐπελθὼν

---

[129]Mt var. ἐν τοῖς οὐρανοῖς
[130]Lk var. πνεῦμα ἅγιον
[131]Mt var. Τότε προσηνέχθη αὐτῷ δαιμονιζόμενος τυφλὸς καὶ κωφός· καὶ ἐθεράπευσεν αὐτόν, ὥστε τὸν κωφὸν λαλεῖν καὶ βλέπειν. καὶ ἐξίσταντο πάντες οἱ ὄχλοι
[132]Mt var. οἱ δὲ Φαρισαῖοι ἀκούσαντες εἶπον οὗτος οὐκ ἐκβάλλει τὰ δαιμόνια εἰ μὴ ἐν τῷ Βεελζεβοὺλ ἄρχοντι τῶν δαιμονίων.
[133]Mt om.
[134]Mt var. εἰδὼς δὲ τὰς ἐνθυμήσεις αὐτῶν
[135]Mt var. μερισθεῖσα
[136]Mt var.καὶ πᾶσα πόλις ἢ οἰκία μερισθεῖσα καθ' ἑαυτῆς οὐ σταθήσεται.
[137]Mt var. καὶ εἰ ὁ Σατανᾶς τὸν Σατανᾶν ἐκβάλλει, ἐφ' ἑαυτὸν ἐμερίσθη·
[138]Mt add. οὖν
[139]Mt om.
[140]Mt var. κριταὶ ἔσονται ὑμῶν
[141]Mt var. πνεύματι θεοῦ

νικήση αυτόν, την πανοπλίαν αυτού αίρει εφ' ή επεποίθει, και τα σκύλα αυτού διαδίδωσιν.¹⁴² ὁ μὴ ὢν μετ' ἐμοῦ κατ' ἐμοῦ ἐστιν, καὶ ὁ μὴ συνάγων μετ' ἐμοῦ σκορπίζει.

## 19. The return of the uncleaned spirit
(Lk 11:24-26=Mt 12:43-45)

Ὅταν¹⁴³ τὸ ἀκάθαρτον πνεῦμα ἐξέλθῃ ἀπὸ τοῦ ἀνθρώπου, διέρχεται δι' ἀνύδρων τόπων ζητοῦν ἀνάπαυσιν, καὶ μὴ εὑρίσκον,¹⁴⁴ τότε λέγει, Ὑποστρέψω εἰς τὸν οἶκόν μου¹⁴⁵ ὅθεν ἐξῆλθον· καὶ ἐλθὸν εὑρίσκει¹⁴⁶ σεσαρωμένον καὶ κεκοσμημένον. τότε πορεύεται καὶ παραλαμβάνει ἕτερα πνεύματα πονηρότερα ἑαυτοῦ ἑπτά,¹⁴⁷ καὶ εἰσελθόντα κατοικεῖ ἐκεῖ, καὶ γίνεται τὰ ἔσχατα τοῦ ἀνθρώπου ἐκείνου χείρονα τῶν πρώτων.

(Ἐγένετο δὲ ἐν τῷ λέγειν αὐτὸν ταῦτα ἐπάρασά τις φωνὴν γυνὴ ἐκ τοῦ ὄχλου εἶπεν αὐτῷ, Μακαρία ἡ κοιλία ἡ βαστάσασά σε καὶ μαστοὶ οὓς ἐθήλασας. αὐτὸς δὲ εἶπεν, Μενοῦν μακάριοι οἱ ἀκούοντες τὸν λόγον τοῦ θεοῦ καὶ φυλάσσοντες Lk 11:27-28).

## 20. The sign of Jonah
(Lk 11:29-32=Mt 12:38-42)¹⁴⁸

Ἡ γενεὰ αὕτη γενεὰ πονηρά ἐστιν· σημεῖον ζητεῖ,¹⁴⁹ καὶ σημεῖον οὐ δοθήσεται αὐτῇ εἰ μὴ τὸ σημεῖον Ἰωνᾶ.¹⁵⁰ καθὼς γὰρ ἐγένετο Ἰωνᾶς τοῖς Νινευίταις σημεῖον,¹⁵¹ οὕτως ἔσται

---

[142] Mt var. ἢ πῶς δύναταί τις εἰσελθεῖν εἰς τὴν οἰκίαν τοῦ ἰσχυροῦ καὶ τὰ σκεύη αὐτοῦ ἁρπάσαι, ἐὰν μὴ πρῶτον δήσῃ τὸν ἰσχυρόν; καὶ τότε τὴν οἰκίαν αὐτοῦ διαρπάσει.

[143] Mt add. δὲ

[144] Mt var. οὐχ εὑρίσκει

[145] Mt var. εἰς τὸν οἶκόν μου ἐπιστρέψω

[146] Mt add. σχολάζοντα,

[147] Mt var. μεθ' ἑαυτοῦ ἑπτὰ ἕτερα πνεύματα πονηρότερα ἑαυτοῦ

[148] Τῶν δὲ ὄχλων ἐπαθροιζομένων ἤρξατο λέγειν Mt var. Τότε ἀπεκρίθησαν αὐτῷ τινες τῶν γραμματέων καὶ Φαρισαίων λέγοντες, Διδάσκαλε, θέλομεν ἀπὸ σοῦ σημεῖον ἰδεῖν. ὁ δὲ ἀποκριθεὶς εἶπεν αὐτοῖς

[149] Mt var. Γενεὰ πονηρὰ καὶ μοιχαλὶς σημεῖον ἐπιζητει

[150] Mt add. τοῦ προφήτου

[151] Mt var. ὥσπερ γὰρ ἦν Ἰωνᾶς ἐν τῇ κοιλίᾳ τοῦ κήτους τρεῖς ἡμέρας καὶ τρεῖς νύκτας, οὕτως ἔσται ὁ υἱὸς τοῦ ἀνθρώπου ἐν τῇ καρδίᾳ τῆς γῆς τρεῖς ἡμέρας καὶ τρεῖς νύκτας.

καὶ ὁ υἱὸς τοῦ ἀνθρώπου τῇ γενεᾷ ταύτῃ.¹⁵² βασίλισσα νότου ἐγερθήσεται ἐν τῇ κρίσει μετὰ τῶν ἀνδρῶν¹⁵³ τῆς γενεᾶς ταύτης καὶ κατακρινεῖ αὐτούς·¹⁵⁴ ὅτι ἦλθεν ἐκ τῶν περάτων τῆς γῆς ἀκοῦσαι τὴν σοφίαν Σολομῶνος, καὶ ἰδοὺ πλεῖον Σολομῶνος ὧδε. ἄνδρες Νινευῖται ἀναστήσονται ἐν τῇ κρίσει μετὰ τῆς γενεᾶς ταύτης καὶ κατακρινοῦσιν αὐτήν· ὅτι μετενόησαν εἰς τὸ κήρυγμα Ἰωνᾶ, καὶ ἰδοὺ πλεῖον Ἰωνᾶ ὧδε.¹⁵⁵

## 21. Concerning the Light
(Lk 11:33-36=Mt 5:15; 6:22-23)

Οὐδεὶς λύχνον ἅψας εἰς κρύπτην τίθησιν οὐδὲ ὑπὸ τὸν μόδιον ἀλλ' ἐπὶ τὴν λυχνίαν,¹⁵⁶ ὁ λύχνος τοῦ σώματός ἐστιν ὁ ὀφθαλμός σου. ὅταν ὁ ὀφθαλμός σου ἁπλοῦς ᾖ, καὶ ὅλον τὸ σῶμά σου φωτεινόν ἐστιν· ἐπὰν δὲ πονηρὸς ᾖ, καὶ τὸ σῶμά σου σκοτεινόν. σκόπει οὖν μὴ τὸ φῶς τὸ ἐν σοὶ σκότος ἐστίν. εἰ οὖν τὸ σῶμά σου ὅλον φωτεινόν, μὴ ἔχον μέρος τι σκοτεινόν, ἔσται φωτεινὸν ὅλον ὡς ὅταν ὁ λύχνος τῇ ἀστραπῇ φωτίζῃ σε.¹⁵⁷

## 22. Woes to the Pharisees
(Lk 11:39-12:3=Mt 23:4-36; 10:26b-28)

εἶπεν δὲ ὁ (Ἰησοῦς) ... Νῦν ὑμεῖς οἱ Φαρισαῖοι τὸ ἔξωθεν τοῦ ποτηρίου καὶ τοῦ πίνακος καθαρίζετε, τὸ δὲ ἔσωθεν ὑμῶν γέμει ἁρπαγῆς καὶ πονηρίας. ἄφρονες, οὐχ ὁ ποιήσας τὸ ἔξωθεν καὶ τὸ ἔσωθεν ἐποίησεν; πλὴν τὰ ἐνόντα δότε ἐλεημοσύνην, καὶ ἰδοὺ πάντα καθαρὰ ὑμῖν ἐστιν.¹⁵⁸

---

¹⁵²Mt has reversed the order.
¹⁵³Mt om.
¹⁵⁴Mt var. αὐτήν
¹⁵⁵Mt has reversed the order of this and the pericope on "The return of the uncleaned spirit".
¹⁵⁶Lk add. (cf . 8:16) ἵνα οἱ εἰσπορευόμενοι τὸ φῶς βλέπωσιν. Mt var. οὐδὲ καίουσιν λύχνον καὶ τιθέασιν αὐτὸν ὑπὸ τὸν μόδιον ἀλλ' ἐπὶ τὴν λυχνίαν, καὶ λάμπει πᾶσιν τοῖς ἐν τῇ οἰκίᾳ.
¹⁵⁷The entire Matthaean version is: Ὁ λύχνος τοῦ σώματός ἐστιν ὁ ὀφθαλμός. ἐὰν οὖν ᾖ ὁ ὀφθαλμός σου ἁπλοῦς, ὅλον τὸ σῶμά σου φωτεινὸν ἔσται· ἐὰν δὲ ὁ ὀφθαλμός σου πονηρὸς ᾖ, ὅλον τὸ σῶμά σου σκοτεινὸν ἔσται. εἰ οὖν τὸ φῶς τὸ ἐν σοὶ σκότος ἐστίν, τὸ σκότος πόσον;
¹⁵⁸Mt var. (23:25f) Οὐαὶ ὑμῖν, γραμματεῖς καὶ Φαρισαῖοι ὑποκριταί, ὅτι καθαρίζετε τὸ ἔξωθεν τοῦ ποτηρίου καὶ τῆς παροψίδος, ἔσωθεν δὲ γέμουσιν ἐξ ἁρπαγῆς καὶ ἀκρασίας. Φαρισαῖε

ἀλλὰ οὐαὶ ὑμῖν τοῖς Φαρισαίοις, ὅτι ἀποδεκατοῦτε τὸ ἡδύοσμον καὶ τὸ πήγανον καὶ πᾶν λάχανον, καὶ παρέρχεσθε τὴν κρίσιν καὶ τὴν ἀγάπην τοῦ θεοῦ· ταῦτα δὲ ἔδει ποιῆσαι κἀκεῖνα μὴ παρεῖναι.[159]

οὐαὶ ὑμῖν τοῖς Φαρισαίοις, ὅτι ἀγαπᾶτε τὴν πρωτοκαθεδρίαν ἐν ταῖς συναγωγαῖς καὶ τοὺς ἀσπασμοὺς ἐν ταῖς ἀγοραῖς.[160]

οὐαὶ ὑμῖν, ὅτι ἐστὲ ὡς τὰ μνημεῖα τὰ ἄδηλα, καὶ οἱ ἄνθρωποι [οἱ] περιπατοῦντες ἐπάνω οὐκ οἴδασιν.[161]

[162]Καὶ ὑμῖν τοῖς νομικοῖς οὐαί, ὅτι φορτίζετε τοὺς ἀνθρώπους φορτία δυσβάστακτα, καὶ αὐτοὶ ἑνὶ τῶν δακτύλων ὑμῶν οὐ προσψαύετε τοῖς φορτίοις.[163]

οὐαὶ ὑμῖν, ὅτι οἰκοδομεῖτε τὰ μνημεῖα τῶν προφητῶν, οἱ δὲ πατέρες ὑμῶν ἀπέκτειναν αὐτούς. ἄρα μάρτυρές ἐστε καὶ συνευδοκεῖτε τοῖς ἔργοις τῶν πατέρων ὑμῶν, ὅτι αὐτοὶ μὲν ἀπέκτειναν αὐτοὺς ὑμεῖς δὲ οἰκοδομεῖτε.[164]

διὰ τοῦτο καὶ ἡ σοφία τοῦ θεοῦ εἶπεν, Ἀποστελῶ εἰς αὐτοὺς προφήτας καὶ ἀποστόλους, καὶ ἐξ αὐτῶν ἀποκτενοῦσιν καὶ διώξουσιν, ἵνα ἐκζητηθῇ τὸ αἷμα πάντων

---

τυφλέ, καθάρισον πρῶτον τὸ ἐντὸς τοῦ ποτηρίου, ἵνα γένηται καὶ τὸ ἐκτὸς αὐτοῦ καθαρόν.

[159]Mt var. (23:23f) Οὐαὶ ὑμῖν, γραμματεῖς καὶ Φαρισαῖοι ὑποκριταί, ὅτι ἀποδεκατοῦτε τὸ ἡδύοσμον καὶ τὸ ἄνηθον καὶ τὸ κύμινον, καὶ ἀφήκατε τὰ βαρύτερα τοῦ νόμου, τὴν κρίσιν καὶ τὸ ἔλεος καὶ τὴν πίστιν· ταῦτα [δὲ] ἔδει ποιῆσαι κἀκεῖνα μὴ ἀφιέναι. ὁδηγοὶ τυφλοί, οἱ διϋλίζοντες τὸν κώνωπα τὴν δὲ κάμηλον καταπίνοντες.

[160]Mt var. (v.23:6f) φιλοῦσιν δὲ τὴν πρωτοκλισίαν ἐν τοῖς δείπνοις καὶ τὰς πρωτοκαθεδρίας ἐν ταῖς συναγωγαῖς καὶ τοὺς ἀσπασμοὺς ἐν ταῖς ἀγοραῖς

[161]Mt var. (v.23:27f) Οὐαὶ ὑμῖν, γραμματεῖς καὶ Φαρισαῖοι ὑποκριταί, ὅτι παρομοιάζετε τάφοις κεκονιαμένοις, οἵτινες ἔξωθεν μὲν φαίνονται ὡραῖοι ἔσωθεν δὲ γέμουσιν ὀστέων νεκρῶν καὶ πάσης ἀκαθαρσίας. οὕτως καὶ ὑμεῖς ἔξωθεν μὲν φαίνεσθε τοῖς ἀνθρώποις δίκαιοι, ἔσωθεν δέ ἐστε μεστοὶ ὑποκρίσεως καὶ ἀνομίας

[162]Lk add. Ἀποκριθεὶς δέ τις τῶν νομικῶν λέγει αὐτῷ, Διδάσκαλε, ταῦτα λέγων καὶ ἡμᾶς ὑβρίζεις. ὁ δὲ εἶπεν

[163]Mt var. (v.23:4) δεσμεύουσιν δὲ φορτία βαρέα καὶ δυσβάστακτα καὶ ἐπιτιθέασιν ἐπὶ τοὺς ὤμους τῶν ἀνθρώπων, αὐτοὶ δὲ τῷ δακτύλῳ αὐτῶν οὐ θέλουσιν κινῆσαι αὐτά.

[164]Mt var. (v.23:29-32) Οὐαὶ ὑμῖν, γραμματεῖς καὶ Φαρισαῖοι ὑποκριταί, ὅτι οἰκοδομεῖτε τοὺς τάφους τῶν προφητῶν καὶ κοσμεῖτε τὰ μνημεῖα τῶν δικαίων, καὶ λέγετε, Εἰ ἤμεθα ἐν ταῖς ἡμέραις τῶν πατέρων ἡμῶν, οὐκ ἂν ἤμεθα αὐτῶν κοινωνοὶ ἐν τῷ αἵματι τῶν προφητῶν. ὥστε μαρτυρεῖτε ἑαυτοῖς ὅτι υἱοί ἐστε τῶν φονευσάντων τοὺς προφήτας. καὶ ὑμεῖς πληρώσατε τὸ μέτρον τῶν πατέρων ὑμῶν.

τῶν προφητῶν τὸ ἐκκεχυμένον ἀπὸ καταβολῆς κόσμου ἀπὸ τῆς γενεᾶς ταύτης, ἀπὸ αἵματος Ἄβελ ἕως αἵματος Ζαχαρίου τοῦ ἀπολομένου μεταξὺ τοῦ θυσιαστηρίου καὶ τοῦ οἴκου· ναί, λέγω ὑμῖν, ἐκζητηθήσεται ἀπὸ τῆς γενεᾶς ταύτης.¹⁶⁵

οὐαὶ ὑμῖν τοῖς νομικοῖς, ὅτι ἤρατε τὴν κλεῖδα τῆς γνώσεως· αὐτοὶ οὐκ εἰσήλθατε καὶ τοὺς εἰσερχομένους ἐκωλύσατε.¹⁶⁶

¹⁶⁷οὐδὲν δὲ συγκεκαλυμμένον ἐστὶν ὃ οὐκ ἀποκαλυφθήσεται, καὶ κρυπτὸν ὃ οὐ γνωσθήσεται. ἀνθ' ὧν ὅσα ἐν τῇ σκοτίᾳ εἴπατε ἐν τῷ φωτὶ ἀκουσθήσεται, καὶ ὃ πρὸς τὸ οὖς ἐλαλήσατε ἐν τοῖς ταμείοις κηρυχθήσεται ἐπὶ τῶν δωμάτων.¹⁶⁸

## VI. PREPARING FOR THE IMMINENT END

### 23. On fearless confession
(Lk 12:4-9, 11f=Mt 6:28-33; 10:19f)

Λέγω δὲ ὑμῖν,¹⁶⁹ μὴ φοβηθῆτε ἀπὸ τῶν ἀποκτεινόντων τὸ σῶμα καὶ μετὰ ταῦτα μὴ ἐχόντων περισσότερόν τι ποιῆσαι. ὑποδείξω δὲ ὑμῖν τίνα φοβηθῆτε· φοβήθητε τὸν μετὰ τὸ ἀποκτεῖναι ἔχοντα ἐξουσίαν ἐμβαλεῖν εἰς τὴν γέενναν· ναί,

---

¹⁶⁵Mt var. (v.23:34-35) διὰ τοῦτο ἰδοὺ ἐγὼ ἀποστέλλω πρὸς ὑμᾶς προφήτας καὶ σοφοὺς καὶ γραμματεῖς· ἐξ αὐτῶν ἀποκτενεῖτε καὶ σταυρώσετε, καὶ ἐξ αὐτῶν μαστιγώσετε ἐν ταῖς συναγωγαῖς ὑμῶν καὶ διώξετε ἀπὸ πόλεως εἰς πόλιν· ὅπως ἔλθῃ ἐφ' ὑμᾶς πᾶν αἷμα δίκαιον ἐκχυννόμενον ἐπὶ τῆς γῆς ἀπὸ τοῦ αἵματος Ἄβελ τοῦ δικαίου ἕως τοῦ αἵματος Ζαχαρίου υἱοῦ Βαραχίου, ὃν ἐφονεύσατε μεταξὺ τοῦ ναοῦ καὶ τοῦ θυσιαστηρίου. ἀμὴν λέγω ὑμῖν, ἥξει ταῦτα πάντα ἐπὶ τὴν γενεὰν ταύτην

¹⁶⁶Mt var. (v. 23:13) Οὐαὶ δὲ ὑμῖν, γραμματεῖς καὶ Φαρισαῖοι ὑποκριταί, ὅτι κλείετε τὴν βασιλείαν τῶν οὐρανῶν ἔμπροσθεν τῶν ἀνθρώπων· ὑμεῖς γὰρ οὐκ εἰσέρχεσθε, οὐδὲ τοὺς εἰσερχομένους ἀφίετε εἰσελθεῖν.

¹⁶⁷Both Mt and Lk seem to have changed the setting of this saying. It is more natural to attach it to the preceeding last woe.

¹⁶⁸The entire Mattaean version (v.10:26-29) is οὐδὲν γάρ ἐστιν κεκαλυμμένον ὃ οὐκ ἀποκαλυφθήσεται, καὶ κρυπτὸν ὃ οὐ γνωσθήσεται. ὃ λέγω ὑμῖν ἐν τῇ σκοτίᾳ εἴπατε ἐν τῷ φωτί, καὶ ὃ εἰς τὸ οὖς ἀκούετε κηρύξατε ἐπὶ τῶν δωμάτων.

¹⁶⁹Lk add. τοῖς φίλοις μου.

λέγω ὑμῖν, τοῦτον φοβήθητε.¹⁷⁰ οὐχὶ πέντε στρουθία πωλοῦνται ἀσσαρίων δύο; καὶ ἓν ἐξ αὐτῶν οὐκ ἔστιν ἐπιλελησμένον ἐνώπιον τοῦ θεοῦ. ἀλλὰ καὶ αἱ τρίχες τῆς κεφαλῆς ὑμῶν πᾶσαι ἠρίθμηνται. μὴ φοβεῖσθε· πολλῶν στρουθίων διαφέρετε.¹⁷¹

¹⁷²Πᾶς ὃς ἂν ὁμολογήσῃ ἐν ἐμοὶ ἔμπροσθεν τῶν ἀνθρώπων, καὶ ὁ υἱὸς τοῦ ἀνθρώπου ὁμολογήσει ἐν αὐτῷ ἔμπροσθεν τῶν ἀγγέλων τοῦ θεοῦ· ὁ δὲ ἀρνησάμενός με ἐνώπιον τῶν ἀνθρώπων ἀπαρνηθήσεται ἐνώπιον τῶν ἀγγέλων τοῦ θεοῦ.¹⁷³

Ὅταν δὲ εἰσφέρωσιν ὑμᾶς ἐπὶ τὰς συναγωγὰς καὶ τὰς ἀρχὰς καὶ τὰς ἐξουσίας, μὴ μεριμνήσητε πῶς ἢ τί ἀπολογήσησθε ἢ τί εἴπητε·¹⁷⁴ δοθήσεται γὰρ ὑμῖν ἐν ἐκείνῃ τῇ ὥρᾳ (Mt10:19b).¹⁷⁵

## 24. On earthly things
### (Lk 12:22-32=Mt 6:25-34)

¹⁷⁶Διὰ τοῦτο λέγω ὑμῖν, μὴ μεριμνᾶτε τῇ ψυχῇ τί φάγητε, μηδὲ τῷ σώματι τί ἐνδύσησθε. ἡ γὰρ ψυχὴ πλεῖόν ἐστιν τῆς τροφῆς καὶ τὸ σῶμα τοῦ ἐνδύματος.¹⁷⁷ κατανοήσατε τοὺς κόρακας ὅτι οὐ σπείρουσιν οὐδὲ θερίζουσιν, οἷς οὐκ ἔστιν ταμεῖον οὐδὲ ἀποθήκη, καὶ ὁ θεὸς τρέφει αὐτούς· πόσῳ μᾶλλον ὑμεῖς διαφέρετε τῶν

---

¹⁷⁰Mt var. καὶ μὴ φοβεῖσθε ἀπὸ τῶν ἀποκτεννόντων τὸ σῶμα, τὴν δὲ ψυχὴν μὴ δυναμένων ἀποκτεῖναι· φοβεῖσθε δὲ μᾶλλον τὸν δυνάμενον καὶ ψυχὴν καὶ σῶμα ἀπολέσαι ἐν γεέννῃ.

¹⁷¹Mt var. οὐχὶ δύο στρουθία ἀσσαρίου πωλεῖται; καὶ ἓν ἐξ αὐτῶν οὐ πεσεῖται ἐπὶ τὴν γῆν ἄνευ τοῦ πατρὸς ὑμῶν. ὑμῶν δὲ καὶ αἱ τρίχες τῆς κεφαλῆς πᾶσαι ἠριθμημέναι εἰσίν. μὴ οὖν φοβεῖσθε· πολλῶν στρουθίων διαφέρετε ὑμεῖς.

¹⁷²Lk add. λέγω δὲ ὑμῖν.

¹⁷³Mt var. πᾶς οὖν ὅστις ὁμολογήσει ἐν ἐμοὶ ἔμπροσθεν τῶν ἀνθρώπων, ὁμολογήσω κἀγὼ ἐν αὐτῷ ἔμπροσθεν τοῦ πατρός μου τοῦ ἐν [τοῖς] οὐρανοῖς.

¹⁷⁴Mt var. ὅταν δὲ παραδῶσιν ὑμᾶς, μὴ μεριμνήσητε πῶς ἢ τί λαλήσητε·

¹⁷⁵Lk var. τὸ γὰρ ἅγιον πνεῦμα διδάξει ὑμᾶς ἐν αὐτῇ τῇ ὥρᾳ ἃ δεῖ εἰπεῖν. Cf. also Mt 10:20 οὐ γὰρ ὑμεῖς ἐστε οἱ λαλοῦντες ἀλλὰ τὸ πνεῦμα τοῦ πατρὸς ὑμῶν τὸ λαλοῦν ἐν ὑμῖν.

¹⁷⁶Lk introduces the pericope with εἶπεν δὲ πρὸς τοὺς μαθητάς αὐτοῦ.

¹⁷⁷Mt var. Διὰ τοῦτο λέγω ὑμῖν, μὴ μεριμνᾶτε τῇ ψυχῇ ὑμῶν τί φάγητε [ἢ τί πίητε,] μηδὲ τῷ σώματι ὑμῶν τί ἐνδύσησθε· οὐχὶ ἡ ψυχὴ πλεῖόν ἐστιν τῆς τροφῆς καὶ τὸ σῶμα τοῦ ἐνδύματος;

πετεινῶν.¹⁷⁸ τίς δὲ ἐξ ὑμῶν μεριμνῶν δύναται ἐπὶ τὴν ἡλικίαν αὐτοῦ προσθεῖναι πῆχυν;¹⁷⁹ εἰ οὖν οὐδὲ ἐλάχιστον δύνασθε, τί περὶ τῶν λοιπῶν μεριμνᾶτε;¹⁸⁰ κατανοήσατε τὰ κρίνα πῶς αὐξάνει· οὐ κοπιᾷ οὐδὲ νήθει·¹⁸¹ λέγω δὲ ὑμῖν, οὐδὲ Σολομῶν ἐν πάσῃ τῇ δόξῃ αὐτοῦ περιεβάλετο ὡς ἓν τούτων. εἰ δὲ ἐν ἀγρῷ τὸν χόρτον ὄντα σήμερον καὶ αὔριον εἰς κλίβανον βαλλόμενον ὁ θεὸς οὕτως ἀμφιέζει, πόσῳ μᾶλλον ὑμᾶς, ὀλιγόπιστοι.¹⁸² καὶ ὑμεῖς μὴ ζητεῖτε τί φάγητε καὶ τί πίητε, καὶ μὴ μετεωρίζεσθε· ταῦτα γὰρ πάντα τὰ ἔθνη τοῦ κόσμου ἐπιζητοῦσιν·¹⁸³ ὑμῶν δὲ ὁ πατὴρ οἶδεν ὅτι χρῄζετε τούτων.¹⁸⁴ πλὴν ζητεῖτε τὴν βασιλείαν αὐτοῦ, καὶ ταῦτα προστεθήσεται ὑμῖν.¹⁸⁵ Μὴ φοβοῦ, τὸ μικρὸν ποίμνιον, ὅτι εὐδόκησεν ὁ πατὴρ ὑμῶν δοῦναι ὑμῖν τὴν βασιλείαν.¹⁸⁶

## 25. On treasures in Heaven
(Lk 12:33f=Mt 6:19-21)

Πωλήσατε τὰ ὑπάρχοντα ὑμῶν καὶ δότε ἐλεημοσύνην· ποιήσατε ἑαυτοῖς βαλλάντια μὴ παλαιούμενα, θησαυρὸν ἀνέκλειπτον ἐν τοῖς οὐρανοῖς, ὅπου κλέπτης οὐκ ἐγγίζει

---

[178] Mt var. ἐμβλέψατε εἰς τὰ πετεινὰ τοῦ οὐρανοῦ ὅτι οὐ σπείρουσιν οὐδὲ θερίζουσιν οὐδὲ συνάγουσιν εἰς ἀποθήκας, καὶ ὁ πατὴρ ὑμῶν ὁ οὐράνιος τρέφει αὐτά· οὐχ ὑμεῖς μᾶλλον διαφέρετε αὐτῶν;

[179] Mt var. τίς δὲ ἐξ ὑμῶν μεριμνῶν δύναται προσθεῖναι ἐπὶ τὴν ἡλικίαν αὐτοῦ πῆχυν ἕνα;

[180] Mt var. καὶ περὶ ἐνδύματος τί μεριμνᾶτε;

[181] Mt var. καταμάθετε τὰ κρίνα τοῦ ἀγροῦ πῶς αὐξάνουσιν· οὐ κοπιῶσιν οὐδὲ νήθουσιν·

[182] Mt var. εἰ δὲ τὸν χόρτον τοῦ ἀγροῦ σήμερον ὄντα καὶ αὔριον εἰς κλίβανον βαλλόμενον ὁ θεὸς οὕτως ἀμφιέννυσιν, οὐ πολλῷ μᾶλλον ὑμᾶς, ὀλιγόπιστοι;

[183] Mt var. μὴ οὖν μεριμνήσητε λέγοντες, Τί φάγωμεν; ἤ, Τί πίωμεν; ἤ, Τί περιβαλώμεθα; 6·32    πάντα γὰρ ταῦτα τὰ ἔθνη ἐπιζητοῦσιν·

[184] Mt var. οἶδεν γὰρ ὁ πατὴρ ὑμῶν ὁ οὐράνιος ὅτι χρῄζετε τούτων ἁπάντων.

[185] Mt var. ζητεῖτε δὲ πρῶτον τὴν βασιλείαν [τοῦ θεοῦ] καὶ τὴν δικαιοσύνην αὐτοῦ, καὶ ταῦτα πάντα προστεθήσεται ὑμῖν. Mt add. μὴ οὖν μεριμνήσητε εἰς τὴν αὔριον, ἡ γὰρ αὔριον μεριμνήσει ἑαυτῆς· ἀρκετὸν τῇ ἡμέρᾳ ἡ κακία αὐτῆς.

[186] Mt om.

οὐδὲ σὴς διαφθείρει· ὅπου γάρ ἐστιν ὁ θησαυρὸς ὑμῶν, ἐκεῖ καὶ ἡ καρδία ὑμῶν ἔσται.[187]

## 26. On readiness and faithfulness
(Lk 12:35-40=Mt 24:42-44)

Ἔστωσαν ὑμῶν αἱ ὀσφύες περιεζωσμέναι καὶ οἱ λύχνοι καιόμενοι, καὶ ὑμεῖς ὅμοιοι ἀνθρώποις προσδεχομένοις τὸν κύριον ἑαυτῶν πότε ἀναλύσῃ ἐκ τῶν γάμων, ἵνα ἐλθόντος καὶ κρούσαντος εὐθέως ἀνοίξωσιν αὐτῷ. μακάριοι οἱ δοῦλοι ἐκεῖνοι, οὓς ἐλθὼν ὁ κύριος εὑρήσει γρηγοροῦντας· ἀμὴν λέγω ὑμῖν ὅτι περιζώσεται καὶ ἀνακλινεῖ αὐτοὺς καὶ παρελθὼν διακονήσει αὐτοῖς. κἂν ἐν τῇ δευτέρᾳ κἂν ἐν τῇ τρίτῃ φυλακῇ ἔλθῃ καὶ εὕρῃ οὕτως, μακάριοί εἰσιν ἐκεῖνοι.[188] τοῦτο δὲ γινώσκετε ὅτι εἰ ᾔδει ὁ οἰκοδεσπότης ποίᾳ ὥρᾳ ὁ κλέπτης ἔρχεται, οὐκ ἂν ἀφῆκεν διορυχθῆναι τὸν οἶκον αὐτοῦ. καὶ ὑμεῖς γίνεσθε ἕτοιμοι, ὅτι ᾗ ὥρᾳ οὐ δοκεῖτε ὁ υἱὸς τοῦ ἀνθρώπου ἔρχεται.[189]

## 27. The Parable of the Good and Wicked Servant
(Lk 12:41-46=Mt 24:45-51)

[190]Τίς ἄρα ἐστὶν ὁ πιστὸς οἰκονόμος ὁ φρόνιμος, ὃν καταστήσει ὁ κύριος ἐπὶ τῆς θεραπείας αὐτοῦ τοῦ διδόναι

---

[187]Mt var. Μὴ θησαυρίζετε ὑμῖν θησαυροὺς ἐπὶ τῆς γῆς, ὅπου σὴς καὶ βρῶσις ἀφανίζει, καὶ ὅπου κλέπται διορύσσουσιν καὶ κλέπτουσιν· θησαυρίζετε δὲ ὑμῖν θησαυροὺς ἐν οὐρανῷ, ὅπου οὔτε σὴς οὔτε βρῶσις ἀφανίζει, καὶ ὅπου κλέπται οὐ διορύσσουσιν οὐδὲ κλέπτουσιν· ὅπου γάρ ἐστιν ὁ θησαυρός σου, ἐκεῖ ἔσται καὶ ἡ καρδία σου.

[188]Cf. the Matthaean parable of the ten virgins (25:1-13).

[189]Mt var. γρηγορεῖτε οὖν, ὅτι οὐκ οἴδατε ποίᾳ ἡμέρᾳ ὁ κύριος ὑμῶν ἔρχεται. ἐκεῖνο δὲ γινώσκετε ὅτι εἰ ᾔδει ὁ οἰκοδεσπότης ποίᾳ φυλακῇ ὁ κλέπτης ἔρχεται, ἐγρηγόρησεν ἂν καὶ οὐκ ἂν εἴασεν διορυχθῆναι τὴν οἰκίαν αὐτοῦ. διὰ τοῦτο καὶ ὑμεῖς γίνεσθε ἕτοιμοι, ὅτι ᾗ οὐ δοκεῖτε ὥρᾳ ὁ υἱὸς τοῦ ἀνθρώπου ἔρχεται.

[190]The entire Matthaean version (24:45-51a) is: Τίς ἄρα ἐστὶν ὁ πιστὸς δοῦλος καὶ φρόνιμος ὃν κατέστησεν ὁ κύριος ἐπὶ τῆς οἰκετείας αὐτοῦ τοῦ δοῦναι αὐτοῖς τὴν τροφὴν ἐν καιρῷ; μακάριος ὁ δοῦλος ἐκεῖνος ὃν ἐλθὼν ὁ κύριος αὐτοῦ εὑρήσει οὕτως ποιοῦντα· ἀμὴν λέγω ὑμῖν ὅτι ἐπὶ πᾶσιν τοῖς ὑπάρχουσιν αὐτοῦ καταστήσει αὐτόν. ἐὰν δὲ εἴπῃ ὁ κακὸς δοῦλος ἐκεῖνος ἐν τῇ καρδίᾳ αὐτοῦ, Χρονίζει μου ὁ κύριος, καὶ ἄρξηται τύπτειν τοὺς συνδούλους αὐτοῦ, ἐσθίῃ δὲ καὶ πίνῃ μετὰ τῶν μεθυόντων, ἥξει ὁ κύριος τοῦ δούλου ἐκείνου ἐν ἡμέρᾳ ᾗ οὐ προσδοκᾷ καὶ ἐν ὥρᾳ ᾗ οὐ γινώσκει, καὶ διχοτομήσει αὐτὸν καὶ τὸ μέρος αὐτοῦ μετὰ τῶν ὑποκριτῶν θήσει.

ἐν καιρῷ [τὸ] σιτομέτριον; μακάριος ὁ δοῦλος ἐκεῖνος, ὃν ἐλθὼν ὁ κύριος αὐτοῦ εὑρήσει ποιοῦντα οὕτως· ἀληθῶς λέγω ὑμῖν ὅτι ἐπὶ πᾶσιν τοῖς ὑπάρχουσιν αὐτοῦ καταστήσει αὐτόν. ἐὰν δὲ εἴπῃ ὁ δοῦλος ἐκεῖνος ἐν τῇ καρδίᾳ αὐτοῦ, χρονίζει ὁ κύριός μου ἔρχεσθαι, καὶ ἄρξηται τύπτειν τοὺς παῖδας καὶ τὰς παιδίσκας, ἐσθίειν τε καὶ πίνειν καὶ μεθύσκεσθαι, ἥξει ὁ κύριος τοῦ δούλου ἐκείνου ἐν ἡμέρᾳ ᾗ οὐ προσδοκᾷ καὶ ἐν ὥρᾳ ᾗ οὐ γινώσκει, καὶ διχοτομήσει αὐτὸν καὶ τὸ μέρος αὐτοῦ μετὰ τῶν ἀπίστων θήσει.[191]

## 28. Divisions in households
(Lk 12:49-53=Mt 10:34-36)

Πῦρ ἦλθον βαλεῖν ἐπὶ τὴν γῆν, καὶ τί θέλω εἰ ἤδη ἀνήφθη...[192] δοκεῖτε ὅτι εἰρήνην παρεγενόμην δοῦναι ἐν τῇ γῇ; οὐχί, λέγω ὑμῖν, ἀλλ' ἢ διαμερισμόν. ἔσονται γὰρ ἀπὸ τοῦ νῦν πέντε ἐν ἑνὶ οἴκῳ διαμεμερισμένοι, τρεῖς ἐπὶ δυσὶν καὶ δύο ἐπὶ τρισίν, διαμερισθήσονται πατὴρ ἐπὶ υἱῷ καὶ υἱὸς ἐπὶ πατρί, μήτηρ ἐπὶ τὴν θυγατέρα καὶ θυγάτηρ ἐπὶ τὴν μητέρα, πενθερὰ ἐπὶ τὴν νύμφην αὐτῆς καὶ νύμφη ἐπὶ τὴν πενθεράν.[193]

## 29. The Signs of the Time
(Lk 12:54-56=Mt 16:2f)

[194]Ὅταν ἴδητε [τὴν] νεφέλην ἀνατέλλουσαν ἐπὶ δυσμῶν, εὐθέως λέγετε ὅτι Ὄμβρος ἔρχεται, καὶ γίνεται οὕτως· καὶ ὅταν νότον πνέοντα, λέγετε ὅτι Καύσων ἔσται, καὶ γίνεται. ὑποκριταί, τὸ πρόσωπον τῆς γῆς καὶ τοῦ οὐρανοῦ οἴδατε δοκιμάζειν, τὸν καιρὸν δὲ τοῦτον πῶς οὐκ οἴδατε δοκιμάζειν;[195]

---

[191]Mt add. ἐκεῖ ἔσται ὁ κλαυθμὸς καὶ ὁ βρυγμὸς τῶν ὀδόντων.

[192]Lk add. βάπτισμα δὲ ἔχω βαπτισθῆναι καὶ πῶς συνέχομαι ἕως ὅτου τελεσθῇ.

[193]Mt var. Μὴ νομίσητε ὅτι ἦλθον βαλεῖν εἰρήνην ἐπὶ τὴν γῆν· οὐκ ἦλθον βαλεῖν εἰρήνην ἀλλὰ μάχαιραν. ἦλθον γὰρ διχάσαι ἄνθρωπον κατὰ τοῦ πατρὸς αὐτοῦ καὶ θυγατέρα κατὰ τῆς μητρὸς αὐτῆς καὶ νύμφην κατὰ τῆς πενθερᾶς αὐτῆς, καὶ ἐχθροὶ τοῦ ἀνθρώπου οἱ οἰκιακοὶ αὐτοῦ.

[194]Cf. the difference in the setting. Mt has ὁ δὲ ἀποκριθεὶς εἶπεν αὐτοῖς; Lk has Ἔλεγεν δὲ καὶ τοῖς ὄχλοις.

[195]Mt textual var. Ὀψίας γενομένης λέγετε, Εὐδία, πυρράζει γὰρ ὁ οὐρανός· καὶ πρωΐ, Σήμερον χειμών, πυρράζει γὰρ στυγνάζων ὁ οὐρανός. τὸ μὲν πρόσωπον τοῦ οὐρανοῦ γινώσκετε διακρίνειν, τὰ δὲ σημεῖα τῶν καιρῶν οὐ δύνασθε.

### 30. The parable of the mustard seed
(Lk 13:18f=Mt 13:31f)

Ἔλεγεν οὖν, Τίνι ὁμοία ἐστὶν ἡ βασιλεία τοῦ θεοῦ, καὶ τίνι ὁμοιώσω αὐτήν; ὁμοία ἐστὶν κόκκῳ σινάπεως, ὃν λαβὼν ἄνθρωπος ἔβαλεν εἰς κῆπον ἑαυτοῦ, καὶ ηὔξησεν καὶ ἐγένετο εἰς δένδρον, καὶ τὰ πετεινὰ τοῦ οὐρανοῦ κατεσκήνωσεν ἐν τοῖς κλάδοις αὐτοῦ.[196]

### 31. The parable of the Leaven
(Lk 13:20-21=Mt 13:33)

Καὶ πάλιν εἶπεν, Τίνι ὁμοιώσω τὴν βασιλείαν τοῦ θεοῦ; ὁμοία ἐστὶν[197] ζύμῃ, ἣν λαβοῦσα γυνὴ [ἐν]έκρυψεν εἰς ἀλεύρου σάτα τρία ἕως οὗ ἐζυμώθη ὅλον.

### 32. Condemnation of Israel and their exclusion from the kingdom
(Lk 13:24-30=Mt 7:13f, 22f; 8:11f; 19:30)

[198]'Ἀγωνίζεσθε εἰσελθεῖν διὰ τῆς στενῆς θύρας, ὅτι πολλοί, λέγω ὑμῖν, ζητήσουσιν εἰσελθεῖν καὶ οὐκ ἰσχύσουσιν.[199] ἀφ' οὗ ἂν ἐγερθῇ ὁ οἰκοδεσπότης καὶ ἀποκλείσῃ τὴν θύραν, καὶ ἄρξησθε ἔξω ἑστάναι καὶ κρούειν τὴν θύραν λέγοντες, Κύριε, ἄνοιξον ἡμῖν· καὶ ἀποκριθεὶς ἐρεῖ ὑμῖν, Οὐκ οἶδα ὑμᾶς πόθεν ἐστέ. τότε ἄρξεσθε λέγειν, Ἐφάγομεν ἐνώπιόν σου καὶ ἐπίομεν, καὶ ἐν ταῖς πλατείαις ἡμῶν ἐδίδαξας· καὶ ἐρεῖ λέγων ὑμῖν, Οὐκ οἶδα [ὑμᾶς] πόθεν

---

[196]Mt var. (conflated with the Marcan par.) Ἄλλην παραβολὴν παρέθηκεν αὐτοῖς λέγων, Ὁμοία ἐστὶν ἡ βασιλεία τῶν οὐρανῶν κόκκῳ σινάπεως, ὃν λαβὼν ἄνθρωπος ἔσπειρεν ἐν τῷ ἀγρῷ αὐτοῦ· ὃ μικρότερον μέν ἐστιν πάντων τῶν σπερμάτων, ὅταν δὲ αὐξηθῇ μεῖζον τῶν λαχάνων ἐστὶν καὶ γίνεται δένδρον, ὥστε ἐλθεῖν τὰ πετεινὰ τοῦ οὐρανοῦ καὶ κατασκηνοῦν ἐν τοῖς κλάδοις αὐτοῦ.

[197]Mt var. Ἄλλην παραβολὴν ἐλάλησεν αὐτοῖς· Ὁμοία ἐστὶν ἡ βασιλεία τῶν οὐρανῶν

[198]Lk introduces the pericope with εἶπεν δέ τις αὐτῷ, Κύριε, εἰ ὀλίγοι οἱ σῳζόμενοι; ὁ δὲ εἶπεν πρὸς αὐτούς·

[199]Mt var. (7:13f) Εἰσέλθατε διὰ τῆς στενῆς πύλης· ὅτι πλατεῖα ἡ πύλη καὶ εὐρύχωρος ἡ ὁδὸς ἡ ἀπάγουσα εἰς τὴν ἀπώλειαν, καὶ πολλοί εἰσιν οἱ εἰσερχόμενοι δι' αὐτῆς· τί στενὴ ἡ πύλη καὶ τεθλιμμένη ἡ ὁδὸς ἡ ἀπάγουσα εἰς τὴν ζωήν, καὶ ὀλίγοι εἰσὶν οἱ εὑρίσκοντες αὐτήν.

ἐστέ· ἀπόστητε ἀπ' ἐμοῦ, πάντες ἐργάται ἀδικίας.²⁰⁰ ἐκεῖ ἔσται ὁ κλαυθμὸς καὶ ὁ βρυγμὸς τῶν ὀδόντων, ὅταν ὄψεσθε Ἀβραὰμ καὶ Ἰσαὰκ καὶ Ἰακὼβ καὶ πάντας τοὺς προφήτας ἐν τῇ βασιλείᾳ τοῦ θεοῦ, ὑμᾶς δὲ ἐκβαλλομένους ἔξω. καὶ ἥξουσιν ἀπὸ ἀνατολῶν καὶ δυσμῶν καὶ ἀπὸ βορρᾶ καὶ νότου καὶ ἀνακλιθήσονται ἐν τῇ βασιλείᾳ τοῦ θεοῦ.²⁰¹ καὶ ἰδοὺ εἰσὶν ἔσχατοι οἳ ἔσονται πρῶτοι, καὶ εἰσὶν πρῶτοι οἳ ἔσονται ἔσχατοι.

### 33. Lamment over Jerusalem
(Lk 13:34f=Mt 23:37-39)

Ἰερουσαλὴμ Ἰερουσαλήμ, ἡ ἀποκτείνουσα τοὺς προφήτας καὶ λιθοβολοῦσα τοὺς ἀπεσταλμένους πρὸς αὐτήν, ποσάκις ἠθέλησα ἐπισυνάξαι²⁰² τὰ τέκνα σου ὃν τρόπον ὄρνις τὴν ἑαυτῆς νοσσιὰν²⁰³ ὑπὸ τὰς πτέρυγας, καὶ οὐκ ἠθελήσατε. ἰδοὺ ἀφίεται ὑμῖν ὁ οἶκος ὑμῶν. λέγω δὲ ὑμῖν, οὐ μὴ ἴδητέ με ἕως [ἥξει ὅτε] εἴπητε,²⁰⁴ εὐλογημένος ὁ ἐρχόμενος ἐν ὀνόματι κυρίου.

## VII. EPILOGUE. THE ESCHATOLOGICAL DISCOURSE
### 34. The coming of the Son of Man
(Lk 17:23-37=Mt 24:23-28)

[Τότε] ἐροῦσιν ὑμῖν, Ἰδοὺ ἐκεῖ· ἤ, Ἰδοὺ ὧδε· μὴ ἀπέλθητε μηδὲ διώξητε.²⁰⁵ ὥσπερ γὰρ ἡ ἀστραπὴ ἀστράπτουσα ἐκ τῆς ὑπὸ τὸν οὐρανὸν εἰς τὴν ὑπ' οὐρανὸν λάμπει, οὕτως ἔσται

---

[200] Mt var. (7:22f) πολλοὶ ἐροῦσίν μοι ἐν ἐκείνῃ τῇ ἡμέρᾳ, Κύριε κύριε, οὐ τῷ σῷ ὀνόματι ἐπροφητεύσαμεν, καὶ τῷ σῷ ὀνόματι δαιμόνια ἐξεβάλομεν, καὶ τῷ σῷ ὀνόματι δυνάμεις πολλὰς ἐποιήσαμεν; καὶ τότε ὁμολογήσω αὐτοῖς ὅτι Οὐδέποτε ἔγνων ὑμᾶς· ἀποχωρεῖτε ἀπ' ἐμοῦ οἱ ἐργαζόμενοι τὴν ἀνομίαν.

[201] Mt var. (8:11f) λέγω δὲ ὑμῖν ὅτι πολλοὶ ἀπὸ ἀνατολῶν καὶ δυσμῶν ἥξουσιν καὶ ἀνακλιθήσονται μετὰ Ἀβραὰμ καὶ Ἰσαὰκ καὶ Ἰακὼβ ἐν τῇ βασιλείᾳ τῶν οὐρανῶν· οἱ δὲ υἱοὶ τῆς βασιλείας ἐκβληθήσονται εἰς τὸ σκότος τὸ ἐξώτερον· ἐκεῖ ἔσται ὁ κλαυθμὸς καὶ ὁ βρυγμὸς τῶν ὀδόντων.

[202] Mt var. ἐπισυναγαγεῖν

[203] Mt var. τὰ νοσσία αὐτῆς

[204] Mt var. λέγω γὰρ ὑμῖν, οὐ μή με ἴδητε ἀπ' ἄρτι ἕως ἂν εἴπητε

[205] Mt var. ἐὰν οὖν εἴπωσιν ὑμῖν, Ἰδοὺ ἐν τῇ ἐρήμῳ ἐστίν, μὴ ἐξέλθητε· Ἰδοὺ ἐν τοῖς ταμείοις, μὴ πιστεύσητε·

ὁ υἱὸς τοῦ ἀνθρώπου ἐν τῇ ἡμέρᾳ αὐτοῦ²⁰⁶ ...²⁰⁷ καὶ καθὼς ἐγένετο ἐν ταῖς ἡμέραις Νῶε, οὕτως ἔσται καὶ ἐν ταῖς ἡμέραις τοῦ υἱοῦ τοῦ ἀνθρώπου·²⁰⁸ ἤσθιον, ἔπινον, ἐγάμουν, ἐγαμίζοντο, ἄχρι ἧς ἡμέρας εἰσῆλθεν Νῶε εἰς τὴν κιβωτόν, καὶ ἦλθεν ὁ κατακλυσμὸς καὶ ἀπώλεσεν πάντας.²⁰⁹ [ὁμοίως καθὼς ἐγένετο ἐν ταῖς ἡμέραις Λώτ· ἤσθιον, ἔπινον, ἠγόραζον, ἐπώλουν, ἐφύτευον, ᾠκοδόμουν· ᾗ δὲ ἡμέρᾳ ἐξῆλθεν Λὼτ ἀπὸ Σοδόμων, ἔβρεξεν πῦρ καὶ θεῖον ἀπ' οὐρανοῦ καὶ ἀπώλεσεν πάντας. κατὰ τὰ αὐτὰ ἔσται ᾗ ἡμέρᾳ ὁ υἱὸς τοῦ ἀνθρώπου ἀποκαλύπτεται. ἐν ἐκείνῃ τῇ ἡμέρᾳ ὃς ἔσται ἐπὶ τοῦ δώματος καὶ τὰ σκεύη αὐτοῦ ἐν τῇ οἰκίᾳ, μὴ καταβάτω ἆραι αὐτά, καὶ ὁ ἐν ἀγρῷ ὁμοίως μὴ ἐπιστρεψάτω εἰς τὰ ὀπίσω. μνημονεύετε τῆς γυναικὸς Λώτ].²¹⁰ ὃς ἐὰν ζητήσῃ τὴν ψυχὴν αὐτοῦ περιποιήσασθαι ἀπολέσει αὐτήν, ὃς δ' ἂν ἀπολέσῃ ζῳογονήσει αὐτήν.²¹¹ λέγω ὑμῖν, ταύτῃ τῇ νυκτὶ ἔσονται δύο ἐπὶ κλίνης μιᾶς, ὁ εἷς παραλημφθήσεται καὶ ὁ ἕτερος ἀφεθήσεται· ἔσονται δύο ἀλήθουσαι ἐπὶ τὸ αὐτό, ἡ μία παραλημφθήσεται ἡ δὲ ἑτέρα ἀφεθήσεται.²¹² καὶ ἀποκριθέντες λέγουσιν αὐτῷ, Ποῦ, κύριε; ὁ δὲ εἶπεν αὐτοῖς,²¹³ Ὅπου τὸ σῶμα, ἐκεῖ καὶ οἱ ἀετοὶ ἐπισυναχθήσονται.²¹⁴

---

²⁰⁶Mt var. ὥσπερ γὰρ ἡ ἀστραπὴ ἐξέρχεται ἀπὸ ἀνατολῶν καὶ φαίνεται ἕως δυσμῶν, οὕτως ἔσται ἡ παρουσία τοῦ υἱοῦ τοῦ ἀνθρώπου.

²⁰⁷Lk add. πρῶτον δὲ δεῖ αὐτὸν πολλὰ παθεῖν καὶ ἀποδοκιμασθῆναι ἀπὸ τῆς γενεᾶς ταύτης.

²⁰⁸Mt var. ὥσπερ γὰρ αἱ ἡμέραι τοῦ Νῶε, οὕτως ἔσται ἡ παρουσία τοῦ υἱοῦ τοῦ ἀνθρώπου.

²⁰⁹Mt var. ὡς γὰρ ἦσαν ἐν ταῖς ἡμέραις [ἐκείναις] ταῖς πρὸ τοῦ κατακλυσμοῦ τρώγοντες καὶ πίνοντες, γαμοῦντες καὶ γαμίζοντες, ἄχρι ἧς ἡμέρας εἰσῆλθεν Νῶε εἰς τὴν κιβωτόν, καὶ οὐκ ἔγνωσαν ἕως ἦλθεν ὁ κατακλυσμὸς καὶ ἦρεν ἅπαντας, οὕτως ἔσται καὶ ἡ παρουσία τοῦ υἱοῦ τοῦ ἀνθρώπου.

²¹⁰Mt om. the Lot incident.

²¹¹Mt var. ὁ εὑρὼν τὴν ψυχὴν αὐτοῦ ἀπολέσει αὐτήν, καὶ ὁ ἀπολέσας τὴν ψυχὴν αὐτοῦ ἕνεκεν ἐμοῦ εὑρήσει αὐτήν.

²¹²Mt var. τότε δύο ἔσονται ἐν τῷ ἀγρῷ, εἷς παραλαμβάνεται καὶ εἷς ἀφίεται· δύο ἀλήθουσαι ἐν τῷ μύλῳ, μία παραλαμβάνεται καὶ μία ἀφίεται.

²¹³Mt om.

²¹⁴Mt var. ὅπου ἐὰν ᾖ τὸ πτῶμα, ἐκεῖ συναχθήσονται οἱ ἀετοί.

## 35. Ending of the Eschatological Discourse (?)²¹⁵
(Lk 21:34-36)

(Προσέχετε δὲ ἑαυτοῖς μήποτε βαρηθῶσιν ὑμῶν αἱ καρδίαι ἐν κραιπάλῃ καὶ μέθῃ καὶ μερίμναις βιωτικαῖς, καὶ ἐπιστῇ ἐφ' ὑμᾶς αἰφνίδιος ἡ ἡμέρα ἐκείνη ὡς παγὶς. ἐπεισελεύσεται γὰρ ἐπὶ πάντας τοὺς καθημένους ἐπὶ πρόσωπον πάσης τῆς γῆς. ἀγρυπνεῖτε δὲ ἐν παντὶ καιρῷ δεόμενοι ἵνα κατισχύσητε ἐκφυγεῖν ταῦτα πάντα τὰ μέλλοντα γίνεσθαι, καὶ σταθῆναι ἔμπροσθεν τοῦ υἱοῦ τοῦ ἀνθρώπου).²¹⁶

## OTHER POSSIBLE Q-SAYINGS
(excluded according to our procedural principles
but usually attributed to the Q-Document by some scholars)

### (<6). Blind guides
(Lk 6:39=Mt 15:14)

Εἶπεν δὲ καὶ παραβολὴν αὐτοῖς· Μήτι δύναται τυφλὸς τυφλὸν ὁδηγεῖν; οὐχὶ ἀμφότεροι εἰς βόθυνον ἐμπεσοῦνται;²¹⁷

### (<6). Disciples and teachers
(Lk 6:40=Mt 10:24f)

οὐκ ἔστιν μαθητὴς ὑπὲρ τὸν διδάσκαλον, κατηρτισμένος δὲ πᾶς ἔσται ὡς ὁ διδάσκαλος αὐτοῦ.²¹⁸

### (<30). Agreement with one's accuser
(Lk 12:58-59=Mt 5:25-26)

ὡς γὰρ ὑπάγεις μετὰ τοῦ ἀντιδίκου σου ἐπ' ἄρχοντα, ἐν τῇ ὁδῷ δὸς ἐργασίαν ἀπηλλάχθαι ἀπ' αὐτοῦ, μήποτε κατασύρῃ σε πρὸς τὸν κριτήν, καὶ ὁ κριτής σε παραδώσει τῷ

---

²¹⁵See also n. 230.
²¹⁶Cf. Mt var. (24:42-44) γρηγορεῖτε οὖν, ὅτι οὐκ οἴδατε ποίᾳ ἡμέρᾳ ὁ κύριος ὑμῶν ἔρχεται. ἐκεῖνο δὲ γινώσκετε ὅτι εἰ ᾔδει ὁ οἰκοδεσπότης ποίᾳ φυλακῇ ὁ κλέπτης ἔρχεται, ἐγρηγόρησεν ἂν καὶ οὐκ ἂν εἴασεν διορυχθῆναι τὴν οἰκίαν αὐτοῦ. διὰ τοῦτο καὶ ὑμεῖς γίνεσθε ἕτοιμοι, ὅτι ᾗ οὐ δοκεῖτε ὥρᾳ ὁ υἱὸς τοῦ ἀνθρώπου ἔρχεται.
²¹⁷Cf. Mt var. ἄφετε αὐτούς· τυφλοί εἰσιν ὁδηγοί [τυφλῶν]· τυφλὸς δὲ τυφλὸν ἐὰν ὁδηγῇ, ἀμφότεροι εἰς βόθυνον πεσοῦνται.
²¹⁸Cf. Mt var. Οὐκ ἔστιν μαθητὴς ὑπὲρ τὸν διδάσκαλον οὐδὲ δοῦλος ὑπὲρ τὸν κύριον αὐτοῦ. ἀρκετὸν τῷ μαθητῇ ἵνα γένηται ὡς ὁ διδάσκαλος αὐτοῦ, καὶ ὁ δοῦλος ὡς ὁ κύριος αὐτοῦ.

πράκτορι, καὶ ὁ πράκτωρ σε βαλεῖ εἰς φυλακήν. λέγω σοι, οὐ μὴ ἐξέλθῃς ἐκεῖθεν ἕως καὶ τὸ ἔσχατον λεπτὸν ἀποδῷς.[219]

## (<34). The Parable of the Great Supper
(Lk 14:16-24=Mt 22:2-14)

Ἄνθρωπός τις ἐποίει δεῖπνον μέγα, καὶ ἐκάλεσεν πολλούς, καὶ ἀπέστειλεν τὸν δοῦλον αὐτοῦ τῇ ὥρᾳ τοῦ δείπνου εἰπεῖν τοῖς κεκλημένοις, Ἔρχεσθε, ὅτι ἤδη ἕτοιμά ἐστιν. καὶ ἤρξαντο ἀπὸ μιᾶς πάντες παραιτεῖσθαι. ὁ πρῶτος εἶπεν αὐτῷ, Ἀγρὸν ἠγόρασα καὶ ἔχω ἀνάγκην ἐξελθὼν ἰδεῖν αὐτόν· ἐρωτῶ σε, ἔχε με παρῃτημένον. καὶ ἕτερος εἶπεν, Ζεύγη βοῶν ἠγόρασα πέντε καὶ πορεύομαι δοκιμάσαι αὐτά· ἐρωτῶ σε, ἔχε με παρῃτημένον. καὶ ἕτερος εἶπεν, Γυναῖκα ἔγημα καὶ διὰ τοῦτο οὐ δύναμαι ἐλθεῖν. καὶ παραγενόμενος ὁ δοῦλος ἀπήγγειλεν τῷ κυρίῳ αὐτοῦ ταῦτα. τότε ὀργισθεὶς ὁ οἰκοδεσπότης εἶπεν τῷ δούλῳ αὐτοῦ, Ἔξελθε ταχέως εἰς τὰς πλατείας καὶ ῥύμας τῆς πόλεως, καὶ τοὺς πτωχοὺς καὶ ἀναπείρους καὶ τυφλοὺς καὶ χωλοὺς εἰσάγαγε ὧδε. καὶ εἶπεν ὁ δοῦλος, Κύριε, γέγονεν ὃ ἐπέταξας, καὶ ἔτι τόπος ἐστίν. καὶ εἶπεν ὁ κύριος πρὸς τὸν δοῦλον, Ἔξελθε εἰς τὰς ὁδοὺς καὶ φραγμοὺς καὶ ἀνάγκασον εἰσελθεῖν, ἵνα γεμισθῇ μου ὁ οἶκος· λέγω γὰρ ὑμῖν ὅτι οὐδεὶς τῶν ἀνδρῶν ἐκείνων τῶν κεκλημένων γεύσεταί μου τοῦ δείπνου.[220]

---

[219]Cf. Mt var. Ἴσθι εὐνοῶν τῷ ἀντιδίκῳ σου ταχὺ ἕως ὅτου εἶ μετ' αὐτοῦ ἐν τῇ ὁδῷ, μήποτέ σε παραδῷ ὁ ἀντίδικος τῷ κριτῇ, καὶ ὁ κριτὴς τῷ ὑπηρέτῃ, καὶ εἰς φυλακὴν βληθήσῃ· ἀμὴν λέγω σοι, οὐ μὴ ἐξέλθῃς ἐκεῖθεν ἕως ἂν ἀποδῷς τὸν ἔσχατον κοδράντην.

[220]Cf. Mt var. Ὡμοιώθη ἡ βασιλεία τῶν οὐρανῶν ἀνθρώπῳ βασιλεῖ, ὅστις ἐποίησεν γάμους τῷ υἱῷ αὐτοῦ. καὶ ἀπέστειλεν τοὺς δούλους αὐτοῦ καλέσαι τοὺς κεκλημένους εἰς τοὺς γάμους, καὶ οὐκ ἤθελον ἐλθεῖν. πάλιν ἀπέστειλεν ἄλλους δούλους λέγων, Εἴπατε τοῖς κεκλημένοις, Ἰδοὺ τὸ ἄριστόν μου ἡτοίμακα, οἱ ταῦροί μου καὶ τὰ σιτιστὰ τεθυμένα, καὶ πάντα ἕτοιμα· δεῦτε εἰς τοὺς γάμους. οἱ δὲ ἀμελήσαντες ἀπῆλθον, ὃς μὲν εἰς τὸν ἴδιον ἀγρόν, ὃς δὲ ἐπὶ τὴν ἐμπορίαν αὐτοῦ· οἱ δὲ λοιποὶ κρατήσαντες τοὺς δούλους αὐτοῦ ὕβρισαν καὶ ἀπέκτειναν. ὁ δὲ βασιλεὺς ὠργίσθη, καὶ πέμψας τὰ στρατεύματα αὐτοῦ ἀπώλεσεν τοὺς φονεῖς ἐκείνους καὶ τὴν πόλιν αὐτῶν ἐνέπρησεν. τότε λέγει τοῖς δούλοις αὐτοῦ, Ὁ μὲν γάμος ἕτοιμός ἐστιν, οἱ δὲ κεκλημένοι οὐκ ἦσαν ἄξιοι· πορεύεσθε οὖν ἐπὶ τὰς διεξόδους τῶν ὁδῶν, καὶ ὅσους ἐὰν εὕρητε καλέσατε εἰς τοὺς γάμους. καὶ ἐξελθόντες οἱ δοῦλοι ἐκεῖνοι εἰς τὰς ὁδοὺς συνήγαγον πάντας οὓς εὗρον, πονηρούς τε καὶ ἀγαθούς· καὶ ἐπλήσθη ὁ γάμος ἀνακειμένων. εἰσελθὼν δὲ ὁ βασιλεὺς θεάσασθαι τοὺς ἀνακειμένους εἶδεν ἐκεῖ ἄνθρωπον οὐκ ἐνδεδυμένον ἔνδυμα γάμου· καὶ λέγει αὐτῷ, Ἑταῖρε, πῶς εἰσῆλθες ὧδε μὴ ἔχων ἔνδυμα γάμου; ὁ δὲ ἐφιμώθη.. τότε ὁ βασιλεὺς εἶπεν τοῖς διακόνοις, Δήσαντες αὐτοῦ πόδας καὶ

### (<34). The conditions of discipleship
(Lk 14:26-27=Mt 10:37-38)

Εἴ τις ἔρχεται πρός με καὶ οὐ μισεῖ τὸν πατέρα ἑαυτοῦ καὶ τὴν μητέρα καὶ τὴν γυναῖκα καὶ τὰ τέκνα καὶ τοὺς ἀδελφοὺς καὶ τὰς ἀδελφάς, ἔτι τε καὶ τὴν ψυχὴν ἑαυτοῦ, οὐ δύναται εἶναί μου μαθητής. [καὶ] ὅστις οὐ βαστάζει τὸν σταυρὸν ἑαυτοῦ καὶ ἔρχεται ὀπίσω μου οὐ δύναται εἶναί μου μαθητής.[221]

### (<34). The parable of salt
(Lk 14:34-35=Mt 5:13)

Καλὸν οὖν τὸ ἅλας· ἐὰν δὲ καὶ τὸ ἅλας μωρανθῇ, ἐν τίνι ἀρτυθήσεται; οὔτε εἰς γῆν οὔτε εἰς κοπρίαν εὔθετόν ἐστιν· ἔξω βάλλουσιν αὐτό. ὁ ἔχων ὦτα ἀκούειν ἀκουέτω.[222]

### (<34). The parable of the lost sheep
(Lk 15:3-7=Mt 18:12-14)

εἶπεν δὲ πρὸς αὐτοὺς τὴν παραβολὴν ταύτην λέγων, Τίς ἄνθρωπος ἐξ ὑμῶν ἔχων ἑκατὸν πρόβατα καὶ ἀπολέσας ἐξ αὐτῶν ἓν οὐ καταλείπει τὰ ἐνενήκοντα ἐννέα ἐν τῇ ἐρήμῳ καὶ πορεύεται ἐπὶ τὸ ἀπολωλὸς ἕως εὕρῃ αὐτό; καὶ εὑρὼν ἐπιτίθησιν ἐπὶ τοὺς ὤμους αὐτοῦ χαίρων, καὶ ἐλθὼν εἰς τὸν οἶκον συγκαλεῖ τοὺς φίλους καὶ τοὺς γείτονας λέγων αὐτοῖς, Συγχάρητέ μοι, ὅτι εὗρον τὸ πρόβατόν μου τὸ ἀπολωλός. λέγω ὑμῖν ὅτι οὕτως χαρὰ ἐν τῷ οὐρανῷ ἔσται ἐπὶ ἑνὶ ἁμαρτωλῷ μετανοοῦντι ἢ ἐπὶ ἐνενήκοντα ἐννέα δικαίοις οἵτινες οὐ χρείαν ἔχουσιν μετανοίας.[223]

---

χεῖρας ἐκβάλετε αὐτὸν εἰς τὸ σκότος τὸ ἐξώτερον· ἐκεῖ ἔσται ὁ κλαυθμὸς καὶ ὁ βρυγμὸς τῶν ὀδόντων. πολλοὶ γάρ εἰσιν κλητοὶ ὀλίγοι δὲ ἐκλεκτοί.

[221]Cf. Mt var. Ὁ φιλῶν πατέρα ἢ μητέρα ὑπὲρ ἐμὲ οὐκ ἔστιν μου ἄξιος· καὶ ὁ φιλῶν υἱὸν ἢ θυγατέρα ὑπὲρ ἐμὲ οὐκ ἔστιν μου ἄξιος· καὶ ὃς οὐ λαμβάνει τὸν σταυρὸν αὐτοῦ καὶ ἀκολουθεῖ ὀπίσω μου, οὐκ ἔστιν μου ἄξιος.

[222]Cf. Mt var. Ὑμεῖς ἐστε τὸ ἅλας τῆς γῆς· ἐὰν δὲ τὸ ἅλας μωρανθῇ, ἐν τίνι ἁλισθήσεται; εἰς οὐδὲν ἰσχύει ἔτι εἰ μὴ βληθὲν ἔξω καταπατεῖσθαι ὑπὸ τῶν ἀνθρώπων.

[223]Cf. Mt var. Τί ὑμῖν δοκεῖ; ἐὰν γένηταί τινι ἀνθρώπῳ ἑκατὸν πρόβατα καὶ πλανηθῇ ἓν ἐξ αὐτῶν, οὐχὶ ἀφήσει τὰ ἐνενήκοντα ἐννέα ἐπὶ τὰ ὄρη καὶ πορευθεὶς ζητεῖ τὸ πλανώμενον; καὶ ἐὰν γένηται εὑρεῖν αὐτό, ἀμὴν λέγω ὑμῖν ὅτι χαίρει ἐπ' αὐτῷ μᾶλλον ἢ ἐπὶ τοῖς ἐνενήκοντα ἐννέα τοῖς μὴ πεπλανημένοις. οὕτως οὐκ ἔστιν θέλημα ἔμπροσθεν τοῦ πατρὸς ὑμῶν τοῦ ἐν οὐρανοῖς ἵνα ἀπόληται ἓν τῶν μικρῶν τούτων.

## (<34). On serving two masters
### (Lk 16:13=Mt 6:24)

Οὐδεὶς οἰκέτης²²⁴ δύναται δυσὶ κυρίοις δουλεύειν· ἢ γὰρ τὸν ἕνα μισήσει καὶ τὸν ἕτερον ἀγαπήσει, ἢ ἑνὸς ἀνθέξεται καὶ τοῦ ἑτέρου καταφρονήσει. οὐ δύνασθε θεῷ δουλεύειν καὶ μαμωνᾷ.

## (<34). Concerning divorce
### (Lk 16:18=Mt 5:32)

Πᾶς ὁ ἀπολύων τὴν γυναῖκα αὐτοῦ καὶ γαμῶν ἑτέραν μοιχεύει, καὶ ὁ ἀπολελυμένην ἀπὸ ἀνδρὸς γαμῶν μοιχεύει.²²⁵

## (<34). On scandals
### (Lk 17:1-2=Mt 18:6-7)

Ἀνένδεκτόν ἐστιν τοῦ τὰ σκάνδαλα μὴ ἐλθεῖν, πλὴν οὐαὶ δι' οὗ ἔρχεται· λυσιτελεῖ αὐτῷ εἰ λίθος μυλικὸς περίκειται περὶ τὸν τράχηλον αὐτοῦ καὶ ἔρριπται εἰς τὴν θάλασσαν ἢ ἵνα σκανδαλίσῃ τῶν μικρῶν τούτων ἕνα.²²⁶

## (<34). On forgiveness
### (Lk 17:3-4=Mt 18:15.21-22)

ἐὰν ἁμάρτῃ ὁ ἀδελφός σου ἐπιτίμησον αὐτῷ, καὶ ἐὰν μετανοήσῃ ἄφες αὐτῷ· καὶ ἐὰν ἑπτάκις τῆς ἡμέρας ἁμαρτήσῃ εἰς σὲ καὶ ἑπτάκις ἐπιστρέψῃ πρὸς σὲ λέγων, Μετανοῶ, ἀφήσεις αὐτῷ.²²⁷

---

²²⁴Mt om.

²²⁵Cf. Mt var. πᾶς ὁ ἀπολύων τὴν γυναῖκα αὐτοῦ παρεκτὸς λόγου πορνείας ποιεῖ αὐτὴν μοιχευθῆναι, καὶ ὃς ἐὰν ἀπολελυμένην γαμήσῃ μοιχᾶται.

²²⁶Cf. Mt var. ῝Ος δ' ἂν σκανδαλίσῃ ἕνα τῶν μικρῶν τούτων τῶν πιστευόντων εἰς ἐμέ, συμφέρει αὐτῷ ἵνα κρεμασθῇ μύλος ὀνικὸς περὶ τὸν τράχηλον αὐτοῦ καὶ καταποντισθῇ ἐν τῷ πελάγει τῆς θαλάσσης. οὐαὶ τῷ κόσμῳ ἀπὸ τῶν σκανδάλων· ἀνάγκη γὰρ ἐλθεῖν τὰ σκάνδαλα, πλὴν οὐαὶ τῷ ἀνθρώπῳ δι' οὗ τὸ σκάνδαλον ἔρχεται.

²²⁷Cf. Mt var. Ἐὰν δὲ ἁμαρτήσῃ [εἰς σὲ] ὁ ἀδελφός σου, ὕπαγε ἔλεγξον αὐτὸν μεταξὺ σοῦ καὶ αὐτοῦ μόνου. ἐάν σου ἀκούσῃ, ἐκέρδησας τὸν ἀδελφόν σου.. . .Τότε προσελθὼν ὁ Πέτρος εἶπεν αὐτῷ, Κύριε, ποσάκις ἁμαρτήσει εἰς ἐμὲ ὁ ἀδελφός μου καὶ ἀφήσω αὐτῷ; ἕως ἑπτάκις; λέγει αὐτῷ ὁ Ἰησοῦς, Οὐ λέγω σοι ἕως ἑπτάκις ἀλλὰ ἕως ἑβδομηκοντάκις ἑπτά.

### (<34). On faith
(Lk 17:6=Mt 17:20)

εἶπεν δὲ ὁ κύριος, Εἰ ἔχετε πίστιν ὡς κόκκον σινάπεως, ἐλέγετε ἂν τῇ συκαμίνῳ [ταύτῃ], Ἐκριζώθητι καὶ φυτεύθητι ἐν τῇ θαλάσσῃ· καὶ ὑπήκουσεν ἂν ὑμῖν.[228]

### (<35). The parable of the talents
(Lk 19:12-26=Mt 25:14-30)

θρωπός τις εὐγενὴς ἐπορεύθη εἰς χώραν μακρὰν λαβεῖν ἑαυτῷ βασιλείαν καὶ ὑποστρέψαι. καλέσας δὲ δέκα δούλους ἑαυτοῦ ἔδωκεν αὐτοῖς δέκα μνᾶς καὶ εἶπεν πρὸς αὐτούς, Πραγματεύσασθε ἐν ᾧ ἔρχομαι. οἱ δὲ πολῖται αὐτοῦ ἐμίσουν αὐτόν, καὶ ἀπέστειλαν πρεσβείαν ὀπίσω αὐτοῦ λέγοντες, Οὐ θέλομεν τοῦτον βασιλεῦσαι ἐφ' ἡμᾶς. Καὶ ἐγένετο ἐν τῷ ἐπανελθεῖν αὐτὸν λαβόντα τὴν βασιλείαν καὶ εἶπεν φωνηθῆναι αὐτῷ τοὺς δούλους τούτους οἷς δεδώκει τὸ ἀργύριον, ἵνα γνοῖ τί διεπραγματεύσαντο. παρεγένετο δὲ ὁ πρῶτος λέγων, Κύριε, ἡ μνᾶ σου δέκα προσηργάσατο μνᾶς. καὶ εἶπεν αὐτῷ, Εὖγε, ἀγαθὲ δοῦλε, ὅτι ἐν ἐλαχίστῳ πιστὸς ἐγένου, ἴσθι ἐξουσίαν ἔχων ἐπάνω δέκα πόλεων. καὶ ἦλθεν ὁ δεύτερος λέγων, Ἡ μνᾶ σου, κύριε, ἐποίησεν πέντε μνᾶς. εἶπεν δὲ καὶ τούτῳ, Καὶ σὺ ἐπάνω γίνου πέντε πόλεων. καὶ ὁ ἕτερος ἦλθεν λέγων, Κύριε, ἰδοὺ ἡ μνᾶ σου ἣν εἶχον ἀποκειμένην ἐν σουδαρίῳ· ἐφοβούμην γάρ σε, ὅτι ἄνθρωπος αὐστηρὸς εἶ, αἴρεις ὃ οὐκ ἔθηκας καὶ θερίζεις ὃ οὐκ ἔσπειρας. λέγει αὐτῷ, Ἐκ τοῦ στόματός σου κρίνω σε, πονηρὲ δοῦλε. ᾔδεις ὅτι ἐγὼ ἄνθρωπος αὐστηρός εἰμι, αἴρων ὃ οὐκ ἔθηκα καὶ θερίζων ὃ οὐκ ἔσπειρα; καὶ διὰ τί οὐκ ἔδωκάς μου τὸ ἀργύριον ἐπὶ τράπεζαν; κἀγὼ ἐλθὼν σὺν τόκῳ ἂν αὐτὸ ἔπραξα. καὶ τοῖς παρεστῶσιν εἶπεν, Ἄρατε ἀπ' αὐτοῦ τὴν μνᾶν καὶ δότε τῷ τὰς δέκα μνᾶς ἔχοντι καὶ εἶπαν αὐτῷ, Κύριε, ἔχει δέκα μνᾶς-λέγω ὑμῖν ὅτι παντὶ τῷ ἔχοντι δοθήσεται, ἀπὸ δὲ τοῦ μὴ ἔχοντος καὶ ὃ ἔχει ἀρθήσεται.[229]

---

[228]Cf. Mt var. ἀμὴν γὰρ λέγω ὑμῖν, ἐὰν ἔχητε πίστιν ὡς κόκκον σινάπεως, ἐρεῖτε τῷ ὄρει τούτῳ, Μετάβα ἔνθεν ἐκεῖ, καὶ μεταβήσεται· καὶ οὐδὲν ἀδυνατήσει ὑμῖν.

[229]Cf. Mt var. Ὥσπερ γὰρ ἄνθρωπος ἀποδημῶν ἐκάλεσεν τοὺς ἰδίους δούλους καὶ παρέδωκεν αὐτοῖς τὰ ὑπάρχοντα αὐτοῦ, καὶ ᾧ μὲν ἔδωκεν πέντε τάλαντα, ᾧ δὲ δύο, ᾧ δὲ ἕν, ἑκάστῳ κατὰ τὴν ἰδίαν δύναμιν, καὶ ἀπεδήμησεν. εὐθέως πορευθεὶς ὁ τὰ πέντε τάλαντα λαβὼν ἠργάσατο ἐν αὐτοῖς καὶ ἐκέρδησεν ἄλλα πέντε· ὡσαύτως ὁ τὰ δύο ἐκέρδησεν ἄλλα δύο. ὁ δὲ τὸ ἓν λαβὼν ἀπελθὼν ὤρυξεν γῆν καὶ ἔκρυψεν τὸ ἀργύριον τοῦ κυρίου αὐτοῦ. μετὰ δὲ

## (>35). The twelve thrones[230]
(Lk 22:28-30=Mt 19:28)

ὑμεῖς δέ ἐστε οἱ διαμεμενηκότες μετ' ἐμοῦ ἐν τοῖς πειρασμοῖς μου· κἀγὼ διατίθεμαι ὑμῖν καθὼς διέθετό μοι ὁ πατήρ μου βασιλείαν ἵνα ἔσθητε καὶ πίνητε ἐπὶ τῆς τραπέζης μου ἐν τῇ βασιλείᾳ μου, καὶ καθήσεσθε ἐπὶ θρόνων τὰς δώδεκα φυλὰς κρίνοντες τοῦ Ἰσραήλ.[231]

---

πολὺν χρόνον ἔρχεται ὁ κύριος τῶν δούλων ἐκείνων καὶ συναίρει λόγον μετ' αὐτῶν. καὶ προσελθὼν ὁ τὰ πέντε τάλαντα λαβὼν προσήνεγκεν ἄλλα πέντε τάλαντα λέγων, Κύριε, πέντε τάλαντά μοι παρέδωκας· ἴδε ἄλλα πέντε τάλαντα ἐκέρδησα. ἔφη αὐτῷ ὁ κύριος αὐτοῦ, Εὖ, δοῦλε ἀγαθὲ καὶ πιστέ, ἐπὶ ὀλίγα ἦς πιστός, ἐπὶ πολλῶν σε καταστήσω· εἴσελθε εἰς τὴν χαρὰν τοῦ κυρίου σου. προσελθὼν [δὲ] καὶ ὁ τὰ δύο τάλαντα εἶπεν, Κύριε, δύο τάλαντά μοι παρέδωκας· ἴδε ἄλλα δύο τάλαντα ἐκέρδησα. ἔφη αὐτῷ ὁ κύριος αὐτοῦ, Εὖ, δοῦλε ἀγαθὲ καὶ πιστέ, ἐπὶ ὀλίγα ἦς πιστός, ἐπὶ πολλῶν σε καταστήσω· εἴσελθε εἰς τὴν χαρὰν τοῦ κυρίου σου. προσελθὼν δὲ καὶ ὁ τὸ ἓν τάλαντον εἰληφὼς εἶπεν, Κύριε, ἔγνων σε ὅτι σκληρὸς εἶ ἄνθρωπος, θερίζων ὅπου οὐκ ἔσπειρας καὶ συνάγων ὅθεν οὐ διεσκόρπισας· καὶ φοβηθεὶς ἀπελθὼν ἔκρυψα τὸ τάλαντόν σου ἐν τῇ γῇ· ἴδε ἔχεις τὸ σόν. ἀποκριθεὶς δὲ ὁ κύριος αὐτοῦ εἶπεν αὐτῷ, Πονηρὲ δοῦλε καὶ ὀκνηρέ, ᾔδεις ὅτι θερίζω ὅπου οὐκ ἔσπειρα καὶ συνάγω ὅθεν οὐ διεσκόρπισα; ἔδει σε οὖν βαλεῖν τὰ ἀργύριά μου τοῖς τραπεζίταις, καὶ ἐλθὼν ἐγὼ ἐκομισάμην ἂν τὸ ἐμὸν σὺν τόκῳ. ἄρατε οὖν ἀπ' αὐτοῦ τὸ τάλαντον καὶ δότε τῷ ἔχοντι τὰ δέκα τάλαντα· τῷ γὰρ ἔχοντι παντὶ δοθήσεται καὶ περισσευθήσεται· τοῦ δὲ μὴ ἔχοντος καὶ ὃ ἔχει ἀρθήσεται ἀπ' αὐτοῦ. καὶ τὸν ἀχρεῖον δοῦλον ἐκβάλετε εἰς τὸ σκότος τὸ ἐξώτερον· ἐκεῖ ἔσται ὁ κλαυθμὸς καὶ ὁ βρυγμὸς τῶν ὀδόντων.

[230]After a second thought this passage seems to be a better ending of the Q-Document.

[231]Cf. Mt var. Ἀμὴν λέγω ὑμῖν ὅτι ὑμεῖς οἱ ἀκολουθήσαντές μοι, ἐν τῇ παλιγγενεσίᾳ, ὅταν καθίσῃ ὁ υἱὸς τοῦ ἀνθρώπου ἐπὶ θρόνου δόξης αὐτοῦ, καθήσεσθε καὶ ὑμεῖς ἐπὶ δώδεκα θρόνους κρίνοντες τὰς δώδεκα φυλὰς τοῦ Ἰσραήλ.

# 6
# EUCHARIST AND Q*

The proper understanding of the Eucharist has always been a stumbling block in Christian theology and life; not only at the start of the Christian community when the church had to struggle against a multitude of mystery cults, but also much later when scholastic theology (mostly in the West) has systematized a latent "sacramentalistic" view of *the* Mystery *par excellence* of the One undivided Holy Catholic and Apostolic Church. In vain distinguished theologians of the East (most notably in the case of Cabasilas) attempted to redefine the Christian sacramental theology on the basis of the Trinitarian theology. Seen from a modern theological perspective, this was a desperate attempt to reject certain tendencies which overemphasized the importance of Christology at the expense - and to the detriment - of the importance of the role of the Holy Spirit. The controversy between East and West on the issues of the *filioque*, the *epiclesis* etc. are well known,[1] though their consequences to the sacramental theology of the Church have yet to be fully and systematically examined. The tragic consequences of those tendencies were in fact felt a few generations after the final Schism between East and West with the further division of Western Christianity. One of the main focuses during the Reformation, and rightly so, was the "sacramentalistic" understanding of the Eucharist in Western Christianity which resulted, among other things, in the departure of the mainstream Protestant theology from the early Christian sacramental theology. The dialectic opposition between "sacramentalism" on the one hand, and "the complete rejection of sacraments" on the other, was the main reason of the tragic secularization of our society and the transformation of the Church into a religion, in some cases a cultic religion. Unfortunately, this mounting sacramentalism of the medieval Catholicism has also influenced Eastern Christianity too, if not in theology at least certainly in piety and liturgical practice.[2]

---

*A lecture—entitled "Eucharist and Q. The Understanding of Eucharist in the Primitive Church"— given to the faculty and post-graduate students of the University of Lund, during my official visit as a guest professor, April-May 1995.

[1] Cf. my "Orthodox Theology Facing the 21st Century," *GOTR* 34 (1990) 139-150; also my "Orthodoxy and the West," *Orthodoxy at the Crossroads*, Thessaloniki 1992, 91ff. (in Greek).

[2] Cf. my "Eucharistic and Therapeutic Spirituality," *GOTR* 42 (1997), pp. 1-23, and (in Greek) in my *Lex Orandi. Studies of Liturgical Theology*, Thessaloniki 1994 107-135.

In a recent study of mine on the Johannine understanding of the Eucharist[3] I came to the following conclusion:

> "In John we have the beginnings of what has become axiomatic in Christian theology: To have eternal life—in other words to live in a true and authentic way and not just live a conventional life—one has to be in communion with Christ. Communion with Christ, however, means participation in the perfect communion, which exists within the Holy Trinity between the Father and the Son *("Just as the living Father sent me, and I live through the Father, he who eats me will live through me"* 6:57). What we have here in John, is in fact a parallel expression to the classic statement of II Peter "θείας φύσεως κοινωνοί" (partakers of the divine nature, 1:4), which has become in later patristic literature the biblical foundation of the doctrine of divinization *(θέωσις)*. In the case of the Gospel of John, however, this idea is expressed in a more descriptive and less abstract way that in II Peter. If we now take this argument a little further, we can say that Johannine theology more fully develops the earlier interpretation of the Eucharist as the continually repeated act of sealing the "new covenant" of God with his new people. This interpretation is evidenced in the synoptic and Pauline tradition, although there the covenantal interpretation of Jesus' death in the phrase *"this is my blood of the covenant"* (Mk 14:24 par and I Cor 11:25), is somewhat hidden by the soteriological formula "which is shed for you" (ibid.).[4]

What comes out of this understanding of the Eucharist by John with its more direct emphasis on the idea of the covenant, of communion, is the transformation of Jeremiah's vision—which was at the same time also a promise—from a marginal to a central feature. Just as in the book of Jeremiah, so also in John it is the ideas of *a new covenant*, of *communion*, and of the Church as *a people*, that are most strongly emphasized. Listen to what the prophet was saying: *"and I will make a **covenant**... a new covenant*,*"* Jer 38.31; and *"I will give them a heart (τοῦ εἰδέναι αὐτούς ἐμέ) to know that I am the Lord....and they shall be unto me **a people**,"* Jer 24.7).

If any conclusion is to be drawn from the....analysis of the Johannine eucharistic understanding, this is an affirmation of the ecclesiological dimension of...the Eucharist as a communion event and not as an act of personal devotion; an expression of the Church as the people of God and as the Body of Christ mystically united with its head, and not a sacramentalist quasi-magical rite.[5] More precisely, the eucharistic

---

[3] "The Understanding of Eucharist in St. John's Gospel," in L. Padovese (ed.), *Atti del VI Simposio di Efeso su S. Giovanni Apostolo,* Rome 1996, pp. 39-52, and (in Greek) in my *Orthodoxy at the Crossroads,* pp. 169-190.

[4] More on this in my *Cross and Salvation,* Thessaloniki 1983 (in Greek), an English summary of which can be found in a paper of mine delivered at the 1984 annual Leuven Colloquium ("Σταυρός: Centre of the Pauline Soteriology and Apostolic Ministry," A. Vanhoye [ed.], *L'Apôtre Paul. Personnalité, Style et Conception du Ministère,* BETL LXXIII, Leuven U.P. 1986, 246-253).

[5] Cf. also J. Zizioulas' affirmation that "when it is understood in its correct and primitive sense—and not how it has come to be regarded even in Orthodoxy under the

theology of the Gospel of John is beyond any notion related to sacramental practices of the ancient Mystery cults. The Eucharist as the unique and primary Sacrament of the Church cannot be related to "sacramentalism"; it is rather an expression of the communion of the people of God, which in turn is a reflection of the communion that exists between the persons of the Holy Trinity.[6]

This understanding of the Eucharist, not so much as a cult or rite, but primarily as a dynamic expression of the people of God and a proleptic manifestation of the Kingdom to come, evidenced at the end of the apostolic era, i.e. at almost the last end of the spectrum of the N.T. literature, if it is to be correct, or at least of some value for discovering the authentic character of Eucharist, has to be tested by reference to the other end of the spectrum, the most ancient stage of primitive Christianity, i.e. the Q-Document.[7]

In a recent survey of the N.T. evidence on the Eucharist in the revised edition of *The Study of Liturgy*,[8] prepared by a the late Cheslyn Jones and slightly revised by C. J. A. Hickling, there is no mention at all the pre-Pauline Christianity. The common view till very recently was that there is no history, or more precisely the *pre*-history,[9] of Eucharist prior to Paul, i.e. prior to the mid-50s. However, there has been recently a great progress in N.T. scholarship, and especially in Q studies. Modern biblical theology more and more focus attention to Q, and the understanding of Church origins has been undoubtedly determined by the hypothesis of the second source of the Synoptic tradition, now lost, which expounds a radically different theological stance from the mainstream kerygmatic expression of the early Church. H. W. Attridge has stated that recent research on Q "has revealed the complexity of early Christian literary

---

influence Western scholasticism—the Eucharist is first of all an assembly (σύναξις), a community, a network of relations..."*(Being as Communion. Studies in Personhood and the Church*, New York, SVS Press 1985, p.60). Cf. also his interesting remark: "the Fourth Gospel identifies eternal life, i.e. life without death, with truth and knowledge, (which) can be accomplished only if the individualization of nature becomes transformed into communion—that is if communion becomes identical with being. Truth, once again, must be communion if it is to be life" (p. 105).

[6] "The Understanding of Eucharist in St. John's Gospel," pp. 51f.

[7] An updated bibliography on Q—though covering only the scholarly research in North America, Great Britain and Germany—is found in the 1991 special issue of *Semeia* 55 (pp. 245-265), which under the title, *Early Christianity, Q and Jesus* , was devoted to the 1983-1989 work of the Q Seminar. A full and updated bibliography on Q is about to be published by the International Q Project.

[8] C. P. M. Jones (revised by C. J. A. Hickling), "The Eucharist: I. The New Testament," *The Study of Liturgy. Revised Edition,* SPCK London 1992, pp. 184-209.

[9] A. C. Couratin, "Liturgy," in *The Pelican Guide to Modern Theology*, vol. 2, *Historical Theology*, 1969, pp. 131-240.

activity and also contributed to a reassessment of the originating impulse(s) of the whole Christian movement."[10]

\*

In a series of articles during the last two decades[11] I have considered the Q-Hypothesis from the literary critical point of view, and have claimed that St. Matthew and St. Luke had used independently of each other another common source beside Mark. This source, which is referred to as *Q* or *Q-Source*, but which is better attested as *Q-Document*, was a *single written document*, consisting of about 200 verses which form a literary whole.

Apart from the historical value of this source, what is more important is its *theological characteristics*. Questions like "What was the document's theological character?" "Was it a document with any christological significance or was just aimed for purely catechetical purposes?" "Is there any relationship between Q and wisdom tradition?" "Is there any relationship between the Q-Document and the Gospel of Mark, our earliest written Gospel?", have puzzled N.T. scholars for more than two generations.[12] And if scholarly research on the various literary characteristics of the Q-Document went through different and sometimes contradictory stages to reach its almost final statement, the same procedure is inevitably to be expected with regard to the debate on its theological character and function. Clues for these are only provided internally. Two points are particularly important: on the one hand, the prevailing view that Q consists almost entirely of sayings material, and on the other, the complete absence of any material concerning the passion Kerygma and the *theologia crucis* in general.

With the relationship between the Q-Document and the Gospel of Mark, a problem that is relevant to our subject, since Mark is considered the best attestation of *theologia crucis,* we dealt in another article.[13] After examining the different solutions proposed in the past, namely (a) The Q-Document's dependence on Mark,[14] (b) Mark's dependence on the Q-

---

[10] H. W. Attridge, "Reflections on Research into Q," *Semeia* 55 (1991) 223-34, p.223.

[11] "Did Q Exist?" Ἐκκλησία καὶ Θεολογία 1 (1980) 287-327; "The Nature and Extent of the Q-Document," *NT* 20 (1978) 49-73. (The above articles are the English versions of my doctoral dissertation in modern Greek: Ἡ περὶ τῆς Πηγῆς τῶν Λογίων θεωρία, Athens 1977. Some paragraphs of what follows is an English version of ch. III of that dissertation); "The Original Order of Q. Some Residual Cases," J. Delobel (ed.), *Logia*, Leuven 1982, 379-387. Cf. chs 1, 2, and 3 in this volume.

[12] P. Vassiliadis, "Prolegomena to a Discussion on the Relationship Between Mark and the Q-Document", Δελτίον Βιβλικῶν Μελετῶν 3 (1975) 31-46. Cf. ch. 4 in this volume.

[13] Ibid.

[14] This view was put forward by J. Wellhausen and A. Jülicher (ibid., pp. 32-33).

Document,[15] (c) mutual independence of Mark and Q,[16] and (d) a compromise solution between b and c,[17] we came to the following conclusion: Despite the almost unanimously prevailed view in recent scholarship about the mutual independence of the two main sources of the synoptic tradition, the whole problem needs radical reconsideration. According to our view:

> "two points at least seem quite clear: Firstly the Q-Document cannot have depended on Mark; and secondly, the relationship between Mark and Q has to be determined on grounds other than literary. The whole problem, therefore, would seem to reduce itself to the following questions: (i) Did St. Mark have any *knowledge of Q-traditions*? (ii) If he did, is there any explicit evidence that he was *acquainted with the Q-Document* itself? (iii) If he was, did he *derive* any material therefrom? and finally (iv) If so, was his attitude to the Q-materials receptive or critical?"[18]

Only such a procedure can lead us to a critically acceptable solution of the Q-Marcan relationships.[19]

The survey of the Q-Marcan relations gives us a taste of the investigation of the more general question on the theology of Q. This question during the last two decades came vigorously to the foreground, with the American school, more precisely the Q Seminar of the Society of Biblical Literature, which under the strong leadership of influential scholars like J. M. Robinson and H. Koester attempted a stratigraphic analysis and redactional division of the various stages or clusters of the entire non Marcan *sayings material* loosely described as Q, most notably in the case of J. S. Kloppenborg.[20]

The history of investigation on the theology of Q is divided into four stages, the turning points of which were the monumental works of A.

---

[15] This was maintained on literary grounds by B. Weiss, A. Loisy, M. Goguel, W. Sanday, B. W. Bacon and F. C. Grant (ibid., pp. 33-36).

[16] This was first maintained by A. Harnack, J. Moffatt, B. H. Streeter and B. H. Throckmorton (ibid., pp. 36-39).

[17] A. Meyer, A. E. J. Rawlinson and T. E. F. Honey have maintained that Mark had used not the Q-Document itself but a source similar to it ($Q^R$, q etc.)

[18] P. Vassiliadis, "Prolegomena...," p. 45.

[19] Cf. also most recently B. L. Mack, "Q and the Gospel of Mark: Revisiting Christian Origins," *Semeia* 55 (1991), pp. 15-39; and J. Schüling, *Studien zum Verhältnis von Logienquelle und Markusevangelium*, Würzburg 1991.

[20] From an extensive list of his studies I put aside his major work *The Formation of Q: Trajectories in Ancient Wisdom Collections*, Philadelphia 1987, which was characterized by Robinson in the forward as the latest word on the Q scholarship; cf. also the special issue of *Semeia* 55 (1991), which under the title, *Early Christianity, Q and Jesus*, was devoted to the 1983-1989 work of the Q Seminar.

Harnack,[21] H. E. Tödt[22] and the joint volume by H. Koester and J. M. Robinson.[23]

The conclusions I reached in my doctoral thesis conducted almost twenty years ago under the supervision of Prof. S. Agouridis, are valid even today, being the consensus of the recent Q research. And they run as follows:[24]

**1.** One definite conclusion from the investigation into the Q-Document is that it can no longer be considered as a *Manual of Ethics*. Apart from the fact that it also includes some narratives, either in integral form (cf. Lk 10.16ff. par), or as framing discourse material Lk 7.19ff. par; Lk 11.14ff. par.), a sufficient number of verses (cf. Lk 10.21f. par, Lk 4.1–13 par, Lk 11.14ff. par, Lk 7.18–35 par, i.e. passages with clear traces of christological coloring) suggest that the interests of the collector/compiler of the Q-Document, as well as of the community that lies behind it, were not didactic or hortatory. In addition, the familiar scene of the inauguration-call of the Prophets seems to have a parallel in the Temptation (and probably Baptism) story (Lk 4.1ff. par.). The similarities, however, of the Q-Document with the O.T. prophetic books does not necessarily mean that Q faithfully follows their pattern[25].

The *eschatological* element, which was neglected by Harnack, but accepted by Manson and so vigorously emphasized by Tödt and W. D. Davies is clearly prominent in Q. This applies both in the wider existentialist sense,[26] i.e. the demand for a decision (cf. Davies' view)[27]. The strong expectation of the coming judgment in which Jesus will appear as Son of Man is to a considerable extent dominant in the Q-Document. Stanton's attack was successful only in diminishing the strength of the argument. The formal evidence of the "eschatological correlative" structure to which Edwards has drawn attention may be adduced as a further argument.

---

[21] *Sprüche und Reden Jesu: Die zweite Quelle des Matthäus und Lukas,* Leipzig, 1907, translated into English under the title *The Sayings of Jesus* , London, 1908.

[22] *Der Menschensohn in der synoptischen Überlieferung,* Gütersloh, 1959, translated into English under the title *The Son of Man in the Synoptic Tradition,* London, 1965. Tödt deals with Q in detail in pp. 232ff.

[23] *Trajectories Through Early Christianity,* Philadelphia, 1971, pp. 71-113

[24] What follows is an almost verbatim translation of the conclusions (pp. 143ff.) of ch. III of my 'Η περὶ τῆς Πηγῆς τῶν Λογίων θεωρία, where I reviewed the scholarship on the theological characteristics of Q up to that period.

[25] See also G. N. Stanton's remarks in his "On the Christology of Q," B. Lindars-S. Smalley (eds.), *Christ and Spirit in the N.T.: Studies in Honour of C. F. D. Moule,* Cambridge 1973, 27-42, p. 39.

[26] We are following here O. Cullmann's terminology *(Salvation in History,* ET, London 1967, pp. 78-79).

[27] According to S. Agouridis *(The Sermon on the Mount,* Athens 1975, in Greek) Jesus demands from his disciples "either all or nothing".

The most important result, however, of Q-research at the present stage is certainly the *christological* significance of the Q-Document. The community behind this document, if not the document itself, was concerned with the vital question "Who was Jesus?". But to detect the answer to this question with any precision is an extremely difficult task. As Stanton has pointed out, the Q-material is so varied that precludes a single solution. On the other hand all Q passages are available only in their Lucan or Matthaean edited form.

In these circumstances all that can be done is to spell out the most characteristic christological implications of Q. And in this respect the most prominent of all is undoubtedly the *Son-of-Man Christology*. As it is well known, from all three kinds of the Son-of-Man sayings of the Gospel tradition, namely those referring to his earthly activity, his future coming and his passion and resurrection, the last one which is so prominent to the Gospel of Mark (and consequently to all our present Synoptics) is entirely absent from Q. However, the problem of the relationship between the Son of Man acting on earth and the coming one has not yet been solved.[28] What we can, therefore, say with a fair amount of certainty is that Christology in Q was of a quite different kind from that of the mainstream primitive Orthodoxy.

To this very important characteristic of the Q-material one can also add the important notion of *Jesus' rejection* by his own people[29]. However, so far as the Q-Document is concerned, this rejection has nothing to do with Jesus' giving voluntarily "his soul as a ransom for many" (Mk 10.45 par.). It is something which can be better understood on the analogy of the O.T. prophets,[30] or even on the analogy of the ancient myth of the personified Wisdom. In Bultmann's words this myth runs as follows: "The pre-existent Wisdom, God's companion at creation, seeks a dwelling on earth among men; but she seeks it in vain; her preaching is rejected. She comes to her own, but her own do not receive her. She returns, therefore, to the

---

[28] Cf. R. H. Fuller, *The New Testament in Current Study*, London 1963, p. 91. Most recently J. M. Robinson ("The Son of Man in the Sayings Gospel Q," C. Elsas and others (eds.), *Tradition and Translation. Festschrift für C. Colpe zum 65. Geburstag,* Walter de Gruyter Berlin & New York 1994, pp. 315-335) has argued that "Q tended to indicate the initial stages of the christological development from a non-titular, non-apocalyptic idiom of a generic meaning, that by implication could have especially the speaker in mind, as used by Jesus" (p. 335).

[29] D. Lührmann, Die *Redaktion der Logienquelle,* Neukirchen 1969, expresses the same view by referring to the tension between Jesus and this generation (ἡ γενεά αὔτη pp. 24ff ).

[30] Cf. O. H. Steck, *Israel und das gewaltsame Geschick der Propheten,* Neukirchen 1967, esp. pp. 253ff.

heavenly world and dwells there in concealment."[31] Of course, the Q community did not fully develop a wisdom Christology, and in addition, the Sophia tradition is limited to only four or five passages (Lk 7.35 par; 10.21f. par; 11.49–51 par; 13.34f. par; and perhaps 11.31 par).[32] It is, however, to these passages, generally agreed to be of a wisdom influence, that the notion of Jesus' rejection is limited, too; and this can hardly be a coincidence. Nevertheless wisdom motifs, although indisputably present in Q, are not of primary significance.

Apart from these most important theological characteristics of the Q-Document, one should not forget that *missionary motifs* have also played a part at least in the collection of some Q materials. By putting the emphasis on the ecumenical character of the Christian message the Q-Document gave a strong impetus on missionary activities in the Early Church.[33] We cannot also ignore that, despite the non-catechetical character of the Q-Document, there is still much in it which presents Jesus as the teacher of the community, thus bringing in mind a parallel situation in the Qumran community. The Q community seems also to have been fully aware of the O.T. thought,[34] but the use of the LXX in Q is very limited.[35] In general, the Q-Document fits better in a Jewish-Syrian milieu, where, in addition, the prestige of John the Baptist was considerably high. We have elsewhere shown that the reference to the Baptist in Q covers about 1/10 of the whole document.[36] But "although John is presented in it as functioning in the context of Heilsgeschichte, he still remains outside the Christian Kerygma with a significance of his own."[37]

**2.** These are the most apparent indications of the theological characteristics of the Q-Document. However, to go any further and give a more accurate account of the theology of Q based solely on the extant readings of Matthew and Luke would be mere postulation. Since the Q sayings are now preserved only within their Matthaean and Lucan

---

[31] R. Bultmann, "Die religionsgeschichtliche Hintergrund des Prologs zum Johannesevagelium," *ΕΥΧΑΡΙΣΤΗΡΙΟΝ: Studien zur Religion und Literatur des Alten und Neuen Testaments. H. Gungel zum 60. Geburtstag II* (1923), pp. 10f.

[32] Cf. F. Christi, *Jesus Sophia: Die Sophia-Christologie bei den Synoptikern*, Zürich 1970, pp. 61f; cf. also Lk 9.58=Mt 8.20.

[33] S. Agouridis, *Introduction to the N.T.*, Athens 1971, p. 108 (in Greek).

[34] J. C. Hawkins, "Probabilities as to the so-called Double Tradition of St. Matthew and St. Luke," W. Sanday (ed.), *Oxford Studies on the Synoptic Problem*, 95-138, p. 128.

[35] The use of LXX apart from Lk 7,27 is limited only to the narrative of Temptation. S. E. Johnson ("The Biblical Quotations in Matthew," *HTR* 36 (1943), 135-53, esp. pp. 144f.) has argued that the Q-Document, before its use by the later Synoptists, had been influenced by LXX. Cf. also idem, "The LXX and the New Testament," *JBL* 56 (1937), 331-45.

[36] P. Vassiliadis, "The Function of John the Baptist in Q and Mark", *Θεολογία* 46 (1975), 405-413, esp. p. 406. Cf. also ch. 6 above.

[37] Ibid. pp. 412, 408.

contexts, it is extremely difficult to know with some degree of certainty whether or not the emphasis, which the author (or the community) of Q put on certain logia, has been accepted by the later Synoptists. N.T. criticism has reached the conclusion that at least in few cases (cf. e.g. Lk 11.49 par; Lk 7.35 par)[38] there are obvious indications of a later redaction by one of the later Synoptists. With that in mind one can also account for certain theological expressions in Q which both the later Synoptists, and independently of each other, modified in the same or different directions. The fact that Q did not serve purely didactic purposes but rather theological ones favors such a view.

One may question the current American trend to argue that the Q-Document should be read through Gnostic spectacles, and therefore be closely connected with later Gnosticism. That it belongs, however, to a tradition alien to what comes out of the Acts and Pauline evidence is a reasonably based hypothesis. Granted that the Q-Document did exist in a written form,[39] the lack of any reference to it in all early Christian literature supports the hypothesis. In addition, the insistence of the Gospel of Thomas, a non orthodox writing, that "ὅστις ἂν τὴν ἑρμηνείαν τῶν λόγων τούτων εὑρίσκῃ, θανάτῳ οὐ μὴ γεύσηται,"[40] as well as the sharp distinction made by Polycarp of Smyrna, an admitted leader of early orthodoxy, between the theology of the Cross and the logia tradition in favor of the former,[41] strongly supports the view that the Q-Document did not develop along the lines of Pauline, or even Jerusalem theology. It is more likely to have been the product of a Christian community which was outside the sphere of the direct influence of the Pauline and Jerusalem churches, i.e. of what has come to be called the Primitive Orthodoxy.

If, however, it is extremely difficult to go beyond the possible redaction made by both Matthew and Luke which could have perhaps enabled us to uncover the hidden theology of Q, there is another legitimate way forward: to consider the *final arrangement and grouping of the Q materials*. According to the procedural principles set up by us[42] and

---

[38] In the first instance St. Matthew has changed the more authentic "ἡ σοφία τοῦ Θεοῦ" (Lk 11.49a) with the word "ἐγώ" (Mt 18.34), thus identifying Jesus with the personified Wisdom. Similarly in the second case "τέκνων" (Lk 7.35) has been replaced by "ἔργων" in Mt 11.19.

[39] Chs. 2 and 3 above: "The Nature and Extent of the Q-Document"; and "The Original Order of Q".

[40] This is the introductory logion of the Gnostic Gospel of St. Thomas, also to be found in Greek in the 654th Oxyrhynchus papyrus; cf. J. A. Fitzmyer, "The Oxyrhynchus Logoi of Jesus and the Coptic Gospel according to Thomas," *TS* 20 (1959) 505-60.

[41] Cf. "ὃς ἂν μὴ ὁμολογῇ τὸ μαρτύριον τοῦ *σταυροῦ*....καὶ ὃς ἂν μεθοδεύῃ τὰ *λόγια* τοῦ Κυρίου" (*Phil* VIII,1; *italics* mine).

[42] "The Nature and Extent of the Q-Document," pp. 66ff.

accepted by J. S. Kloppenborg,[43] the Q-Document must have run as follows: It starts with a reference to the Baptist's appearance followed by a short account of his eschatological teaching, and a confession of Jesus' higher authority. This authority of Jesus is tested by a number of temptations which in fact bear witness to his origin (Son of God). After that confirmation, Jesus addresses the crowd with his authoritative teaching. The response of the people is immediate, ranging from some Gentiles to John's disciples and other individuals. Those who follow him and accept his teaching are involved in a mission to the world which also includes the healing of the sick. Jesus rejoices at the success of that mission. He thanks his Father, blesses his followers, and teaches them how to pray, ensuring at the same time God's response. On the other hand, those who reject him are confronted with him in a series of controversies which culminate with Jesus' denunciation of the scribes and Pharisees. This confrontation brings, in effect, crisis to Israel, the climax of which is to come at the End of the time, involving heavy persecutions for those who have followed him. Jesus exhorts them to stand firm and to confess fearlessly, and advises them not to care about earthly things; and of course, "to be ready, because the Son of Man will come at an hour, when (they) are not expecting him" (Lk 12.40=Mt 24.44). Jesus makes this clear in a series of parables and isolated sayings, at the end of which he weeps over Jerusalem because of the disobedience of her people. The entire document ends with an eschatological discourse which refers to the soon expected Day of the Son of Man.[44]

From the above reconstruction and classification of its material the Q-Document does not seem to reveal the historical interest our canonical four Gospels show. Its most important feature is the complete *lack of the passion narrative*. And not only that; it also *lacks all references to the passion*, either as direct predictions (Mk 8.31 par; 9.31 par; 10.33f par) or as indirect hints (Mk 10.38 par etc.). This is almost an evidence (though *ex silentio*) that the collector/compiler of the Q-Document had no interest on the historical basis of the Christian message which culminates according to almost all canonical evidence to Jesus' Cross and Resurrection. It is also quite characteristic that the essential term εὐαγγέλιον,[45] which in both the

---

[43] *The Formation of Q*, pp. 83ff.("sound and responsible criteria", p. 84; "application of the criteria suggested by Vassiliadis lead to the conclusion..", p. 88).

[44] The above construction of the document shows how indispensable the Q-Hypothesis is. For the order of the sections is quite intelligible; each section shows affinities with both the preceding and the following one. "Moreover, all sections end in the same formal way (namely with sayings which sum up the whole section) making the passing from one section to the other natural and smooth" ("The Nature and Extent of the Q-Document," pp. 72f. and n. 128; also above ch. 2).

[45] Cf. 1 Cor 15.1; Gal 1.11; 1 Thess 1.5 etc. Also the use of the terms "εὐαγγέλιον" (in Mark and Matthew) and "εὐαγγελίζεσθαι" (in Luke).

Pauline and the canonical Synoptic tradition is connected with the kerygma about Jesus' earthly life, his Cross and Resurrection, is nowhere to be found in Q. Similarly, the Q-Document never refers to "the twelve,"[46] either by name or as a term designating the historical dimension of the Christian message. In other words, *the center of gravity in Q's theology is the eschatological dimension of the Christian movement.*

\*

At the first glance we get the impression that there is no reference to the Eucharist in Q. But this can hardly be a strong argument against, since even the 4th Evangelist, who is rightly considered as the sacramental theologian *par excellence,*[47] omits e.g. the words of institution of the Eucharist.[48] After all, we have to remind ourselves that in the entire N.T. we have only a skeletal pre-history of the liturgical praxis of the primitive church, based on small pieces of evidence, to be pieced together "knowing that many of the bits are irretrievably lost."[49]

The issue at stake here is whether the understanding of what is viewed as the expression the church's identity as a koinonia of the eschata, i.e. the Eucharist, is at all related to the "sacramentalistic" views both of the ancient, contemporary to the early Church, Hellenistic Mystery Cults, and also of some later "Christian" practice. And with this in mind one should consider the place of Eucharist in Q on a different level. The reconstruction of the Q-Document, we attempted above, if it is viewed as a guiding principle for uncovering the theological characteristics of the community behind it, it can also provide some hints for what we broadly call Eucharist.

---

[46] Cf. A. Harnack, *The Sayings,* p. 153.

[47] Cf. O. Cullmann, *Les Sacraments dans l'Evangile Johannique* 1951, incorporated in his *Early Christian Worship,* 1953. The rediscovery of the sacramental characteristics in St. John's Gospel has in fact a long history in modern biblical scholarship; cf. C. T. Craig, "Sacramental Interest in the Fourth Gospel," *JBL* 58 (1939) 31-41; also J. M. Creed, "Sacraments in the Fourth Gospel," *The Modern Churchman* 16 (1926) 363-372. More on this in my "The Understanding of Eucharist in St. John's Gospel."

[48] One can only read carefully the reference to the new commandment of love (13:34-35), and will immediately recall the institution narrative, since the ἐντολή καινή (the new commandment) sounds very similar to the καινή διαθήκη (the new testament) of the synoptic tradition. Furthermore the symbolism of the vine and the branches in the "Farewell Discourse" (ch. 15), the washing of the disciples feet (ch. 13), which actually replaces the synoptic account of the so-called Institution of the Eucharist, the flow of blood and water from the pierced side of the crucified Jesus (19:34) and above all Chapter 6 with its "Eucharistic Discourse" (especially 6:51b-58); they all make the sacramental, or rather eucharistic, character of the Fourth Gospel more than inescapable. Not to mention, of course, the miraculous change of the water into wine at the Wedding in Cana (2:1-11) at the outset of Jesus' earthly ministry, as well as many other cases.

[49] Cf. A. C. Couratin, "Liturgy," pp. 154f.

Exegetes, as well as liturgists, are still puzzled[50] about what it appears as a seeming dissimilarity between the N.T. evidence and our earliest account in the post-apostolic period, with regard to the process of events in the celebration of the Eucharist: first the eucharistic meal and then an extended period of common prayer and praise and of teaching (Synoptic Last Supper accounts and Paul, at least in Corinth), or the other way around (Justin, and the Church's practice thereafter). Jones-Hickling have stated that "how and when this reversal took place we do not know; it turned out to be universal, and so it may have happened quite early, early enough to be reflected in Luke 24.25–35 and possibly in John 6, where extended teaching precedes the allusion to the Eucharist (if such it is) at vv. 51–58."[51]

The structure of the Q-Document exhibits a striking parallel with the church's "celebration" of the Eucharist, as first described by Justin Martyr in his *1st Apology* 65, where the celebration was preceded by biblical readings, sermon and intercession. If we take the entire section of Q on Jesus' Teaching together with the one on Response to Jesus' Teaching as the universal Christian liturgical rite which precedes the Eucharist proper, i.e. The Liturgy of the Word, then all one has to find is some connection of the following section (Jesus and his Disciples) with the Eucharistic Liturgy. It is indeed striking that Jesus' Thanksgiving *(eucharistia)* to the Father (Lk 10.21f. par) not only resembles to the liturgical *anaphora* of the later Christian Eucharistic rite, but it is also structured in regard to the *Lord's Prayer* in exactly the same way with the post-anaphora rites. Both in the Q-Document and in the Eucharistic Liturgy the Lord's Prayer follows the *Anaphora*.

The question which arises is whether the evidence allows the argument that the Q-Document is throughout structured according to the primitive church's eucharistic practice. The answer to that question should be definitely no; but if we take the Eucharist neither as a cult nor as a ritual, but as "the living expression of the ecclesiological identity of the early Christian community as the koinonia of the eschata,"[52] in other words as the vivid act of the community by which the faithful proleptically lived the coming Kingdom of God, then the answer could be: yes there some connection between the most eschatologically oriented document of the

---

[50] See C. P. M. Jones (revised by C. J. A. Hickling), "The Eucharist: I. The New Testament," p. 204.

[51] Ibid.

[52] P. Vassiliadis, "The Biblical Background of the Eucharistic Ecclesiology," *Lex Orandi. Studies of Liturgical Theology,* Thessaloniki EKO 9 1994, 29-53, p. 49 (in Greek). In this article, contrary to the wider held scholarly view, I have argued for the "holistic" or "eschatological" consecration of the Sacrament of the Eucharist, not for the "linear" one, which is based on the so-called "institutional sayings" of Jesus (p.50).

N.T. tradition (Q) and the most eschatological act of the Christian community (Eucharist).⁵³

---

⁵³ On the eschatological character of the Eucharist see J. Zizioulas, *Being as Communion;* and D. Passakos, *The Eucharist in the Pauline Mission. Sociological Approach,* Thessaloniki, 1995 [2nd edition *Eucharist and Mission. Sociological Presuppositions of the Pauline Theology,* Athens 1997].

# APPENDIX
## The Structure of Q
(with details of the "Eucharistic" Section)

I. Prologue ...

II. Jesus' Teaching ...              (
                                     )(=The Liturgy of the Word?)
III. Response to Jesus' Teaching...(
                                     .
                                     .

IV. Jesus and his Disciples ......    (=The Eucharistic Liturgy?)

a. *The mission charge*

ἔλεγεν δὲ πρὸς αὐτούς, Ὁ μὲν θερισμὸς πολύς, οἱ δὲ ἐργάται ὀλίγοι· δεήθητε οὖν τοῦ κυρίου τοῦ θερισμοῦ ὅπως ἐργάτας ἐκβάλῃ εἰς τὸν θερισμὸν αὐτοῦ. ὑπάγετε· ἰδοὺ ἀποστέλλω ὑμᾶς ὡς ἄρνας ἐν μέσῳ λύκων [γίνεσθε οὖν φρόνιμοι ὡς οἱ ὄφεις καὶ ἀκέραιοι ὡς αἱ περιστεραί] μὴ βαστάζετε βαλλάντιον, μὴ πήραν, μὴ ὑποδήματα, καὶ μηδένα κατὰ τὴν ὁδὸν ἀσπάσησθε. εἰς ἣν δ᾽ ἂν εἰσέλθητε οἰκίαν, πρῶτον λέγετε, Εἰρήνη τῷ οἴκῳ τούτῳ. καὶ ἐὰν ἐκεῖ ᾖ υἱὸς εἰρήνης, ἐπαναπαήσεται ἐπ᾽ αὐτὸν ἡ εἰρήνη ὑμῶν· εἰ δὲ μή γε, ἐφ᾽ ὑμᾶς ἀνακάμψει. ἐν αὐτῇ δὲ τῇ οἰκίᾳ μένετε, ἐσθίοντες καὶ πίνοντες τὰ παρ᾽ αὐτῶν, ἄξιος γὰρ ὁ ἐργάτης τοῦ μισθοῦ αὐτοῦ. μὴ μεταβαίνετε ἐξ οἰκίας εἰς οἰκίαν. [καὶ εἰς ἣν ἂν πόλιν εἰσέρχησθε καὶ δέχωνται ὑμᾶς, ἐσθίετε τὰ παρατιθέμενα ὑμῖν,] καὶ θεραπεύετε τοὺς ἐν αὐτῇ ἀσθενεῖς, καὶ λέγετε αὐτοῖς, Ἤγγικεν ἐφ᾽ ὑμᾶς ἡ βασιλεία τοῦ θεοῦ. εἰς ἣν δ᾽ ἂν πόλιν εἰσέλθητε καὶ μὴ δέχωνται ὑμᾶς, ἐξελθόντες εἰς τὰς πλατείας αὐτῆς εἴπατε, καὶ τὸν κονιορτὸν τὸν κολληθέντα ἡμῖν ἐκ τῆς πόλεως ὑμῶν εἰς τοὺς πόδας ἀπομασσόμεθα ὑμῖν· πλὴν τοῦτο γινώσκετε ὅτι ἤγγικεν ἡ βασιλεία τοῦ θεοῦ. λέγω ὑμῖν ὅτι Σοδόμοις ἐν τῇ ἡμέρᾳ ἐκείνῃ ἀνεκτότερον ἔσται ἢ τῇ πόλει ἐκείνῃ.

b. *Woes to the towns of Galilee*

Οὐαί σοι, Χοραζίν· οὐαί σοι, Βηθσαιδά· ὅτι εἰ ἐν Τύρῳ καὶ Σιδῶνι ἐγενήθησαν αἱ δυνάμεις αἱ γενόμεναι ἐν ὑμῖν, πάλαι ἂν ἐν σάκκῳ καὶ σποδῷ καθήμενοι μετενόησαν. πλὴν Τύρῳ καὶ Σιδῶνι ἀνεκτότερον ἔσται ἐν τῇ κρίσει ἢ ὑμῖν. καὶ σύ, Καφαρναούμ,
       μὴ ἕως οὐρανοῦ ὑψωθήσῃ;
          ἕως τοῦ ᾅδου καταβήσῃ.
Ὁ ἀκούων ὑμῶν ἐμοῦ ἀκούει, καὶ ὁ ἀθετῶν ὑμᾶς ἐμὲ ἀθετεῖ· ὁ δὲ ἐμὲ ἀθετῶν ἀθετεῖ τὸν ἀποστείλαντά με...

c. *Jesus' Thanksgiving to the Father* } (=The Anaphora?)

Ἐν αὐτῇ τῇ ὥρᾳ ἠγαλλιάσατο (ὁ Ἰησοῦς) ... καὶ εἶπεν,
Ἐξομολογοῦμαί σοι, πάτερ,
   κύριε τοῦ οὐρανοῦ καὶ τῆς γῆς,
     ὅτι ἀπέκρυψας ταῦτα ἀπὸ σοφῶν καὶ συνετῶν,
     καὶ ἀπεκάλυψας αὐτὰ νηπίοις·
ναί, ὁ πατήρ, ὅτι οὕτως εὐδοκία ἐγένετο ἔμπροσθέν σου.
Πάντα μοι παρεδόθη ὑπὸ τοῦ πατρός μου,
   καὶ οὐδεὶς γινώσκει τίς ἐστιν ὁ υἱὸς εἰ μὴ ὁ πατήρ,
   καὶ τίς ἐστιν ὁ πατὴρ εἰ μὴ ὁ υἱὸς
   καὶ ᾧ ἐὰν βούληται ὁ υἱὸς ἀποκαλύψαι.

d. *Jesus' Blessing of his Disciples*

Μακάριοι οἱ ὀφθαλμοὶ οἱ βλέποντες ἃ βλέπετε. λέγω γὰρ ὑμῖν ὅτι πολλοὶ προφῆται καὶ βασιλεῖς ἠθέλησαν ἰδεῖν ἃ ὑμεῖς βλέπετε καὶ οὐκ εἶδαν, καὶ ἀκοῦσαι ἃ ἀκούετε καὶ οὐκ ἤκουσαν.

e. *The Lord's Prayer*           (=The Post-anaphora Lord's Prayer?)

Πάτερ,
   ἁγιασθήτω τὸ ὄνομά σου·
     ἐλθέτω ἡ βασιλεία σου·
τὸν ἄρτον ἡμῶν τὸν ἐπιούσιον
   δίδου ἡμῖν τὸ καθ' ἡμέραν·
καὶ ἄφες ἡμῖν τὰς ἁμαρτίας ἡμῶν,
   καὶ γὰρ αὐτοὶ ἀφίομεν παντὶ ὀφείλοντι ἡμῖν·
   καὶ μὴ εἰσενέγκῃς ἡμᾶς εἰς πειρασμόν.

f. *God's answering of Prayer*

[κἀγὼ ὑμῖν λέγω,] αἰτεῖτε, καὶ δοθήσεται ὑμῖν· ζητεῖτε, καὶ εὑρήσετε· κρούετε, καὶ ἀνοιγήσεται ὑμῖν. πᾶς γὰρ ὁ αἰτῶν λαμβάνει, καὶ ὁ ζητῶν εὑρίσκει, καὶ τῷ κρούοντι ἀνοιγήσεται. τίνα δὲ ἐξ ὑμῶν τὸν πατέρα αἰτήσει ὁ υἱὸς ἰχθύν, καὶ ἀντὶ ἰχθύος ὄφιν αὐτῷ ἐπιδώσει; ἢ καὶ αἰτήσει ᾠόν, ἐπιδώσει αὐτῷ σκορπίον; εἰ οὖν ὑμεῖς πονηροὶ ὑπάρχοντες οἴδατε δόματα ἀγαθὰ διδόναι τοῖς τέκνοις ὑμῶν, πόσῳ μᾶλλον ὁ πατὴρ ὁ ἐξ οὐρανοῦ δώσει ἀγαθὰ τοῖς αἰτοῦσιν αὐτόν.

         ·
         ·
         ·

V. Jesus and his Opponents ....

VI. The Time of Crisis and Preparation for it....

VII. Epilogue. The Eschatological Discourse (The Coming of the Son of Man).

# 7
# THE FUNCTION OF JOHN THE BAPTIST IN Q AND MARK

*1. Introduction*

In his detailed treatment of the figure of John the Baptist from a redaction-critical point of view, W. Wink,[1] starting from the important role of John the Baptist in the Gospel tradition, came to the conclusion that "the church stood at the center of John's movement from the very beginning and became its one truly great survivor and heir."[2] Although this conclusion might not be completely justified, it directs attention to the relations between John and the Christian movement at a very early stage. Wink[3] went on to show—and this in my view is more convincing—how the Christian conception about John—without any sign of antagonism between the Church and John's sect being prominent in the four Gospels and Acts[4]—went through a process of development. This development is traced from the image of "Elijah-incognito" in Mark to that of Jesus' ally against the hostile front of Judaism in Matthew, to the traditional figure of the forerunner in the panoramic conception of Heilsgeschichte in Luke, to reach in the Fourth Gospel its climax with a complete christianization of John.[5] Wink's study, however, did not include any thorough examination and comparison of the figure of John in Mark and Q, and it is with this that we shall be concerned here, starting with Q.

---

[1] *John the Baptist in the Gospel Tradition,* Cambridge 1968. Wink's study was based on previous suggestions mainly by M. Dibelius, *Die urchristliche Überlieferung von Johannes dem Täufer,* Göttingen 1911; W. Marxsen, *Mark the Evangelist,* ET, New York 1969; C. H. Kraeling, *John the Baptist,* USA 1951; W. Trilling, "Die Täufertradition bei Matthäus," *BZ* 3 (1959), pp. 271-89; E. Käsemann, "The Disciples of John the Baptist in Ephesus," in *Essays on New Testament Themes,* ET, London 1964, pp. 36-48; Other major contributions on the Baptist studies are the monographs: M. Goguel, *Au seuil l' évangile Jean Baptist,* Payot 1928; E. Lohmeyer, *Das Urchristentum. I Buch: Johannes der Täufer,* Göttingen 1932; C. H. H. Scobie, *John the Baptist,* London 1964. For further bibliography see these books. See also G. S. Gratseas, *John the Baptist according to the Sources,* Athens 1968 (in Greek).

[2] *Op. cit.,* p. 110.

[3] Ibid., pp. 110-11.

[4] Wink insists on the "fundamental error of regarding the two groups (Church and Baptist's sect) as separate and alien! (ibid.).

[5] In fact the process of the incorporation of John into the christian theology of history had already started in Matthew (ibid., p. 40).

## 2. John the Baptist in the Q-Document

Accounts of John's ministry and his relationship with Jesus in Q are to be found in Lk 3.7–9,16–18=Mt 3.7–12, and in Lk 7.18–35=Mt 11.2–11,16–19. There is also a reference to John in Lk 11.1 where one of Jesus' disciples asked him to teach them how to pray, «καθὼς καὶ Ἰωάννης ἐδίδαξεν τοὺς μαθητὰς αὐτοῦ»; this, in my view, is not likely to have been taken by St. Luke from Q; it has been supplied rather by St. Luke himself.[6] This material, amounting to no less than 20 verses in a document consisting of about 200 verses, (i.e. one tenth of the entire document), indicates that John and his relation to Jesus played some part in the thought of the community reflected in Q.[7] This becomes more evident if we take seriously into account the location in Q of Lk 7.18–35 par., the main body of Q's references to John. For if we are right in classifying this passage along with Lk 7.2ff. par. and Lk. 9.57ff par. under the heading, "Response to Jesus' Teaching,"[8] then a very revealing situation emerges with regard to the relations between the Q community and John's disciples. And this situation can be described neither as favorable to nor as hostile to John's disciples, but rather as one of mutual understanding.

To seek for various strata in Q is as legitimate as in the Gospels, and in any of their sources.[9] If we compare the children-in-the-market parable (which concludes with the sophia-logion), with the preceding verses, the existence of various strata may be discerned in this very group of sayings (Lk 7.10–35 par.). In Lk 7.31–35 par. both John and Jesus are wisdom's envoys and they are both referred to, or at least they were referred to at an early stage, as equals.[10] This becomes more evident if we read «Ἰησοῦς» instead of «υἱὸς τοῦ ἀνθρώπου» in 7.34 par[11]. The collector/compiler of the Q-Document has given the parable a christological significance by ascribing to Jesus the august title "son of man".[12] In Lk 7. 18–30, on the

---

[6] *Op. cit.*, p.18, n.1. Wink speaks of Q "not so much as a 'redaction' but as a collection, a miscellany of logia without sufficiently clear or extensive editorial data (in most cases)".

[7] Cf. B. H. Streeter, *The Four Gospels*, London 1924, p. 292.

[8] Cf. F. C. Grant, *The Gospels*, London 1957), pp. 59f. The other suggestion by T. W. Manson, *The Sayings of Jesus*, London 1949, pp. 39-71, adopted also by M. J. Suggs, *Wisdom, Christology, and Law in Matthew's Gospel*, Massachusetts 1970, p. 38, that the material up to Lk 7.35 should be classified under the head "Jesus and John the Baptist, " though it does not affect our argument (it rather strengthens it), nevertheless it poses a lot of difficulties when we consider the classification of Q as a whole.

[9] Despite his hesitation as to the type of the Q-Document (cf. n. 6 above) Wink himself accepts different strata in some cases *(op. cit.,* pp. 13ff)*.

[10] Cf. M.J. Suggs, *op. cit.*, pp. 33ff.

[11] Ibid., p. 44.

[12] We can go even further: v 34 can be taken not as an integral part of the parable, as J. Jeremias takes it, but as a secondary interpretation already taken up in Q (cf. M. J. Suggs, *op. cit.*, p. 34).

other hand, Jesus is identified with the Messiah (vv. 22f)[13] by means of Is. 61.1f.[14] whereas John is given the characterization of a prophet or "more than a prophet" (v 26);[15] in other words he is the forerunner (ἄγγελος)[16] of the Messiah, being thus subordinate to Jesus (cf. also v 28b). Even so, he is still the "greatest born of women'"(v 28a).

But even in Lk 7.28=Mt 11.11 itself it is possible to discern two different strata of tradition: a pro-Baptist logion (v 28a) and a Christian commentary on it (v 28b).[17]

The other unit concerning John in the earlier part of the Q-Document, i.e. the continuous verses Lk 3.7–9, 16–18=Mt 3.7–12, shows affinities with both strata. On the one hand, John appears as an eschatological figure[18] with a significance of his own proclaiming the divine judgment to come, and warning people "to flee from the wrath to come" for "the ax is already laid to the root of the trees". On the other hand, it accords with Lk 7.24–28 par. in that he proclaims the coming of the "mightier one," though the two figures referred to in Lk 7.22 par. and Lk 3.6–18 par. can hardly be equated. In Lk 3.16–18 the "mightier one," who "will baptize with the (Holy) Spirit and with fire,"[19] could easily be identified with a Son-of-Man-

---

[13] Although both St. Luke and St. Matthew understood this saying as an enumeration of miracles performed by Jesus (cf. τὰ ἔργα τοῦ Χριστοῦ Ἰησοῦ in Mt 11.2 and the entire verse in Lk 7.21), in Q the original saying was understood as an eschatological cry of joy for the dawn of the time of salvation, as in Is. 61.1f. Lk 7.22f=Mt 11.5f is indeed a free combination of Is. 35.5 ff and 29.18f. with Is. 61.1f., and if we contrast, as J. Jeremias, *New Testament Theology*, Vol. I, ET. London 1971, p. 104, the Tannaitic list in Ned. 64b Bar "Four are compared with a dead man: the lame, the blind, the leper, and the childless," the analogy becomes more evident. Now, if we read this situation through another O.T. saying also from Isaiah (52.7), we can say with some hesitation that Jesus was understood in Q as the Messiah.

[14] G. N. Stanton, "On the Christology of Q," in *Christ and the Spirit in the New Testament* (Festschrift to C. F. D. Moule, ed. by B. Lindars and S. S. Smalley Cambridge, 1974), pp. 27-42, maintains that Is. 61.1f has influenced deeply the Q-material.

[15] It is quite clear that in Q John is designated προφήτης in the sense of a forerunner of the Messiah (for a detailed investigation of the title "prohpet" see O. Cullmann, *The Christology of the N.T.*, ET. London 1959, pp. 13-50, where also bibliography). Nevertheless it is possible that the collector/ compiler has used sayings in which John appeared as a Prophet in the sense of the forerunner of God himself (cf. n. 18 below).

[16] Both in Mal 3.1 and in Ex 22.23 ἄγγελος corresponds to "angel, " but in Q it clearly indicates the "forerunner".

[17] W. Wink, *op. cit.*, pp. 23f. and bibliography there. I find this explanation better than that proposed by O. Cullmann, "ὁ ὀπίσω μου ἐρχόμενος," in *The Early Church*, ET, London 1956, pp.175-182, esp. p. 180, which takes the μικρότερος to refer to Jesus (as a disciple of John): "He who is least (i.e. Jesus as a disciple of John) is greater than he (i.e. John) in the kingdom of God."

[18] Lk 3.7-9 par. is very close to the characterization of John as the forerunner of God himself, and it is not unlikely to have originally had that sense.

[19] It is not unlikely that in the pre-Q original form the saying (Lk. 3.17 par) lacked the reference to the Holy Spirit, but there is no question of its being present in the Q form [However, in a later short study of mine ("'Ερμηνευτικὴ προσέγγιση στὸ Λουκ 3.16. Ἡ

type of figure whose function is always placed somewhere in the future; but the Messiah implied by Lk 7.22f par. is definitely a present reality.

Further examination of Lk 3. 7–9,16–18=Mt 3.7–12[20] makes possible again a further distinction of two strata as in Lk 7.28=Mt 11.11: an earlier one derived perhaps from a Baptist source (Lk 3.7–9=Mt 3.7–10), and a later Christian addition (Lk 3.16–18=Mt 3.11–12).

In any case, whatever the meaning of the separate small units may have originally been, the function of John at the last stage of the tradition, as this was conceived by the collector/compiler of the Q-Document, is quite clear: *he was the forerunner of the Messiah; and yet he was still an autonomous figure with a significance of his own.*

## 3. John the Baptist in the Gospel of Mark

In Mark references to John and his relationship with Jesus are to be found at the beginning of his Gospel, 1.1–11, 14; in 6.14–29; and in 9.9–13; some scattered mention being found also in 2.18; 8.28; and 11.30ff. Verses 2.18 and 11.30ff—about the fasting of John, and the derivation of John's baptism respectively—both belong to pre-Marcan sources and they have been preserved unchanged, at least in so far as the Baptist himself is concerned.[21]

The key, and indeed the only one, for recovering the Marcan understanding of John the Baptist is 9.9–13. Wink has rightly pointed out its importance;[22] Even though his interpretation of the crucial verse 9.12 is doubtful,[23] his main point that in Mark John was identified with Elijah is fully justified.[24] St. Mark, however, has taken a further step; he has given

---

ἁγιοπνευματικὴ διάστασῃ τοῦ χριστιανισμοῦ" =Hermeneutical Approach to Lk 3:16. The Pneumatological Dimension of Christianity, Γρηγόριος ὁ Παλαμᾶς 68 1985, pp. 61ff in Greek) I have argued that the original saying of John the Baptist had only «πνεῦμα» in an eschatological and not pneumatological meaning, predicting Jesus' final judgment].

[20] That all these verses stem form Q forming a unity is unquestionable.

[21] It is striking, however, that both these references belong to the same sort of material (conflict-stories) alleged to have originally formed a single collection; cf. M. Albertz, *Die Synoptischen Streitgespräche*, Berlin 1921, pp. 5-36; but see also W. L. Knox, *The Sources of the Synoptic Gospels. I* Oxford 1953, pp. 8ff.

[22] W. Marxsen, *op. cit.,* pp. 30-53 has paid no attention to the significance of Mk 9.31-33, limiting his investigation only to the opening verses of Mark.

[23] Wink has taken the Son of Man in 9.12 to refer to Elijah (=John), following a suggestion by C. C. Richardson : "Elijah does come first to restore all things; and how is it written of that son of man (Elijah), that he should suffer many things..." *(op. cit.,* p. 14, n.). However, this interpretation poses a lot of difficulties; mainly because, in my view, the word πολλά reflects clearly the first prediction in 8.31. Cf. also H. E. Tödt, *The Son of Man in the Synoptic Tradition*, ET. London 1965, pp. 169,196.

[24] This is made clear by the omission in Luke both of Mk 9.9-13 and 6.17-29. This deliberate act by Luke is also found in John in explicit form (v.1.21). Matthew, on the other hand, has retained the analogy.

the title the suffering-motif[25] so prominent in his theology. It was for this reason that he placed the "bazaar rumor"[26]-story about John's death at this point in his Gospel.[27] If now 9.11–13, namely the idea of a *suffering- Elijah*[28] who "will restore all things", is the starting point for the part John the Baptist plays in Mark, it becomes quite clear why the ministry of Jesus has been prefaced with a brief reference to the ministry of John which ends with his being handed over shortly before the start of Jesus' ministry, and why the two ministries have been so sharply divided chronologically in v.14.[29]

We have seen that John's function was perceived by Q as that of the forerunner of the Messiah. The wilderness motif,[30] the quotation from Mal 3.1,[31] and the logion about the coming of the mightier one,[32] as well as the tension in the relations between John and Jesus prominent in every reference to John, all belonged to Q. St. Mark maintained all these, but he took on his part a further step: he identified the ἄγγελος of Malachi (v. 3.1) with Elijah, probably by the use also of Malachi (v. 4.5f), and this could be explained as a revision by St. Mark of the Q picture in the light of his own understanding of John as Elijah, to be found in 9.11–13.[33]

W. Marxsen[34] has stated that "there is no reason for departing from the conclusion of K. L. Schmidt,[35] who regards the introduction (to Mark's

---

[25] There does not seem to be a non-Christian tradition, at least known to us, which speaks of the suffering of Elijah; moreover it is completely alien to the Jewish Elijah-belief (cf. W. Wink, *op. cit.*, p.14).

[26] In A. E. J. Rawlinson's term *(The Gospel according to St. Mark,* London 1947[7], p. 82).

[27] Cf. the analogy between Elijah as the victim of Ahab and Jezebel (I Kg 16.29 ff) and John as the victim of Herod and Herodias (Mk 6.17-29). This is a further indication that John was thought of by St. Mark as Elijah.

[28] In fact the idea of rejection of John *is* found in Q (cf. Lk 7.33=Mt 11.18), but this is to be understood against a wisdom background, and has nothing to do with the more advanced suffering theology of Mark.

[29] Marxsen has shown throughout his study on John the Baptist *(op. cit.,* pp. 30 ff.) how the evangelist uses statements which in themselves were chronological and topological for theological purposes.

[30] Cf. Lk 7.24=Mt 11.7.

[31] Cf. Lk 7.27=Mt 11.10.

[32] Cf. Lk 3.16-18=Mt 3.11-12.

[33] It is generally held that Mark and Q were mutually independent of each other, and that the detection of the Marcan theology from the way the author of the second Gospel used and revised the Q-Document is an unsafe criterion (cf. R. H. Stein, "The Proper Methodology for Ascertaining a Marcan Redaction History," *NT* 13 (1971), pp. 181-198, esp. p.189, n.2 ). This view, however, has to be reconsidered to a considerable extent (see my "Prolegomena to a Discussion on the Relationship between Mark and the Q-Document," *ΔBM* 3 (1975), pp. 31-46). Without suggesting a literary dependence of Mark on Q, we must allow at least some acquaintance by St. Mark of the traditions current in the community that lies behind Q.

[34] *Op. cit.,* p. 32.

[35] *Der Rahmen der Geschichte Jesu,* Berlin, 1919, pp. 18-19.

Gospel) as the evangelist's own composition." I accept this view, at least in its general outline; it is more suggestive and plausible than E. Lohmeyer's assumption that Mark is reproducing a traditional unit.[36] Marxsen has also suggested that Mark was composed backward.[37] However true this may be for the entire Gospel, it does not apply to the opening verses.[38] Mk 1.1–11 can be better explained as an expansion by St. Mark of earlier views, evidenced in Q, about the Baptist and his relationship with Jesus, by means of the identification of John and Elijah. The genesis in detail of the Marcan introduction may be rebuilt as follows.[39]

Verse **2** can be accounted for by Q (Mt 10.11=Lk 7.27).[40] The same is true for verses **7–8** preserved in Mark without the crucial word πυρί and the following "fan"-verse (cf. Lk 3.16–18=Mt 3.11–12).[41] In v. **6** details about John's dressing are deliberately introduced in order to equate John with Elijah according to 2 Kg 1.8 and Zech 13. 4;[42] his diet is also given to accord with the notion of the wilderness, also to be accounted for by Q (Lk 7. 24=Mt 11.7). Verse **3**, the O.T. quotation from Is. 40.3, is a further example of St. Mark's supplying scriptural evidence of John's role in accordance with the wilderness motif.[43] Verse **4**, a brief report of John's function (βαπτίζων ἐν τῇ ἐρήμῳ), and his proclamation (κηρύσσων) of a "baptism of repentance for the remission of sins," and verse **5**, the description of the mass response by the people (πᾶσα, πάντες), are information given by St. Mark, so that the John-Elijah analogy can be further illuminated.[44] The remaining verses **9–11** describe Jesus' Baptism.

---

[36] *Das Evangelium des Markus,* Göttingen 1937, pp. 10ff.

[37] In Marxsen's view it is the resurrection that gives meaning to the passion which in turn makes meaningful the healings, exorcisms and parables; in the same way it is the ministry that has given birth to the introduction *(op. cit.,* p. 32).

[38] According to Marxsen, *(op. cit.,* pp. 32f.) vv. 1.9-11 point back to vv. 1.4-8, and so on. Wink also is in disagreement with Marxsen's thesis in some cases *(op. cit.,* p. 4).

[39] B. W. Bacon, "The Prologue of Mark,"*JBL* 26 (1908), pp. 84-106, had earlier suggested that the opening verses of Mark seem to be echoing or abridging Q.

[40] A. E. J. Rawlinson, *(op. cit.,* p. 6) ; V. Taylor, *The Gospel according to St. Mark,* London 1952, p. 153 (there also a list of other supporters before 1952); and J.A.T. Robinson, "Elijah, John and Jesus," *NTS* 4 (1957-58) pp. 263-81, esp. p. 268, have all considered it a later interpolation (in Robinson's view under the influence of Lk 7.27=Mt 11.10). However, since there is no textual evidence this explanation should be excluded.

[41] C. K. Barrett, *The Gospel according to St. John,* London 1960, p. 144, wrongly prefers the D reading which omits the phrase "and had a leather girdle around his waist," having in mind that the identification of John and Elijah is secondary.

[42] In any case, it is unanimously agreed that the Q-version is prior to the Marcan one. If, however, the latter is to be taken as redaction, it becomes clear how St. Mark tried to weaken the emphasis on the future activity of Jesus and lay more emphasis on the past.

[43] We are not concerned here with the question of the existence of such testimonies (i. e. vv. 2 and 3) prior to Mark but only with their use by St. Mark.

[44] In Judaism this restoration came to be conceived of as a mass repentance. "If 'all' have now repented at the word of John, is he not Elijah who is to come?" (Wink, *op. cit.,* p. 3, where there is further bibliography).

We are not concerned here with a detailed discussion of its origin and christological meaning; what concerns us only is the relationship between Jesus and John, and to that purpose this passage is exceedingly important. In Q the entire passage, Lk 7.18–35=Mt 11.2–19, leaves the reader still puzzled as to the degree of superiority between the two figures. St. Mark in a very carefully structured passage in 1.9ff[45] has settled the problem: John has been given a comparatively high function; he was Jesus' baptizer and yet Jesus remained totally autonomous and independent of John.[46] What happened at the baptism cannot be described as due to a relation between John and Jesus, but as an interrelation between the Father and the Son, John's participation being limited to the minimum.

If, however, all the passages concerning John, can be thus accounted for, is it possible to account for the omissions, too? For St. Mark appears to have had other information available to him (cf. 2.18; 11.32), but he has not made use of them possibly because they were not related sufficiently to the idea of fulfillment;[47] since his conception is built upon 9.11, John concerns him in what *he is*, not in what *he says or does*.[48]

## 4. Conclusions

To sum up: The Q-Document, in so far as the figure of John and his relationship with Jesus are concerned, already discloses signs of a theological development, but although John is presented in it as functioning in the context of *Heilsgeschichte* he still remains outside the Christian *kerygma* with a significance of his own. *It was St. Mark who took the step to incorporate John in the kerygma by identifying him with Elijah and depriving him of any significance of his own.*

In this he was followed by all his successors. His further step, however, of introducing the concept of the suffering Elijah[49] was not reproduced by all the evangelists in the same way.[50]

---

[45] It is very important that it was Jesus who took the initiative and responsibility for his baptism. He "went" (ἦλθεν), he "was baptized" (ἐβαπτίσθη), he "saw" (εἶδεν) what took place, and finally he was addressed *privately:* "σὺ εἶ ὁ υἱός μου...". In that very important detail Mark was not followed by the other Synoptics; perhaps because the problem of the relations of John with Jesus had already been settled by then.

[46] It is not a coincidence that «ὑπὸ Ἰωάννου» has been put at the end of the whole sentence.

[47] J. M. Robinson, *The Problem of History in Mark*, London, 1957, p. 25.

[48] Wink, *op. cit.,* p. 4.

[49] Paul, on the other hand, is even more radical. From the data we attain from the authentic epistles of St. Paul (I take Acts 13.24f; 19.3f as due to St. Luke's hand), he appears to keep the Baptist outside the *kerygma* which he confines solely to Jesus' death and resurrection. Thus, Mark seems to be standing in the mean position between Q and Paul, in so far as the function of John the Baptist is concerned.

[50] Wink also speaks of a "Elijanic secret" (Elijah incognito,) but this is not very clear in the text (ibid., pp. 16-7).

# 8
# THE CHALLENGE OF Q.
# THE CYNIC HYPOTHESIS

## I

There is no doubt that Christian theology is heavily indebted to Pauline theology. What is, however, of even more significance is that any serious attempt to reconstruct the origins of Christianity depends to a considerable extent on the information and data which we gain from his authentic so-called great (or proto-Pauline) epistles, the earliest extant written documents of Christianity. St. John Chrysostom, the well-known Antiochean exegete and perhaps one of the greatest theologians of the Church of all time, acknowledges St. Paul the apostle as the most accurate and authentic interpreter of the Historical Jesus.

This picture has been actually reinforced with slight variations in our recent critical era. It is an almost assured result of modern criticism that our Gospel accounts—at least the Synoptic ones and more precisely that of St. Mark—form the basis for the quest of the life and teaching of the Historical Jesus. Some isolated sayings, of course, from the Sayings Source (Q) of the synoptic tradition entered into the scene, but they were always considered within the Marcan framework, which as a matter of fact depends on the theological understanding of the Christ event by that great apostle, more precisely on his dynamic interpretation of Jesus' death on the cross.

The undisputed historical fact of Jesus' death, coupled with his eschatological teaching, have undoubtedly played an important part in shaping the fundamental basics of the faith of the early Christian community, which were expanded with secondary contemporary (greco-roman, hellenistic, oriental etc.) elements to form what can be very loosely called "Christ cult".

However, this picture which dominated biblical scholarship for almost a century has started to be challenged by the most recent results of N.T. scholarship, the focal point being the unexpected great progress that has taken place in the field of the Q research. Modern biblical theology more and more turned its attention to Q, and the understanding of Christian and/or Church origins has been undoubtedly determined by the scientific data of the second source of the Synoptic tradition, now lost, which seems to expound a radically different theological stance from the mainstream kerygmatic expression of the early Church.[1]

In fact, the challenge of Q to the conventional picture of Christian origins, and by extension also to the quest of the Historical Jesus and the predominance of the Pauline interpretation of the Christ event, is more far-reaching than the making of a little room for yet "another gospel," another early Christian community. If Q is taken seriously into account the entire landscape of early Christianity with all that it entails may need to be radically revised, at least thoroughly reconsidered. Before I come to this point, however, allow me first to review the entire issue of the Q-Hypothesis, as I journeyed it during the last two decades.

## II

Early in the '70s I set up in a scholarly journey into the mysteries of synoptic scholarship with a hidden intention to disprove the Q-Hypothesis in its widely held form.[2] After almost five years of research, during which I considered the Q-Hypothesis from all literary critical angles, I was won to that hypothesis and became a fervent supporter of it. In my dissertation[3] I aligned to the view—now accepted by the almost all serious biblical scholars, at least by many more than in the '70s—that St. Matthew and St. Luke had used independently of each other another common source beside Mark. Reviewing the state of scholarly discussion up to that moment I come to the conclusion that this source "did not develop along the lines of Pauline, or even Jerusalem theology." It is more likely to have been the product of a Christian community which was outside the sphere of the direct influence of the Pauline and Jerusalem churches, i.e. of what has come to be called the Primitive Orthodoxy."[4] My own suggestion, on the basis of the final arrangement and grouping of Q at its final stage, was "that the center of gravity in Q's theology is the eschatological dimension of the Christian movement."[5]

The most serious result of the Q research since the time I finished my thesis is the affirmation that, if we accept the existence of a Q-Document to explain away the literary, historical, and theological problems of the synoptic tradition, it is not only legitimate but also imperative to study it

---

[1] H. W. Attridge has rightly stated that recent research on Q "has revealed the complexity of early Christian literary activity and also contributed to a reassessment of the originating impulse(s) of the whole Christian movement " ("Reflections on Research into Q," *Semeia* 55 (1991) 223-34, p.223).

[2] Cf. my first scholarly contribution "Behind Mark: Towards a Written Source," *NTS* 20 (1974), pp. 52-60.

[3] *The Q-Document Hypothesis. A Critical Examination of Today's Literary and Theological Problems Concerning the Q-Document*, Athens 1977 (in Greek).

[4] Ibid., pp. 121ff.

[5] Ibid., p. 149.

*in its own merit.* Let alone that the Q tradition—better than any other existing tradition of the early Christian literature—fills the gap of the most lively and normative period between the life and teaching of the Historical Jesus and the emergence of our narrative gospels (and to some extent also the rest of the N.T. literature), which later gave the Church, but also modern scholarship, the official and standard account of Christian origins. The Q-Document is a well organized unit with an integral theological outlook, which can eventually offer a more plausible explanation of the twilight period of the emergence of Christianity and its advance to conquer the Greco-roman world. The picture it gives is complete enough to reconstruct the history of the early Church to the extent no other document from the earliest times has done, at least to this moment.

In my view, this present development in biblical scholarship at the end of this century, with the enormous consequence for Christian origins (as well as the quest for the Historical Jesus) it entails, can only be compared with the great and far-reaching shift in paradigm caused by such scholars as J. Weiss[6] and A. Schweitzer[7] around the turn of the 20th century. They were both instrumental in redirecting attention from a Jesus of Nazareth as a teacher of humane ethic to a Jesus as an apocalyptic prophet, a radical visionary of the cataclysmic end of the world. At the other end on the liberal side A. Harnack ironically tried to use Q for his counter attack in 1907 in his *Sprüche und Reden Jesu.* Weiss and Schweitzer's suggestion to the scholarly world has prevailed throughout the century and was further substantiated on both literary-historical and theological grounds by prominent, though diverse, scholars such as R. Bultmann[8] and C. H. Dodd,[9] both of whom assumed that Jesus' message was essentially apocalyptic.[10] One can also easily recall E. Käsemann's widely discussed conclusion that "the apocalyptic is the matrix of all Christian theology."[11]

---

[6] *Die Predigt Jesu vom Reiche Gottes* (ET. *Jesus' Proclamation of the Kingdom of God,* Philadelphia 1971), the first (1892) edition of which contained only 67 pages.

[7] *Vom Reimarus zu Wrede* (ET. with the brilliant title *The Quest of the Historical Jesus)* 1906.

[8] Cf. his consideration of christian origins in his classical works: (a) *Die Geschichte der synoptischen Tradition,* Göttingen 1921 from a historical critical point of view, and (b) *Jesus,* Berlin 1926 from a theological perspective, where he gave a privileged place to apocalyptic sayings and explained most of the wisdom material as later Church additions.

[9] Cf. his *The Parables of the Kingdom,* London 1935¹, 1961².

[10] Cf. also the classical and balanced work of N. Perrin, *Rediscovering the Teaching of Jesus,* London 1967, which summarizes the mainstream scholarly research on the issue just before the reopening of the Q question.

[11] E. Käsemann, "Die Anfänge christlicher Theologie," *ZTK* 57 (1960) 162-85; and "Zur Thema der christlichen Apokalyptik," *ZTK* 58 (1962) 257-84; both translated into English under the title "The Beginnings of Christian Theology," and "On the Subject of Primitive Christian Apocalyptic," *New Testament Questions of Today,* London 1969, pp. 82- 107 and 108-137 respectively.

What, however, puzzled the N.T. scholars ever since the consolidation of this scholarly view, was the existence among the so-called "authentic"— or rather undisputed—dominical logia of both *apocalyptic* announcements and *wisdom* sayings. In fact, in all reconstructions of the teaching of Jesus—based both on Q but also on the rest of the synoptic tradition—a quite substantial number of the sayings can better be classed as *wisdom* than *apocalyptic*. The obvious question is how an apocalyptic hero announcing the end of the present world can offer at the same time instruction for living in it. The famous "interim Ethik" of A. Schweitzer is well known as the first, though unsuccessful, attempt to offer a solution to the problem.[12]

However, the languages of *wisdom* and *apocalyptic* assume different views of the world, the literary genre of sophiology is on its basics different from that of the apocalyptic literature, and the apocalyptic prophets as a class are very often distinguished from the sages, the former being better known for their predictions of judgment while the latter normally offer individual instructions and propose ways of social health and healing. Raymond Brown underlined their difference by pointing out that "they differed in many ways almost to the point of opposition."[13]

It is not accidental, therefore, that biblical scholars found extremely difficult to imagine how Jesus have merged both the apocalyptic and wisdom element and language in a single message, more so in view of the fact that in Q these two components constitute the basis of Jesus' language and teaching. Naturally, then, historians "invested enormous energy in the investigation of the ancient near eastern literatures of proverbial wisdom and apocalyptic vision, seeking to understand each world view and looking for ways in which each may have been related to the other."[14]

From the mid 70's, the time I completed my research, the Q studies have experienced a dramatic development, which was actually the result of the tension between these two basic—if not exclusive—elements of the Q traditions, i.e. sapiential and apocalyptic, in terms both of form and of content. Inevitably the focal point in Q research has shifted from the field of the *theology* of Q in its final form to its *redaction*, i.e. the previous editions (layers, stages etc.) of its existence; from the end-document which was used by the authors of our later Synoptics to the field of the *pre-history* of the Q-Document.[15] Although D. Lührmann[16] on this side of the

---

[12] The question was in force even from the early period of the pauline mission (cf. 1 Cor 7. 29-31 etc.).

[13] R. E. Brown, *An Introduction to New Testament Christology*, New York 1994, pp. 205ff.

[14] B. L. Mack, *The Lost Gospel. The Book of Q and Christian Origins*, San Francisco 1993, pp.31f.

[15] Early in the 80s I was stating that "N.T. scholars are becoming...reluctant to pay much attention to minor literary questions. The majority of them are quite rightly

*The Challenge of Q* 145

Atlantic was the first to introduce into Q studies the layering by postulating a conscious editing by the editor(s) of Q of heterogeneous saying material, it was the American scholars, more precisely the Q Seminar of the Society of Biblical Literature, which under the chairmanship of J. M. Robinson attempted a stratigraphic analysis and redactional division of the various stages and clusters of the entire non Marcan *sayings material* (loosely described as Q) most notably in the case of J. S. Kloppenborg.[17] The question, therefore, of the theology of Q in the last two decades has shifted to a completely new area, which affected also the picture of origins of Christianity, and consequently the quest of the Historical Jesus. It is quite characteristic that back in Europe P. Hoffmann, from the Catholic University of Bamberg in Germany (who is also engaged in the International Q Project together with Robinson and Kloppenborg[18]), has recently published his minor Q studies,[19] in "an attempt to repair," as he himself states, "to a deficit in (his) Habilitationschrift, *Studien zur Theologie der Logienquelle."* [20]

The major breakthrough in the "wisdom or apocalyptic" dilemma undoubtedly occurred in 1964 with J. M. Robinson,[21] who underlined the formal similarity of Q with such early Christian documents as the Gnostic *Gospel of Thomas,* the *Didache,* but also with smaller units of sayings material of the synoptic tradition, like the parables in Mark 4 etc. The

---

turning their attention to the more important, and to some extent more fascinating, issues of theology and redaction of the oldest source of our Gospel accounts" ("The Original Order of Q: Some Residual Cases," J. Delobel [ed.], *Logia,* Leuven 1982, 379-387, p. 379; also above ch. 3).

[16] *Die Redaktion der Logienquelle,* Neukirchen 1969; cf. also O. H. Steck, *Israel und das gewaltsame Geschick der Propheten,* Neukirchen 1967, whose conclusion concerning the Deuteronomic redaction motif (on the basis of the Q=Lk 6.23, 11.49-51, 13.34f sayings) in early christianity has gained unanimous support among Q scholars.

[17] His major monograph, *The Formation of Q: Trajectories in Ancient Wisdom Collections,* Philadelphia 1987, is characterized by Robinson in the forward (p. xi) as the latest word on the Q scholarship; Kloppenborg was actually based on a previous important remark he made in an article on the methodology of the discussion of the composition and redaction of Q, that both form-critical and tradition-historical analysis have to be overcome in dealing with Q, since they are inadequate to assist in answering the crucial question posed above

[18] Under preparation by the International Q Project is a complete list of the Q bibliography and a critical edition of Q text, together with a classified and assessed presentation of all the scholarly contributions during the last two centuries, a periodically published series under the title *Documenta Q,* Leiden 1996ff.

[19] *Tradition und Situation. Studien zur Jesusüberlieferung in der Logienquelle und den synoptischen Evangelien,* Münster 1995.

[20] Münster 1982³. The quotation from p. 159 of his recent article "The Redaction of Q and the Son of Man: A Preliminary Sketch," R. A. Piper (ed.), *The Gospel Behind the Gospels. Current Studies on Q,* Leiden 1995, 159-198.

[21] "ΛΟΓΟΙ ΣΟΦΩΝ: Zur Gattung der Spruchquelle Q," *Zeit und Geschichte. Dankesgabe an Rudolf Bultmann,* Tübingen 1964, 77-96; also presented in an English version in *Trajectories Through Early Christianity,* Philadelphia, 1971.

inevitable conclusion of his approach was that the literary genre of Q was that of the wisdom literatures of the Old Testament, the near East and the ancient Egypt, that the sayings of the Q Document were «λόγοι σοφῶν» (cf. Prov 22.17), that the idiom of wisdom and not of apocalyptic was fundamental to the collection, and that Jesus' disciples (at least those of the Q community) understood them as instructions of a sage teacher, not of an apocalyptic prophet. Of equal significance at this point was H. Koester's observation that Q most probably has experienced a shift in its generic trajectory, beginning with one genre and moving through a redactional process to another.[22] These findings in fact rekindled the issue of reconsideration of the theological character of Q. However, the prevailing among scholars view, first presented in 1969 with sound argumentation by Lührmann,[23] was that the prophetic and apocalyptic logia in Q were not marginal, secondary or peripheral in the overall structure of the document, but they form an integral part in its editing, with the theme of judgment functioning as an organizational principle for the entire Q material.

For almost two decades the priority of the apocalyptic over the sapiential element in Q was been confirmed or at least accepted with minor variations in a number of scholarly works,[24] until J. S. Kloppenborg set out to scrutinize the entire hypothetical end-document of Q. Having reconstructed the Q-Document on the basis mainly of our procedural principles[25] he came to the following significant conclusion: the wisdom sayings in Q on strictly literary grounds cannot be secondary to the apocalyptic ones, since they were all formed without the slightest interest in, or knowledge of, the theme of judgment; even more significant was his conclusion, that almost all prophetic and apocalyptic material either presuppose or clearly incorporated the wisdom sayings. The prophetic

---

[22] This is clearly implied from his articles included in the jointly with J. M. Robinson published volume *Trajectories Through Early Christianity*, Philadelphia, 1971; cf. also his later *Ancient Christian Gospels. Their History and Development*, SCM London, TPI Philadelphia 1990, esp. pp. 128ff..

[23] *Die Redaktion* .

[24] Cf. A. D. Jacobson, *Wisdom Christology in Q*, Ph.D. at Claremont 1978 (also his *The First Gospel. An Introduction to Q*, Sonoma 1992); D. Zeller, *Kommentar zur Logienquelle*, Stuttgart 1984; Ph.E.Sellew, *Early Collections of Jesus' Words: The Development of Dominical Discourses*, Ph.D. at Harvard 1986; L. Vaage, *Q: The Ethos and Ethic of an Itinerant Intelligence*, Ph.D. at Claremont 1987; and basically M. Sato, *Q und Prophetie. Studien zur Gattungs and Traditions-geschichte der Quelle Q*, Ph.D under U.Luz, Tübingen 1988.

[25] Kloppenborg characterized them "sound and responsible criteria",*(The Formation of Q*, p. 84); and concluded his reconstruction chapter with the following statement: "rigorous examination of the Matt-Luke agreements and application of the criteria suggested by Vassiliadis lead to the conclusion that essentially Q was composed of sayings and chriae", p. 88).

apocalyptic material, he argued, were definitely added to Q at a later stage of its composition.[26]

The implications of Kloppenborg's findings—if the shift from wisdom to apocalyptic be explained—can also have some consequences for the quest of the historical Jesus and a fresh look at Christian origins. Indeed, B. L. Mack himself in his fascinating—though not entirely justified from a scholarly perspective[27]—book *The Lost Gospel,* a brilliant book intended for non-technical readership, has taken these findings to their extreme, arguing that "as for Jesus," it would mean that he had probably been more the sage, less the prophet. And as for Christian origins, it would mean that something other than an apocalyptic message and motivation may have impelled the new movement and defined its fundamental attraction".[28] And moving a further step he (and a few others) suggested the so-called *Cynic alternative.* This is a new interpretation of Christian origins and a new alternative of understanding the Historical Jesus, which slowly but steadily is gaining support in scholarly circles on both sides of the Atlantic.[29] All the more because of the wide acceptance of the rhetoric approach to the N.T. literature, and the tendency to look more and more to Hellenistic rather than Jewish parallels for Christian origins. I myself do not align with those who all-too-hasty dismiss any consideration of the roots of the early Christian tradition other than the established and widely accepted one.[30] Even though the notorious "Jesus Seminar"[31] has given rise to justified reactions, especially after the radical popular books on the Historical Jesus that have recently come out.[32]

As far as Q is concerned, the cynic parallels, both formal and in content, are indeed striking. The aphoristic style in many of the Q material, especially in its earliest edition ($Q^1$, or first stage), the imperatives, injunctions and instructions, maxims, admonitions and lores, sometimes in

---

[26] According to Kloppenborg the Temptation story was developed at a later (3rd stage). It is not without significance the he started with those clusters of sayings where the motif of judgment appears quite prominent (pp. 102ff.), and then with the sapiential speeches in Q (pp. 171ff.).

[27] More on that below.

[28] B. L. Mack, *The Lost Gospel*, p. 37.

[29] Beside Mack cf. also H.-D. Betz, "Jesus and the Cynics: Survey and Analysis of an Hypothesis," *JR* 74 (1994); F. G. Downing, "Quite like 'Q'. The 'Lives' of Cynic Philosophers," *Biblica* 69 (1988) 196-224; "Cynics and Christians," *NTS* 30 (1984) 584-93. Also the collective works *Christ and the Cynics. Jesus and Other Radical Preachers in First-Century Tradition* , Sheffield 1988; and *Cynics and Christian Origins,* Edinburgh 1992. L. Vaage, *Q: The Ethos and Ethic of an Itinerant Intelligence,* Ph. D Claremont 1987.

[30] Cf. P. Perkins, "Jesus before Christianity. Cynic and Sage?" *ChrCen* 110 (1993) 749-51.

[31] Cf. the product of the 74 members of that seminar: *The Five Gospels,* Macmillan 1993 (the 5th being the Gospel of Thomas).

[32] L. D. Crossan's *Jesus: A Revolutionary Biography,* Harper San Francisco 1993. B. L. Mack's *The Lost Gospel* may be counted among those, but not quite.

a keen, pungent, terse character, as well as the unconditional discipleship demanded in the most authentic dominical sayings, together with the unconventional behavior (begging, absurdity, unsocial living, voluntary poverty, renunciation of needs and critique of riches, pretension and hypocrisy etc.), are all signs that make the Jesus' movement, it is argued, resemble not to the prophetic apocalyptic (traditional view), not even to the traditional proverbial wisdom (Robinson's view[33]), but rather to the popular cynic philosophy. If this interpretation is proved true, then early Christianity has to dissociated from either the "reformation" model (and also the "sectarian" one: "true Israel," authentic "people of God" etc.) or the "revolutionary" (or even the "utopian") explanation of Jesus' and the early Church's teaching and overall behavior. The cynic alternative demands a total dismantling of the traditional picture.

If one takes in mind that the prevailed modern view of the term "cynic," "cynical" etc. does not represent accurately what the ancient cynics really were, and sees the cynics more or less as the Greek analog of the O.T. Hebrew prophets, then one may think that no much difference would be caused if Jesus' words (at least those stemming from Q) are read against the background of the O.T. prophets or against the background of the Greek cynics. The problem, however, is much more complex if one goes further and deeper into Jesus' message and to the effect it has for the social and community life. For the cynics' general attitude to the social evil is romantic and naturalistic and by no means radical and dynamic. In short, it was a call for *individuals* to live against the stream, an invitation to swim against the social currents that threatened to overwhelm and silence human dynamism; not a program offered for the reformation of the *society*. The cynics' critique of cultural conventions rest not on society as a system but on the shoulders of the individual. It may not be too much an exaggeration, if one characterizes the "cynic alternative" as a spiritual child of the Enlightenment and the values of the western individualism. For social institutions were not under attack by the cynics; the cynics rather invited the individual to live "according to nature". The striking indeed evidence of the picture one gets from the earlier strata of the sayings material of the Gospels (and more precisely from the most primitive version of Q) was what made Mack declare that, on the basis of the evidence of Q, "Jesus was much more like a Cynic-teacher than a Christ-savior or messiah with a program for the reformation of the second-temple Jewish society and religion".[34]

---

[33] A sage has to be differentiated from a cynic, hence the "sapiential" alternative with regard to Q - and by extension to christian origins and the quest of the Historical Jesus - is not to be confused with the "cynic" one.

[34] B. L. Mack, *The Lost Gospel*, p. 245.

In a recent article J. M. Robinson,[35] refuted from a scholarly perspective and through various ankles (history of religions, translation, rhetoric, historical [the cynic getup], redactional [the editions of Q] etc.) Mack's cynic hypothesis, characterizing his book "an eminently readable, indeed fascinating and entertaining, achievement in popular scholarship,"[36] which nevertheless "makes the Cynic hypothesis too easy for the popular audience and too difficult for the critical scholar".[37]

However, the problem of the origins of early Christianity is still there. The challenge to the conventional picture of the Historical Jesus, based mainly on the Pauline interpretation, is still under question by the almost universal acceptance of Q as the earliest written, though in successive stages, account of Gospel tradition. And we are only at the beginning.

### III

Fr. Benedict Viviano in a recent article[38] suggested that from the examination of the doubly attested sayings of the synoptic tradition (Q-Mark) one can almost reach the same (with the one prevailing at the moment in scholarship and in Christian tradition in general) conclusion, with the exception perhaps of the Eucharist. On my part I am not so optimist; and in addition it seems to me that one should start from exactly the opposite end; and Eucharist and Q are by no means irreconcilable entities.

In my contribution to last year's VI Symposium on John the Apostle in Ephesos[39], presenting the Johannine view of the Eucharist, I argued for the Eucharist as a communion event and a proleptic manifestation of the eschata, i.e. for its ecclesial and diaconal dimension, and the anti-sacramentalistic character of it at almost the last end of the spectrum of the N.T. literature.[40] And this understanding of the Eucharist, not so much as a cult or rite, but primarily as a dynamic expression of the people of God and a glimpse and foretaste of the Kingdom to come, I also tested by reference to the other end of the spectrum, the most ancient stage of primitive Christianity, i.e. the Q-Document.[41]

---

[35] "The History-of-Religions Taxonomy of Q. The Cynic Hypothesis," H. Preissler-H. Seiwer [eds.], *Gnosisforschung und Religionsgeschichte*, Marburg 1995, pp.247-65.

[36] Ibid., p. 247.

[37] Ibid., p.265.

[38] B. Viviano, "The Historical Jesus in the Doubly Attested Sayings: An Experiment," *Revue Biblique* 103 (1996) 367-410.

[39] "The Understanding of Eucharist in St. John's Gospel," L. Padovese (ed.), *Atti del VI Simposio di Efeso su S.Giovanni Apostolo,* Rome 1996, 39-52.

[40] Ibid., pp. 51f.

[41] Cf. my "Eucharist and Q", *Scholarly Annual of the Theological Department of the University of Thessaloniki*, vol. 6 (1996) pp. 111-130. I had finished this article, which I then presented to the University of Lund, when I came across an extremely important treatment of the subject by Bruce Chilton under the title *A Feast of Meanings. Eucharistic Theologies from Jesus through Johannine Circles*, Leiden 1994. Chilton

In a recent survey of the N.T. evidence on the Eucharist in the revised edition of *The Study of Liturgy*,[42] there is no mention at all of the pre-Pauline Christianity. The common view till very recently was that there is no history, or more precisely *pre*-history,[43] of Eucharist prior to Paul, i.e. prior to the mid-50s. At a first glance we get the impression that there is no reference to the Eucharist in Q. But in the N.T. we have only a skeletal pre-history of the liturgical praxis of the primitive church, based on small pieces of evidence, to be pieced together "knowing that many of the bits are irretrievably lost".[44] But as I argued,[45] one should consider the place of Eucharist in Q on a different level. The reconstruction of the Q-Document, we referred to above, if it is viewed as a guiding principle for uncovering the theological characteristics of the community behind it, it can also provide some hints for what we broadly call Eucharist.

Exegetes, as well as liturgists, are still puzzled[46] about what it appears as a seeming dissimilarity between the N.T. evidence and our earliest account in the post-apostolic period, with regard to the process of events in the celebration of the Eucharist: first the eucharistic meal and then an extended period of common prayer and praise and of teaching (Synoptic Last Supper accounts and Paul, at least in Corinth), or the other way around (Justin, and the church's practice thereafter). Jones-Hickling have stated that "how and when this reversal took place we do not know; it turned out to be universal, and so it may have happened quite early, early enough to be reflected in Luke 24.25–35 and possibly in John 6, where extended teaching precedes the allusion to the Eucharist (if such it is) at vv. 51–58".[47]

I have shown[48] that he structure of the Q-Document exhibits a striking parallel with the Church's "celebration" of the Eucharist, as first described by Justin Martyr in his *1st Apology* 65, where the celebration was preceded by biblical readings, sermon and intercession. If we take the entire section of Q on "Jesus' Teaching" together with the one on "Response to Jesus' Teaching" as the universal Christian liturgical rite which precedes the Eucharist proper, i.e. the Liturgy of the Word, then all one has to find is

---

argues for a similar understanding of the Eucharist at the early stages of its development.

[42] C. P. M. Jones (revised by C. J. A. Hickling), "The Eucharist: I. The New Testament," *The Study of Liturgy. Revised Edition,* SPCK London 1992, pp. 184-209.

[43] A. C. Couratin, "Liturgy," in *The Pelican Guide to Modern Theology*, vol. 2, *Historical Theology,* 1969, pp. 131-240.

[44] Cf. A. C. Couratin, "Liturgy," pp.154f.

[45] "Eucharist and Q," pp. 126ff. Also above ch. 6.

[46] See C. P. M. Jones (revised by C. J. A. Hickling), "The Eucharist: I. The New Testament," p.204.

[47] Ibid.

[48] "Eucharist and Q," pp. 127ff.

some connection of the following section ("Jesus and his Disciples") with the Eucharistic Liturgy.[49] It is indeed striking that Jesus' Thanksgiving *(eucharistia)* to the Father (Lk 10.21f. par) not only resembles to the liturgical *anaphora* of the later Christian Eucharistic rite, but it is also structured with regard to the *Lord's Prayer* in exactly the same way as the post-anaphora liturgical rites. Both in the Q-Document and in the Eucharistic Liturgy the Lord's Prayer follows the *anaphora*.

The question which arises is whether the evidence allows the argument that the Q-Document is throughout structured according to the primitive Church's eucharistic practice. The answer to that question should be definitely "no"; but if we take the Eucharist neither as a cult nor as a mere ritual, but as "the living expression of the ecclesial identity of the early Christian community as a koinonia of the eschata", a proleptic manifestation of the Kingdom of God (an idea that plays a significant part even from the first stage of the Q-Document [$Q^1$]),[50] in other words as the vivid act of the community by which the faithful proleptically lived the coming new world, then the answer could be: yes, there is some connection between the most eschatologically oriented document—though not apocalyptic—of the N.T. tradition (Q) and the most eschatological act of the Christian community (Eucharist).[51]

In my view this is the only effective and legitimate defense against the dismantling for Christian theology development in recent synoptic (Q) scholarship. Of course, a widely accepted solution to the problem of the "paradigm shift" in early Christian (Pauline?) theology is pending, but this is subject for another paper. For me it is a problem closely connected to methodology. Personally I am quite convinced that the time has come for scholarly research to distance itself as much as possible from the dominant to modern scholarship syndrome of the priority of the texts over the experience, of theology over ecclesiology. There are many scholars who cling to the dogma, imposed by the post-Enlightenment and post-Reformation hegemony over all scholarly theological outlook (and not only in the field of biblical scholarship or of Protestant theology), which can be summarized as follows: what constitutes the basis of any historical investigation, the core of Christian faith, cannot be extracted but from given texts (and/or archeological evidence), from the expressed theological views, from a certain *depositum fidei*—be it the Bible, the Church (or apostolic) Tradition etc.; very rarely is there any serious reference to the

---

[49] See the Appendix in "Eucharist and Q," pp. 128ff..

[50] 7-9 times the term appears in $Q^1$; Mack tried to play down the evidence by paraphrasing it in some places and taking it to mean neutral, non-messianic/ eschatological situations!

[51] On the eschatological character of the Eucharist see J. Zizioulas, *Being as Communion;* and D. Passakos, *Eucharist and Mission. Sociological Presuppositions of the Pauline Theology,* Athens, 1997.

eucharistic/eschatological experience that preceded them, in fact from the communion-event which was responsible and produced these texts and views.

One has, of course, to admit that very early, even from the time of St. Paul, there has been a shift—no matter for what reasons[52]—of the center of gravity from the *(eucharistic) experience* to the *(Christian) message*, from *eschatology* to *christology* (and further and consequently to *soteriology)*, from the *event* (the *Kingdom of God)*, to the *bearer and center* of this event *(Christ,* and more precisely his sacrifice on the cross).[53] Although some theologians consider this second concept, which was mingled with the original biblical/semitic thought, as stemming from Greek philosophers (Stoics and others), nevertheless it is more than clear that the horizontal-eschatological view was the predominant one in the early church, both in the New Testament and in subsequent christian literature. The vertical-soteriological (and pauline) view was always understood within the context of the horizontal-eschatological perspective as supplemental and complementary.[54]

---

[52] D. Passakos in his recent doctoral dissertation tried to analyze this "paradigm shift" at that crucial moment of early christianity and claimed that "the Eucharist in Paul" was understood not only as an icon of the eschata, but also as a missionary event with cosmic and social consequences. The Eucharist for him was not only the sacrament of the Church, but also the sacrament of the world. Within the pauline communities the Eucharist had a double orientation (in contrast to the overall eschatological and otherworldly dimension of it in earlier tradition): towards the world as *diastolic* movement, and towards God as a *systolic* movement" *(Eucharist and Mission,* p. 267). According to Passakos«the Eucharist for Paul is at the same time an experience of the eschata and a movement toward the eschata" (p. 268). Bruce Chilton (*A Feast of Meanings)* has discerned six such paradigm shifts from Jesus' time to the johannine circles.

[53] Cf. my *Cross and Salvation,* 1983 (in Greek), an English summary of which can be found in a paper of mine delivered at the 1984 annual Leuven Colloquium ("Σταυρός: Centre of the Pauline Soteriology and Apostolic Ministry," A. Vanhoye [ed.], *L'Apôtre Paul. Personnalité, Style et Conception du Ministère,* Leuven 1986, pp. 246-253).

[54] This is why the liturgical experience of the early Church is incomprehensible without its social dimension (see Acts 2.42ff., 1 Cor 11.1ff., Heb 13.10-16; Justin, *1 Apology* 67; Irenaeus, *Adver. Her.* 18.1, etc.).

*EXCURSUS*

# 9
# BEHIND MARK.
# TOWARDS A WRITTEN SOURCE

The problem of the sources underlying Mark[1] is not new; it emerged at the beginning of this century after the hypothesis of the priority of Mark.[2] First suggested by C. Lachmann[3] and developed by B. Weiss[4] and H. J. Holtzmann,[5] it reached its completion in the four-document hypothesis of B. H. Streeter.[6] However, the attempts to recover a source nearer to the Jesus of history were abandoned before the outbreak of the second World War just as similar attempts to write the "Life of Jesus" had ceased before the first World War under the influence of A. Schweitzer's brilliant *Von Reimarus zu Wrede* (1906).[7]

The Ur-Markus hypothesis proposed by H. von Söden,[8] E. Wendling,[9] W. Bussmann[10] and some English scholars[11] seems to have been given its quietus by Streeter's work.[12] The work, however, which undoubtedly ended all other attempts[13] to get behind our present Mark was that of R. Bultmann,[14] M. Dibelius[15] and other form-critics,[16] who drew attention to

---

[1] In the following: Mark=the second Gospel; St. Mark=the author; Mk=the source Mark. Similarly for the other Gospels.

[2] The attempts of some scholars (see B. C. Butler, "The Synoptic problem," in *New Catholic Commentary on Holy Scripture*; London, 1969, where there is also a summary of their arguments, and W. R. Farmer, *The Synoptic Problem*, London 1964, to establish the priority of Matthew, must be regarded as unsuccessful since they make the whole synoptic problem more and more complicated. Cf. N. Perrin, *Rediscovering the Teaching of Jesus*, London 1967, p. 34. [More on these in the previous chapters].

[3] *Studien und Kritiken*, 1835, p. 574.

[4] *Lehrbuch der Einleitung in das N.T.*, 1886, pp. 473ff.

[5] *Die Synoptiker*, 1901, pp. 10-20.

[6] *The Four Gospels: A Study of Origins*, London 1924.

[7] This literary genre reappeared only in 1956 in G. Bornkamm's *Jesus von Nazareth* and in a completely different guise.

[8] *Die wichtigsten Fragen im Leben Jesu*, 1907².

[9] *Ur-Markus* (1905), and *Die Entstehung des Markusevangeliums*, 1908.

[10] *Synoptische Studien I-III* (1925-31).

[11] Cf. the works of A. Wright, N. P. Williams, W. W. Holdsworth, etc.

[12] See A. M. Hunter, *Interpreting the NT. 1900-1950*, London 1951, p. 41.

[13] Cf. the Redaction-Hypotheses of J. Weiss, J. G. Hawkins V. S. Stanton, and the Compilation-Hypotheses of E. Meyer, A. J. Gadoux, J. M. G. Crum; see V. Taylor, *The Gospel according to St. Mark*, London 1952, pp. 72f.

[14] *Die Geschichte der synoptischen Tradition*, 1921.

[15] *Die Formgeschichte des Evangeliums*, 1919.

[16] K. L. Schmidt, M. Albertz, V. Taylor, R. H. Lightfoot, etc.

the separate units of material, the *pericopae,* which must have circulated in the period of oral tradition.[17]

Moreover the increasing interest in investigating the Aramaic background, in order to provide a criterion to determine the authenticity of the isolated sayings,[18] after the work of G. Dalman,[19] C. F. Burney,[20] and M. Black[21] had shown the way, as well as the insight provided by the redaction-critics[22] as to the decisive role of the evangelists in shaping and manipulating the Gospel material, redirected the efforts of modern scholars.

Since that time onwards there has been no systematic work on the sources used by St. Mark.[23] Only here and there can one discern an originally existing group of parables in Mk 4.3–9, 13–20, 26–32.[24] Similarly V. Taylor[25] tried to recover the original version of the Passion narrative as it existed in the Roman Community (previous attempts have been made by M. Dibelius, R. Bultmann, H. Lietzmann, E. Klostermann, M. Goguel, R. H. Lightfoot, etc.). We pass over Mk 13 since there is no unanimous agreement among the scholars about the kind and the extent of the sources used.[26] All the other scattered attempts including W. Knox's posthumous book[27] deal with the small complexes of Mark in a way rather parallel to that of the form-critics.

The present writer was not initially concerned with examining this material, and what follows is really a by-product of his investigation of Mk 13.

The source, the existence of which the present writer advances as a hypothesis, consists of sayings of Jesus introduced by the formula «βλέπετε». Βλέπετε (in the sense of warning) forms an introductory formula to Jesus' sayings only in Mk.[28] It is to be found five times in Mark (4.26, 12.36,

---

[17] H. Conzelmann, *An Outline of the Theology of the N. T.*, London 1969, remarks: "Form criticism showed that each individual piece of tradition had christological significance in itself", p. 140.

[18] Cf. J. Jeremias, R. H. Fuller, etc.

[19] *Die Worte Jesu*, 1898.

[20] *The Poetry of our Lord*, Oxford 1925.

[21] *An Aramaic Approach to the Gospels and Acts*, Oxford, 1967².

[22] G. Bornkamm, H. Conzelmann, E. Haenchen, W. Marxsen, etc.

[23] Parker's *(The Gospel before Mark,* 1953) proposed K source used by both St. Mark and St. Matthew is equated with proto-Matthew, and therefore it is to be classified along with the attempts to establish the priority of Matthew (see n. 2).

[24] Cf. J. Jeremias, *The Parables of Jesus*, London, 1963), pp. 92ff.

[25] *Op. cit.*, pp. 653ff.

[26] Moreover G. R. Beasley-Murray, *Jesus and the Future,* London 1954, insists, but with reservations (see also *A Commentary on Mk. XIII,* London, 1957, p. 11 n. 1), on its authenticity.

[27] *The Sources of the Synoptic Gospels, I: St. Mark,* edited by H. Chadwick, Cambridge, 1953.

[28] It is to be found nowhere in Q, M, L.

13.5,9, 33) ; once in Matthew (24.4=Mk 13.5) and twice in Luke (8.18=Mk 4. 24.; and 21.8=Mk 13.5). Also to be considered is Mk 8.15 which is introduced by «ὁρᾶτε βλέπετε». But the most significant fact is that in all these passages «βλέπετε» is followed by a link-phrase—sometimes like a short précis or a title of the logion which comes after. Let us examine each case with care.[29]

1. Mk 13:5bf. «Βλέπετε μή τις ὑμᾶς πλανήσῃ· πολλοὶ ἐλεύσονται ἐπὶ τῷ ὀνόματί μου λέγοντες ὅτι Ἐγώ εἰμι, καὶ πολλοὺς πλανήσουσιν». Βλέπετε is the introductory formula, μή τις ὑμᾶς πλανήσῃ the link-phrase and πολλοὶ ἐλεύσονται ἐπὶ τῷ ὀνόματί μου λέγοντες ὅτι Ἐγώ εἰμι,[30] καὶ πολλοὺς πλανήσουσιν the original logion.

2. Mk 13.9f.: «Βλέπετε δὲ ὑμεῖς ἑαυτούς· παραδώσουσιν ὑμᾶς εἰς συνέδρια καὶ εἰς συναγωγὰς...». Βλέπετε the introductory formula and ὑμεῖς ἑαυτούς the link-phrase reflecting παραδώσουσιν ὑμᾶς. What follows deals with the persecution of the disciples and has been formed by the collector of the sayings and expanded to relate to the whole community.[31]

3. Mk 13.33f.: «Βλέπετε ἀγρυπνεῖτε· οὐκ οἴδατε γὰρ πότε ὁ καιρός ἐστιν. ὡς ἄνθρωπος...». Βλέπετε the introductory formula, ἀγρυπνεῖτε (and perhaps οὐκ οἴδατε γὰρ πότε ὁ καιρός ἐστιν) the link-phrase, a short précis of the following parable of the Doorkeeper in a developed form.[32]

4. Mk 4:24f. «Βλέπετε τί ἀκούετε. ἐν ᾧ μέτρῳ μετρεῖτε...». Again βλέπετε the formula and τί ἀκούετε the link-phrase followed by two similes. The whole passage (v. 4.24f.) as it stands is a warning against false prophets and teachers, though its original meaning[33] was obviously different. What is certain, according to our view, is that τί ἀκούετε reflects a different meaning of the verb ἀκούειν from that which it has in the preceding verses.[34] Otherwise why did St. Mark use «τί»?[35] It is also obvious that the two similes have been misunderstood, although the collector may have used

---

[29] We start with the passages in Mk 13 where this phenomenon is evident.

[30] λέγοντες ὅτι ἐγώ εἰμι must rather be considered as a parenthetical insertion by St. Mark.

[31] It is reasonable to suppose that genuine sayings in v. 6 - this saying is also to be found in another form, perhaps taken from another source, in Mk 13.21f. - and v. 9.f. had been expanded in the course of time and under the increasing influence of the apocalyptic world of ideas by addition of inauthentic sayings before reaching St. Mark. Otherwise we have to accept a great number of sources for the composition of one and the same chapter, and therefore to attribute to St. Mark an extremely difficult task even in our own day and age.

[32] Cf. C. H. Dodd, *The Parables of the Kingdom*, London, 1971, pp. 120-24. Also J. Jeremias, *op. cit.*, pp. 53f.

[33] We are not concerned here as to whether these two similes are *ipsissima verba* of Jesus or not (cf. R. Bultmann, *op. cit.*, ET. by J. Marsh, Oxford 1963, p.112), nor do we discuss their original meaning.

[34] Mk 4.3, 9, 12, 16, 18, 20, 23.

[35] Cf. the meaning of βλέπειν+the prepositions πῶς, τί, etc.

logia transmitted as authentic sayings of Jesus to build up his catechetical collection in a way similar to the Jewish midrash.

5. Mk 12.38bf. : Βλέπετε ἀπὸ τῶν γραμματέων τῶν θελόντων ἐν στολαῖς περιπατεῖν... Βλέπετε the introductory formula, ἀπὸ τῶν γραμματέων the link-phrase like a title of the following saying concerned with the behavior of the scribes. That ἀπὸ τῶν γραμματέων is actually the link-phrase is shown by the difference of the structure between v. 38b (τῶν θελόντων) and v. 40 (οἱ κατεσθίοντες).[36] The collector may have had at his disposal both verbs in the nominative, perhaps in a form similar to the οὐαί-sayings in Q but when forming his βλέπετε-collection he changed the case of the first participle to agree with τῶν γραμματέων.[37] On the other hand the name of the scribes alone must have been sufficient for his readers.

6. In Mk 8.15b finally there is another saying introduced in a quite different way by Ὁρᾶτε βλέπετε.[38] Both verbs, ὁρᾶτε and βλέπετε, mean exactly the same: they correspond to the English verb "to see" literally— or "to take heed" figuratively in this particular case—so that they seem to form a pleonasm. The whole passage Ὁρᾶτε, βλέπετε ἀπὸ τῆς ζύμης τῶν Φαρισαίων καὶ τῆς ζύμης Ἡρῴδου[39] in its present context is an insertion by St. Mark[40] reflecting the previous discussion between Jesus and the Pharisees.[41] R. Bultmann includes it among the *Gesetzworte und Gemeinderegeln,* observing that its original form and meaning are almost beyond recovery."[42] None the less it is possible for this verse (8.15b) to have been the beginning (the formula + the link-phrase?) of a longer logion —since lost—which St. Mark preserved, inserting it in another context

---

[36] W. C. Allen, *The Gospel according to St. Mark,* London, 1915, suggested the careless translation of an Aramaic participle in v. 40; but we can hardly accept his suggestion since the first participle (τῶν θελόντων) has been translated correctly.

[37] E. Lohmeyer, *Das Evangelium des Markus,* Göttingen, 1937, p. 263; V. Taylor, *op. cit.,* p. 495 and D. E. Nineham, *St. Mark,* Harmondsworth 1963, pp. 333f maintain that v. 40 forms a self contained saying with no connection originally with the scribes; this however can hardly stand, see J. Jeremias, *Jerusalem in the Time of Jesus,* London 1969, p. 114; also J. Duncan M. Derrett, "Eating up the Houses of Widows: Jesus' comment on Lawyers?" *NT* 18 (1972) pp. 1-9, who gives the following interpretation: "...those that 'eat away' the estates of widows, and, with such an end in view, indulge in lengthy prayers: they shall suffer a heavier sentence", (p. 8).

[38] D, Θ and some other MSS omit «Ὁρᾶτε», but we shall go too far if we support their originality.

[39] The reading Ἡρωδιανῶν (instead of Ἡρῴδου) of p45, W, Θ and other MSS does not affect our argument and therefore we pass it over.

[40] So D. E. Nineham, *op. cit.,* p. 213. On the other hand V. Taylor, *op. cit.,* p. 385 prefers a pre-Marcan composition for the whole passage because, as he asserts, St. Mark does not insert sayings like St. Matthew, but adds them at the end.

[41] Mk 8.11f.

[42] *Op. cit.,* p. 131.

using the word ζύμη[43] as a catchword. It would only have been possible to consider it as a detached part of Mk 12.38bf.[44] if we had been able to equate scribes with Pharisees.[45]

To sum up: one of the sources which St. Mark had at his disposal was the (βλέπετε-source with the following characteristics:

(a) an introductory formula (=βλέπετε),

(b) a link-phrase, like a short précis or a title of the main logion, after the introductory formula and before the logion proper, and

(c) a possibly genuine logion but in a quite developed or expanded form following the introductory formula and link-phrase. We can see therefore in this particular case three different stages *(Sitz im Leben)* in the transmission of the tradition until the composition of Mark: (a) Jesus; (b) the collector (=the impersonal Church in general); (c) St. Mark. In our first examined passage (Mk 13.5bf.) for instance: (a) Jesus = πολλοὶ ἐλεύσονται..., (b) the collector=«Βλέπετε μή τις ὑμᾶς πλανήσῃ· πολλοὶ ἐλεύσονται..» (c) St. Mark = the whole passage 13.5bf. within the context of Mk 13 and with special reference to the End.

We are unable to determine whether this source was limited to these six sayings or extended to a larger document. We can however discern a *catechetical* tone in it.[46]

The problem which arises is whether these sayings had formed a fixed *written* source before they reached St. Mark, and therefore whether both «Βλέπετε» and the link-phrase are due to the collector, or both these are to be attributed either to Jesus himself or to the evangelist. There is no clear evidence, but certain considerations favor the former solution.

First of all the use of a standard introductory formula—this can also be found in the collections of sayings in the *Gospel of Thomas* and in the papyri found at Oxyrhynchus in the form «λέγει ᾽Ιησοῦς».[47]

---

[43] For ζύμη in a bad sense see H. L. Strack-P. Billerbeck, *Kommentar zum N. T. aus Talmud und Midrash,* 1922, vol. I, pp. 728f.

[44] C. G. Montefiore, *The Synoptic Gospels, I,* 1927, I, asked whether the saying referred to the Pharisees only and τῆς ζύμης ῾Ηρώδου had been added.

[45] Cf. J. Jeremias, *Jerusalem,* pp. 93f.

[46] See below.

[47] It is also remarkable that in John the ἀμήν-logia of Jesus are always introduced by the formula ἀμήν-ἀμήν, whereas in the Synoptics the ἀμήν λέγω formula is always to be found. I am grateful to the Rev. A. E. Harvey for pointing this out to me and also for some other valuable suggestions.

Secondly the fact that the verb «βλέπειν»[48] in a sense of warning occurs only once in the remainder of the Synoptic Gospels (in Mk 13.23) besides these 9 passages.[49]

Thirdly the use of the link-phrase (précis) always after «βλέπετε», sometimes redundant (13.5), sometimes in a different setting (4.25), and sometimes spoiling the structure of the following saying (12.36).

Finally the fact that all these sayings are to be found without any connection with the preceding and following passages in their original setting seems to support the hypothesis.[50]

At first glance, besides these formal characteristics there is nothing else suggesting explicitly the unity of the proposed source; we can, however, discern that all these sayings are hortatory warnings against either the Jewish teaching class (logia 4, 5, 6) or the apocalyptic pseudo-prophecy (logia 1, 3), or those in power (logia 2, 6) : namely against the most dangerous opponents of the primitive Church.

We have no clear evidence also as to whether the language of the source before it came into the hands of St. Mark was Greek or Aramaic. But if we attribute Mk 13.14–23 to an Aramaic source where a parallel (vv. 21–23) to Mk 13.5bf. is to be found,[51] and if we take into account the fact that the division of the night in Mk 13.35 follows the Roman reckoning instead of the Jewish one in its parallel (Lk 12.38), then we can assume that it has been written at least outside Palestine and presumably in *Greek*. On the other hand, as J. H. Moulton[52] has correctly shown, under no circumstances does βλέπετε (=beware) reflect a Hebraism or an Aramaism;[53] on the contrary it has been found in a Greek papyrus (thought to date from AD. 41)[54] and in many Greek writings[55] besides the Pauline epistles.

---

[48] The frequency of the use of the verb «βλέπειν» in the Synoptic Tradition is: Mark 15, Matthew 20, Luke 17; but only 10 times in a sense of warning.

[49] In that particular case it seems to us that βλέπετε as a warning has been preferred by St. Mark - since the verse is clearly Marcan - under the influence of the above source very often used (9 times) for the composition of Mark 13.

[50] It must also be borne in mind that no linguistic peculiarities characteristic of St. Mark are to be found in these passages.

[51] Cf. V. Taylor, *op. cit.*, pp. 641f.

[52] *Grammar of N.T. Greek, II*, Edinburgh 1929, p. 31.

[53] The phrase «βλέπειν ἀπὸ» has been explained by F. Blass, *Grammatik des Neutestamentlichen Griechisch*, p. 127, as Hebrew, and by J. Wellhausen, *Einleitung in die drei ersten Evangelien*, Berlin, 1911, p. 32, as Semitic.

[54] «Βλέπε σατόν (=σαυτόν) ἀπὸ τῶν Ἰουδαίων» in *BGU* 1079.34, which was certainly not written by a Jew.

[55] Cf. βλέπειν in *VGT* and other vocabularies and lexica.

None the less, the apparent Semitic color in many cases[56] convinces us of the use of isolated logia originally uttered or even written in Aramaic, and if so it is highly probable that they go back to Jesus himself.

If the above argument is at all sound then it may be supposed that the elements St. Mark used to compose his Gospel—this strange "phenomenon in the history of literature," as R. Bultmann brilliantly remarks[57]—were of a quite different kind and they subserved other than historical aims; in this particular case catechetical or apologetic, or both—since no sharp line between them could be drawn at so early a period. But on the other hand we must not overlook the fact that St. Mark treated his sources with such faithfulness that he incorporated them *in situ* in his Gospel, even using them in a totally different context—sometimes spoiling his structure and literary form.

---

[56] See ζύμη in v. 8.15, the rhythm in v. 4.26b, the antithetical parallelism in v. 4.25, the rhythm and antithetical parallelism together in v. 13.9f. etc.

[57] *Op. cit.,* p. 348.

# South Florida Studies in the History of Judaism

| | | |
|---|---|---|
| 240001 | Lectures on Judaism in the Academy and in the Humanities | Neusner |
| 240002 | Lectures on Judaism in the History of Religion | Neusner |
| 240003 | Self-Fulfilling Prophecy: Exile and Return in the History of Judaism | Neusner |
| 240004 | The Canonical History of Ideas: The Place of the So-called Tannaite Midrashim, Mekhilta Attributed to R. Ishmael, Sifra, Sifré to Numbers, and Sifré to Deuteronomy | Neusner |
| 240005 | Ancient Judaism: Debates and Disputes, Second Series | Neusner |
| 240006 | The Hasmoneans and Their Supporters: From Mattathias to the Death of John Hyrcanus I | Sievers |
| 240007 | Approaches to Ancient Judaism: New Series, Volume One | Neusner |
| 240008 | Judaism in the Matrix of Christianity | Neusner |
| 240009 | Tradition as Selectivity: Scripture, Mishnah, Tosefta, and Midrash in the Talmud of Babylonia | Neusner |
| 240010 | The Tosefta: Translated from the Hebrew: Sixth Division Tohorot | Neusner |
| 240011 | In the Margins of the Midrash: Sifre Ha'azinu Texts, Commentaries and Reflections | Basser |
| 240012 | Language as Taxonomy: The Rules for Using Hebrew and Aramaic in the Babylonia Talmud | Neusner |
| 240013 | The Rules of Composition of the Talmud of Babylonia: The Cogency of the Bavli's Composite | Neusner |
| 240014 | Understanding the Rabbinic Mind: Essays on the Hermeneutic of Max Kadushin | Ochs |
| 240015 | Essays in Jewish Historiography | Rapoport-Albert |
| 240016 | The Golden Calf and the Origins of the Jewish Controversy | Bori/Ward |
| 240017 | Approaches to Ancient Judaism: New Series, Volume Two | Neusner |
| 240018 | The Bavli That Might Have Been: The Tosefta's Theory of Mishnah Commentary Compared With the Bavli's | Neusner |
| 240019 | The Formation of Judaism: In Retrospect and Prospect | Neusner |
| 240020 | Judaism in Society: The Evidence of the Yerushalmi, Toward the Natural History of a Religion | Neusner |
| 240021 | The Enchantments of Judaism: Rites of Transformation from Birth Through Death | Neusner |
| 240022 | Åbo Addresses | Neusner |
| 240023 | The City of God in Judaism and Other Comparative and Methodological Studies | Neusner |
| 240024 | The Bavli's One Voice: Types and Forms of Analytical Discourse and their Fixed Order of Appearance | Neusner |
| 240025 | The Dura-Europos Synagogue: A Re-evaluation (1932-1992) | Gutmann |
| 240026 | Precedent and Judicial Discretion: The Case of Joseph ibn Lev | Morell |
| 240027 | Max Weinreich *Geschichte der jiddischen Sprachforschung* | Frakes |
| 240028 | Israel: Its Life and Culture, Volume I | Pedersen |
| 240029 | Israel: Its Life and Culture, Volume II | Pedersen |
| 240030 | The Bavli's One Statement: The Metapropositional Program of Babylonian Talmud Tractate Zebahim Chapters One and Five | Neusner |

| | | |
|---|---|---|
| 240031 | The Oral Torah: The Sacred Books of Judaism: An Introduction: Second Printing | Neusner |
| 240032 | The Twentieth Century Construction of "Judaism:" Essays on the Religion of Torah in the History of Religion | Neusner |
| 240033 | How the Talmud Shaped Rabbinic Discourse | Neusner |
| 240034 | The Discourse of the Bavli: Language, Literature, and Symbolism: Five Recent Findings | Neusner |
| 240035 | The Law Behind the Laws: The Bavli's Essential Discourse | Neusner |
| 240036 | Sources and Traditions: Types of Compositions in the Talmud of Babylonia | Neusner |
| 240037 | How to Study the Bavli: The Languages, Literatures, and Lessons of the Talmud of Babylonia | Neusner |
| 240038 | The Bavli's Primary Discourse: Mishnah Commentary: Its Rhetorical Paradigms and their Theological Implications | Neusner |
| 240039 | Midrash Aleph Beth | Sawyer |
| 240040 | Jewish Thought in the 20th Century: An Introduction in the Talmud of Babylonia Tractate Moed Qatan | Schweid |
| 240041 | Diaspora Jews and Judaism: Essays in Honor of, and in Dialogue with, A. Thomas Kraabel | Overman/MacLennan |
| 240042 | The Bavli: An Introduction | Neusner |
| 240043 | The Bavli's Massive Miscellanies: The Problem of Agglutinative Discourse in the Talmud of Babylonia | Neusner |
| 240044 | The Foundations of the Theology of Judaism: An Anthology Part II: Torah | Neusner |
| 240045 | Form-Analytical Comparison in Rabbinic Judaism: Structure and Form in *The Fathers* and *The Fathers According to Rabbi Nathan* | Neusner |
| 240046 | Essays on Hebrew | Weinberg |
| 240047 | The Tosefta: An Introduction | Neusner |
| 240048 | The Foundations of the Theology of Judaism: An Anthology Part III: Israel | Neusner |
| 240049 | The Study of Ancient Judaism, Volume I: Mishnah, Midrash, Siddur | Neusner |
| 240050 | The Study of Ancient Judaism, Volume II: The Palestinian and Babylonian Talmuds | Neusner |
| 240051 | Take Judaism, for Example: Studies toward the Comparison of Religions | Neusner |
| 240052 | From Eden to Golgotha: Essays in Biblical Theology | Moberly |
| 240053 | The Principal Parts of the Bavli's Discourse: A Preliminary Taxonomy: Mishnah Commentary, Sources, Traditions and Agglutinative Miscellanies | Neusner |
| 240054 | Barabbas and Esther and Other Studies in the Judaic Illumination of Earliest Christianity | Aus |
| 240055 | Targum Studies, Volume I: Textual and Contextual Studies in the Pentateuchal Targums | Flesher |
| 240056 | Approaches to Ancient Judaism: New Series, Volume Three, Historical and Literary Studies | Neusner |
| 240057 | The Motherhood of God and Other Studies | Gruber |
| 240058 | The Analytic Movement: Hayyim Soloveitchik and his Circle | Solomon |
| 240059 | Recovering the Role of Women: Power and Authority in Rabbinic Jewish Society | Haas |

| | | |
|---|---|---|
| 240060 | The Relation between Herodotus' *History* and Primary History | Mandell/Freedman |
| 240061 | The First Seven Days: A Philosophical Commentary on the Creation of Genesis | Samuelson |
| 240062 | The Bavli's Intellectual Character: The Generative Problematic: In Bavli Baba Qamma Chapter One And Bavli Shabbat Chapter One | Neusner |
| 240063 | The Incarnation of God: The Character of Divinity in Formative Judaism: Second Printing | Neusner |
| 240064 | Moses Kimhi: Commentary on the Book of Job | Basser/Walfish |
| 240066 | Death and Birth of Judaism: Second Printing | Neusner |
| 240067 | Decoding the Talmud's Exegetical Program | Neusner |
| 240068 | Sources of the Transformation of Judaism | Neusner |
| 240069 | The Torah in the Talmud: A Taxonomy of the Uses of Scripture in the Talmud, Volume I | Neusner |
| 240070 | The Torah in the Talmud: A Taxonomy of the Uses of Scripture in the Talmud, Volume II | Neusner |
| 240071 | The Bavli's Unique Voice: A Systematic Comparison of the Talmud of Babylonia and the Talmud of the Land of Israel, Volume One | Neusner |
| 240072 | The Bavli's Unique Voice: A Systematic Comparison of the Talmud of Babylonia and the Talmud of the Land of Israel, Volume Two | Neusner |
| 240073 | The Bavli's Unique Voice: A Systematic Comparison of the Talmud of Babylonia and the Talmud of the Land of Israel, Volume Three | Neusner |
| 240074 | Bits of Honey: Essays for Samson H. Levey | Chyet/Ellenson |
| 240075 | The Mystical Study of Ruth: *Midrash HaNe'elam* of the Zohar to the Book of Ruth | Englander |
| 240076 | The Bavli's Unique Voice: A Systematic Comparison of the Talmud of Babylonia and the Talmud of the Land of Israel, Volume Four | Neusner |
| 240077 | The Bavli's Unique Voice: A Systematic Comparison of the Talmud of Babylonia and the Talmud of the Land of Israel, Volume Five | Neusner |
| 240078 | The Bavli's Unique Voice: A Systematic Comparison of the Talmud of Babylonia and the Talmud of the Land of Israel, Volume Six | Neusner |
| 240079 | The Bavli's Unique Voice: A Systematic Comparison of the Talmud of Babylonia and the Talmud of the Land of Israel, Volume Seven | Neusner |
| 240080 | Are There Really Tannaitic Parallels to the Gospels? | Neusner |
| 240081 | Approaches to Ancient Judaism: New Series, Volume Four, Religious and Theological Studies | Neusner |
| 240082 | Approaches to Ancient Judaism: New Series, Volume Five, Historical, Literary, and Religious Studies | Basser/Fishbane |
| 240083 | Ancient Judaism: Debates and Disputes, Third Series | Neusner |
| 240084 | Judaic Law from Jesus to the Mishnah | Neusner |
| 240085 | Writing with Scripture: Second Printing | Neusner/Green |
| 240086 | Foundations of Judaism: Second Printing | Neusner |

| | | |
|---|---|---|
| 240087 | Judaism and Zoroastrianism at the Dusk of Late Antiquity | Neusner |
| 240088 | Judaism States Its Theology | Neusner |
| 240089 | The Judaism behind the Texts I.A | Neusner |
| 240090 | The Judaism behind the Texts I.B | Neusner |
| 240091 | Stranger at Home | Neusner |
| 240092 | Pseudo-Rabad: Commentary to Sifre Deuteronomy | Basser |
| 240093 | FromText to Historical Context in Rabbinic Judaism | Neusner |
| 240094 | Formative Judaism | Neusner |
| 240095 | Purity in Rabbinic Judaism | Neusner |
| 240096 | Was Jesus of Nazareth the Messiah? | McMichael |
| 240097 | The Judaism behind the Texts I.C | Neusner |
| 240098 | The Judaism behind the Texts II | Neusner |
| 240099 | The Judaism behind the Texts III | Neusner |
| 240100 | The Judaism behind the Texts IV | Neusner |
| 240101 | The Judaism behind the Texts V | Neusner |
| 240102 | The Judaism the Rabbis Take for Granted | Neusner |
| 240103 | From Text to Historical Context in Rabbinic Judaism V. II | Neusner |
| 240104 | From Text to Historical Context in Rabbinic Judaism V. III | Neusner |
| 240105 | Samuel, Saul, and Jesus: Three Early Palestinian Jewish Christian Gospel Haggadoth | Aus |
| 240106 | What is Midrash? And a Midrash Reader | Neusner |
| 240107 | Rabbinic Judaism: Disputes and Debates | Neusner |
| 240108 | Why There Never Was a "Talmud of Caesarea" | Neusner |
| 240109 | Judaism after the Death of "The Death of God" | Neusner |
| 240110 | Approaches to Ancient Judaism | Neusner |
| 240112 | The Judaic Law of Baptism | Neusner |
| 240113 | The Documentary Foundation of Rabbinic Culture | Neusner |
| 240114 | Understanding Seeking Faith, Volume Four | Neusner |
| 240115 | Paul and Judaism: An Anthropological Approach | Laato |
| 240116 | Approaches to Ancient Judaism, New Series, Volume Eight | Neusner |
| 240119 | Theme and Context in Biblical Lists | Scolnic |
| 240120 | Where the Talmud Comes From | Neusner |
| 240121 | The Initial Phases of the Talmud, Volume Three: Social Ethics | Neusner |
| 240122 | Are the Talmuds Interchangeable? Christine Hayes's Blunder | Neusner |
| 240123 | The Initial Phases of the Talmud, Volume One: Exegesis of Scripture | Neusner |
| 240124 | The Initial Phases of the Talmud, Volume Two: Exemplary Virtue | Neusner |
| 240125 | The Initial Phases of the Talmud, Volume Four: Theology | Neusner |
| 240126 | From Agnon to Oz | Bargad |
| 240127 | Talmudic Dialectics, Volume I: Tractate Berakhot and the Divisions of Appointed Times and Women | Neusner |
| 240128 | Talmudic Dialectics, Volume II: The Divisions of Damages and Holy Things and Tractate Niddah | Neusner |
| 240129 | The Talmud: Introduction and Reader | Neusner |
| 240130 | Gesher Vakesher: Bridges and Bonds The Life of Leon Kronish | Green |
| 240131 | Beyond Catastrophe | Neusner |

| | | |
|---|---|---|
| 240132 | Ancient Judaism, Fourth Series | Neusner |
| 240133 | Formative Judaism, New Series: Current Issues and Arguments Volume One | Neusner |
| 240134 | Sects and Scrolls | Davies |
| 240135 | Religion and Law | Neusner |
| 240136 | Approaches to Ancient Judaism, New Series, Volume Nine | Neusner |
| 240137 | Uppsala Addresses | Neusner |
| 240138 | Jews and Christians in the Life and Thought of Hugh of St. Victor | Moore |
| 240140 | Jews, Pagans, and Christians in the Golan Heights | Gregg/Urman |
| 240141 | Rosenzweig on Profane/Secular History | Vogel |
| 240142 | Approaches to Ancient Judaism, New Series, Volume Ten | Neusner |
| 240143 | Archaeology and the Galilee | Edwards/McCullough |
| 240144 | Rationality and Structure | Neusner |
| 240145 | Formative Judaism, New Series: Current Issues and Arguments Volume Two | Neusner |
| 240146 | Ancient Judaism, Religious and Theological Perspectives First Series | Neusner |
| 240147 | The Good Creator | Gelander |
| 240148 | The Mind of Classical Judaism, Volume IV, The Philosophy and Political Economy of Formative Judaism: The Mishnah's System of the Social Order | Neusner |
| 240149 | The Mind of Classical Judaism, Volume I, Modes of Thought:: Making Connections and Drawing Conclusions | Neusner |
| 240150 | The Mind of Classical Judaism, Volume II, From Philosophy to Religion | Neusner |
| 241051 | The Mind of Classical Judaism, Volume III, What is "Israel"? Social Thought in the Formative Age | Neusner |
| 240152 | The Tosefta, Translated from the Hebrew: Fifth Division, Qodoshim, The Order of Holy Things | Neusner |
| 240153 | The Theology of Rabbinic Judaism: A Prolegomenon | Neusner |
| 240154 | Approaches to Ancient Judaism, New Series, Volume Eleven | Neusner |
| 240155 | Pesiqta Rabbati: A Synoptic Edition of Pesiqta Rabbati Based upon all Extant Manuscripts and the Editio Princeps, V. I | Ulmer |
| 240156 | The Place of the Tosefta in the Halakhah of Formative Judaism: What Alberdina Houtman Didn't Notice | Neusner |
| 240157 | "Caught in the Act," Walking on the Sea, and The Release of Barabbas Revisited | Aus |
| 240158 | Approaches to Ancient Judaism, New Series, Volume Twelve | Neusner |
| 240159 | The Halakhah of the Oral Torah, A Religious Commentary, Introduction and Volume I, Part One, Between Israel and God | Neusner |
| 240160 | Claudian Policymaking and the Early Imperial Repression of Judaism at Rome | Slingerland |
| 240161 | Rashi's Commentary on Psalms 1–89 with English Translation, Introducion and Notes | Gruber |
| 240162 | Peace, In Deed | Garber/Libowitz |
| 240163 | Mediators of the Divine | Berchman |
| 240164 | Approaches to Ancient Judaism, New Series, Volume Thirteen | Neusner |
| 240165 | Targum Studies, Volume Two: Targum and Peshitta | Flesher |
| 240166 | The Text and I: Writings of Samson H. Levey | Chyet |

| | | |
|---|---|---|
| 240167 | The Documentary Form-History of Rabbinic Literature, I. The Documentary Forms of Mishnah | Neusner |
| 240168 | Louis Finkelstein and the Conservative Movement | Greenbaum |
| 240169 | Invitation to the Talmud: A Teaching Book | Neusner |
| 240170 | Invitation to Midrash: The Workings of Rabbinic Bible Interpretation, A Teaching Book | Neusner |
| 240171 | The Documentary Form-History of Rabbinic Literature, II. The Aggadic Sector:Tractate Abot, Abot deRabbi Natan, Sifra, Sifré to Numbers and Sifré to Deuteronomy | Neusner |
| 240172 | The Documentary Form-History of Rabbinic Literature, III. The Aggadic Sector: Mekhilta Attributed to R. Ishmael and Genesis Rabbah | Neusner |
| 240173 | The Documentary Form-History of Rabbinic Literature, IV. The Aggadic Sector: Leviticus Rabbah and Pesiqta deRab Kahana | Neusner |
| 240174 | The Documentary Form-History of Rabbinic Literature, V. The Aggadic Sector: Song of Songs Rabbah, Ruth Rabbah, Lamentations Rabbati, and Esther Rabbah I | Neusner |
| 240175 | The Documentary Form-History of Rabbinic Literature, VI. The Halakhic Sector: The Talmud of the Land of Israel A. Tractates Berakhot and Shabbat through Taanit | Neusner |
| 240176 | The Documentary Form-History of Rabbinic Literature, VI. The Halakhic Sector: The Talmud of the Land of Israel B. Tractates Megillah through Qiddushin | Neusner |
| 240177 | The Documentary Form-History of Rabbinic Literature, VI. The Halakhic Sector: The Talmud of the Land of Israel C. Tractates Sotah through Horayot and Niddah | Neusner |
| 240178 | The Documentary Form-History of Rabbinic Literature, VII. The Halakhic Sector: The Talmud of the Land of Israel A. Tractates Berakhot and Shabbat through Pesahim | Neusner |
| 240179 | The Documentary Form-History of Rabbinic Literature, VII. The Halakhic Sector: The Talmud of Babylonia B. Tractates Yoma through Ketubot | Neusner |
| 240180 | The Documentary Form-History of Rabbinic Literature, VII. The Halakhic Sector: The Talmud of Babylonia C. Tractates Nedarim through Baba Mesia | Neusner |
| 240181 | The Documentary Form-History of Rabbinic Literature, VII. The Halakhic Sector: The Talmud of Babylonia D. Tractates Baba Batra through Horayot | Neusner |
| 240182 | The Documentary Form-History of Rabbinic Literature, VII. The Halakhic Sector: The Talmud of Babylonia E. Tractates Zebahim through Bekhorot | Neusner |
| 240183 | The Documentary Form-History of Rabbinic Literature, VII. The Halakhic Sector: The Talmud of Babylonia F. Tractates Arakhin through Niddah and Conclusions | Neusner |
| 240184 | Messages to Moscow: And Other Current Lectures on Learning and Community in Judaism | Neusner |
| 240185 | The Economics of the Mishnah | Neusner |
| 240186 | Approaches to Ancient Judaism, New Series, Volume Fourteen | Neusner |
| 240187 | Jewish Law from Moses to the Mishnah | Neusner |
| 240188 | The Language and the Law of God | Calabi |

| | | |
|---|---|---|
| 240189 | Pseudo-Rabad: Commentary to Sifre Numbers | Basser |
| 240190 | How Adin Steinstalz Misrepresents the Talmud | Neusner |
| 240191 | How the Rabbis Liberated Women | Neusner |
| 240192 | From Scripture to 70 | Neusner |
| 240193 | The Levites: Their Emergence as a Second-Class Priesthood | Nurmela |
| 240194 | Sifra | Ginsberg |
| 240195 | Approaches to Ancient Judaism, New Series, Volume Fifteen | Neusner |
| 240196 | What, Exactly, Did the Rabbinic Sages Mean by the "Oral Torah"? | Neusner |
| 240197 | The Book of Job with a Commentary for Our Times | Sacks |
| 240198 | Symbol and Theology in Early Judaism | Neusner |

## South Florida Academic Commentary Series

| | | |
|---|---|---|
| 243001 | The Talmud of Babylonia, An Academic Commentary, Volume XI, Bavli Tractate Moed Qatan | Neusner |
| 243002 | The Talmud of Babylonia, An Academic Commentary, Volume XXXIV, Bavli Tractate Keritot | Neusner |
| 243003 | The Talmud of Babylonia, An Academic Commentary, Volume XVII, Bavli Tractate Sotah | Neusner |
| 243004 | The Talmud of Babylonia, An Academic Commentary, Volume XXIV, Bavli Tractate Makkot | Neusner |
| 243005 | The Talmud of Babylonia, An Academic Commentary, Volume XXXII, Bavli Tractate Arakhin | Neusner |
| 243006 | The Talmud of Babylonia, An Academic Commentary, Volume VI, Bavli Tractate Sukkah | Neusner |
| 243007 | The Talmud of Babylonia, An Academic Commentary, Volume XII, Bavli Tractate Hagigah | Neusner |
| 243008 | The Talmud of Babylonia, An Academic Commentary, Volume XXVI, Bavli Tractate Horayot | Neusner |
| 243009 | The Talmud of Babylonia, An Academic Commentary, Volume XXVII, Bavli Tractate Shebuot | Neusner |
| 243010 | The Talmud of Babylonia, An Academic Commentary, Volume XXXIII, Bavli Tractate Temurah | Neusner |
| 243011 | The Talmud of Babylonia, An Academic Commentary, Volume XXXV, Bavli Tractates Meilah and Tamid | Neusner |
| 243012 | The Talmud of Babylonia, An Academic Commentary, Volume VIII, Bavli Tractate Rosh Hashanah | Neusner |
| 243013 | The Talmud of Babylonia, An Academic Commentary, Volume V, Bavli Tractate Yoma | Neusner |
| 243014 | The Talmud of Babylonia, An Academic Commentary, Volume XXXVI, Bavli Tractate Niddah | Neusner |
| 243015 | The Talmud of Babylonia, An Academic Commentary, Volume XX, Bavli Tractate Baba Qamma | Neusner |
| 243016 | The Talmud of Babylonia, An Academic Commentary, Volume XXXI, Bavli Tractate Bekhorot | Neusner |
| 243017 | The Talmud of Babylonia, An Academic Commentary, Volume XXX, Bavli Tractate Hullin | Neusner |

| | | |
|---|---|---|
| 243018 | The Talmud of Babylonia, An Academic Commentary, Volume VII, Bavli Tractate Besah | Neusner |
| 243019 | The Talmud of Babylonia, An Academic Commentary, Volume X, Bavli Tractate Megillah | Neusner |
| 243020 | The Talmud of Babylonia, An Academic Commentary, Volume XXVIII, Bavli Tractate Zebahim A. Chapters I through VII | Neusner |
| 243021 | The Talmud of Babylonia, An Academic Commentary, Volume XXI, Bavli Tractate Baba Mesia, A. Chapters I through VI | Neusner |
| 243022 | The Talmud of Babylonia, An Academic Commentary, Volume XXII, Bavli Tractate Baba Batra, A. Chapters I through VI | Neusner |
| 243023 | The Talmud of Babylonia, An Academic Commentary, Volume XXIX, Bavli Tractate Menahot, A. Chapters I through VI | Neusner |
| 243024 | The Talmud of Babylonia, An Academic Commentary, Volume I, Bavli Tractate Berakhot | Neusner |
| 243025 | The Talmud of Babylonia, An Academic Commentary, Volume XXV, Bavli Tractate Abodah Zarah | Neusner |
| 243026 | The Talmud of Babylonia, An Academic Commentary, Volume XXIII, Bavli Tractate Sanhedrin, A. Chapters I through VII | Neusner |
| 243027 | The Talmud of Babylonia, A Complete Outline, Part IV, The Division of Holy Things; A: From Tractate Zabahim through Tractate Hullin | Neusner |
| 243028 | The Talmud of Babylonia, An Academic Commentary, Volume XIV, Bavli Tractate Ketubot, A. Chapters I through VI | Neusner |
| 243029 | The Talmud of Babylonia, An Academic Commentary, Volume IV, Bavli Tractate Pesahim, A. Chapters I through VII | Neusner |
| 243030 | The Talmud of Babylonia, An Academic Commentary, Volume III, Bavli Tractate Erubin, A. ChaptersI through V | Neusner |
| 243031 | The Talmud of Babylonia, A Complete Outline, Part III, The Division of Damages; A: From Tractate Baba Qamma through Tractate Baba Batra | Neusner |
| 243032 | The Talmud of Babylonia, An Academic Commentary, Volume II, Bavli Tractate Shabbat, Volume A, Chapters One through Twelve | Neusner |
| 243033 | The Talmud of Babylonia, An Academic Commentary, Volume II, Bavli Tractate Shabbat, Volume B, Chapters Thirteen through Twenty-four | Neusner |
| 243034 | The Talmud of Babylonia, An Academic Commentary, Volume XV, Bavli Tractate Nedarim | Neusner |
| 243035 | The Talmud of Babylonia, An Academic Commentary, Volume XVIII, Bavli Tractate Gittin | Neusner |
| 243036 | The Talmud of Babylonia, An Academic Commentary, Volume XIX, Bavli Tractate Qiddushin | Neusner |

| | | |
|---|---|---|
| 243037 | The Talmud of Babylonia, A Complete Outline, Part IV, The Division of Holy Things; B: From Tractate Berakot through Tractate Niddah | Neusner |
| 243038 | The Talmud of Babylonia, A Complete Outline, Part III, The Division of Damages; B: From Tractate Sanhedrin through Tractate Shebuot | Neusner |
| 243039 | The Talmud of Babylonia, A Complete Outline, Part I, Tractate Berakhot and the Division of Appointed Times A: From Tractate Berakhot through Tractate Pesahim | Neusner |
| 243040 | The Talmud of Babylonia, A Complete Outline, Part I, Tractate Berakhot and the Division of Appointed Times B: From Tractate Yoma through Tractate Hagigah | Neusner |
| 243041 | The Talmud of Babylonia, A Complete Outline, Part II, The Division of Women; A: From Tractate Yebamot through Tractate Ketubot | Neusner |
| 243042 | The Talmud of Babylonia, A Complete Outline, Part II, The Division of Women; B: From Tractate Nedarim through Tractate Qiddushin | Neusner |
| 243043 | The Talmud of Babylonia, An Academic Commentary, Volume XIII, Bavli Tractate Yebamot, A. Chapters One through Eight | Neusner |
| 243044 | The Talmud of Babylonia, An Academic Commentary, XIII, Bavli Tractate Yebamot, B. Chapters Nine through Seventeen | Neusner |
| 243045 | The Talmud of the Land of Israel, A Complete Outline of the Second, Third and Fourth Divisions, Part II, The Division of Women, A. Yebamot to Nedarim | Neusner |
| 243046 | The Talmud of the Land of Israel, A Complete Outline of the Second, Third and Fourth Divisions, Part II, The Division of Women, B. Nazir to Sotah | Neusner |
| 243047 | The Talmud of the Land of Israel, A Complete Outline of the Second, Third and Fourth Divisions, Part I, The Division of Appointed Times, C. Pesahim and Sukkah | Neusner |
| 243048 | The Talmud of the Land of Israel, A Complete Outline of the Second, Third and Fourth Divisions, Part I, The Division of Appointed Times, A. Berakhot, Shabbat | Neusner |
| 243049 | The Talmud of the Land of Israel, A Complete Outline of the Second, Third and Fourth Divisions, Part I, The Division of Appointed Times, B. Erubin, Yoma and Besah | Neusner |
| 243050 | The Talmud of the Land of Israel, A Complete Outline of the Second, Third and Fourth Divisions, Part I, The Division of Appointed Times, D. Taanit, Megillah, Rosh Hashannah, Hagigah and Moed Qatan | Neusner |
| 243051 | The Talmud of the Land of Israel, A Complete Outline of the Second, Third and Fourth Divisions, Part III, The Division of Damages, A. Baba Qamma, Baba Mesia, Baba Batra, Horayot and Niddah | Neusner |
| 243052 | The Talmud of the Land of Israel, A Complete Outline of the Second, Third and Fourth Divisions, Part III, The Division of Damages, B. Sanhedrin, Makkot, Shebuot and Abldah Zarah | Neusner |

| | | |
|---|---|---|
| 243053 | The Two Talmuds Compared, II. The Division of Women in the Talmud of the Land of Israel and the Talmud of Babylonia, Volume A, Tractates Yebamot and Ketubot | Neusner |
| 243054 | The Two Talmuds Compared, II. The Division of Women in the Talmud of the Land of Israel and the Talmud of Babylonia, Volume B, Tractates Nedarim, Nazir and Sotah | Neusner |
| 243055 | The Two Talmuds Compared, II. The Division of Women in the Talmud of the Land of Israel and the Talmud of Babylonia, Volume C, Tractates Qiddushin and Gittin | Neusner |
| 243056 | The Two Talmuds Compared, III. The Division of Damages in the Talmud of the Land of Israel and the Talmud of Babylonia, Volume A, Tractates Baba Qamma and Baba Mesia | Neusner |
| 243057 | The Two Talmuds Compared, III. The Division of Damages in the Talmud of the Land of Israel and the Talmud of Babylonia, Volume B, Tractates Baba Batra and Niddah | Neusner |
| 243058 | The Two Talmuds Compared, III. The Division of Damages in the Talmud of the Land of Israel and the Talmud of Babylonia, Volume C, Tractates Sanhedrin and Makkot | Neusner |
| 243059 | The Two Talmuds Compared, I. Tractate Berakhot and the Division of Appointed Times in the Talmud of the Land of Israel and the Talmud of Babylonia, Volume B, Tractate Shabbat | Neusner |
| 243060 | The Two Talmuds Compared, I. Tractate Berakhot and the Division of Appointed Times in the Talmud of the Land of Israel and the Talmud of Babylonia, Volume A, Tractate Berakhot | Neusner |
| 243061 | The Two Talmuds Compared, III. The Division of Damages in the Talmud of the Land of Israel and the Talmud of Babylonia, Volume D, Tractates Shebuot, Abodah Zarah and Horayot | Neusner |
| 243062 | The Two Talmuds Compared, I. Tractate Berakhot and the Division of Appointed Times in the Talmud of the Land of Israel and the Talmud of Babylonia, Volume C, Tractate Erubin | Neusner |
| 243063 | The Two Talmuds Compared, I. Tractate Berakhot and the Division of Appointed Times in the Talmud of the Land of Israel and the Talmud of Babylonia, Volume D, Tractates Yoma and Sukkah | Neusner |
| 243064 | The Two Talmuds Compared, I. Tractate Berakhot and the Division of Appointed Times in the Talmud of the Land of Israel and the Talmud of Babylonia, Volume E, Tractate Pesahim | Neusner |
| 243065 | The Two Talmuds Compared, I. Tractate Berakhot and the Division of Appointed Times in the Talmud of the Land of Israel and the Talmud of Babylonia, Volume F, Tractates Besah, Taanit and Megillah | Neusner |
| 243066 | The Two Talmuds Compared, I. Tractate Berakhot and the Division of Appointed Times in the Talmud of the Land of Israel and the Talmud of Babylonia, Volume G, Tractates Rosh Hashanah and Moed Qatan | Neusner |
| 243067 | The Talmud of Babylonia, An Academic Commentary, Volume XXII, Bavli Tractate Baba Batra, B. Chapters VII through XI | Neusner |
| 243068 | The Talmud of Babylonia, An Academic Commentary, Volume XXIII, Bavli Tractate Sanhedrin, B. Chapters VIII through XII | Neusner |

| | | |
|---|---|---|
| 243069 | The Talmud of Babylonia, An Academic Commentary, Volume XIV, Bavli Tractate Ketubot, B. ChaptersVII through XIV | Neusner |
| 243070 | The Talmud of Babylonia, An Academic Commentary, Volume IV, Bavli Tractate Pesahim, B. Chapters VIII through XI | Neusner |
| 243071 | The Talmud of Babylonia, An Academic Commentary, Volume XXIX, Bavli Tractate Menahot, B. Chapters VII through XIV | Neusner |
| 243072 | The Talmud of Babylonia, An Academic Commentary, Volume XXVIII, Bavli Tractate Zebahim B. Chapters VIII through XV | Neusner |
| 243073 | The Talmud of Babylonia, An Academic Commentary, Volume XXI, Bavli Tractate Baba Mesia, B. Chapters VIII through XI | Neusner |
| 243074 | The Talmud of Babylonia, An Academic Commentary, Volume III, Bavli Tractate Erubin, A. ChaptersVI through XI | Neusner |
| 243075 | The Components of the Rabbinic Documents: From the Whole to the Parts, I. Sifra, Part One | Neusner |
| 243076 | The Components of the Rabbinic Documents: From the Whole to the Parts, I. Sifra, Part Two | Neusner |
| 243077 | The Components of the Rabbinic Documents: From the Whole to the Parts, I. Sifra, Part Three | Neusner |
| 243078 | The Components of the Rabbinic Documents: From the Whole to the Parts, I. Sifra, Part Four | Neusner |
| 243079 | The Components of the Rabbinic Documents: From the Whole to the Parts, II. Esther Rabbah I | Neusner |
| 243080 | The Components of the Rabbinic Documents: From the Whole to the Parts, III. Ruth Rabbah | Neusner |
| 243081 | The Components of the Rabbinic Documents: From the Whole to the Parts, IV. Lamemtations Rabbah | Neusner |
| 243082 | The Components of the Rabbinic Documents: From the Whole to the Parts, V. Song of Songs Rabbah, Part One | Neusner |
| 243083 | The Components of the Rabbinic Documents: From the Whole to the Parts, V. Song of Songs Rabbah, Part Two | Neusner |
| 243084 | The Components of the Rabbinic Documents: From the Whole to the Parts, VI. The Fathers According to Rabbi Nathan | Neusner |
| 243085 | The Components of the Rabbinic Documents: From the Whole to the Parts, VII. Sifré to Deuteronomy, Part One | Neusner |
| 243086 | The Components of the Rabbinic Documents: From the Whole to the Parts, VII. Sifré to Deuteronomy, Part Two | Neusner |
| 243087 | The Components of the Rabbinic Documents: From the Whole to the Parts, VII. Sifré to Deuteronomy, Part Three | Neusner |
| 243088 | The Components of the Rabbinic Documents: From the Whole to the Parts, VIII. Mekhilta Attributed to Rabbi Ishmael, Part One | Neusner |
| 243089 | The Components of the Rabbinic Documents: From the Whole to the Parts, VIII. Mekhilta Attributed to Rabbi Ishmael, Part Two | Neusner |
| 243090 | The Components of the Rabbinic Documents: From the Whole to the Parts, VIII. Mekhilta Attributed to Rabbi Ishmael, Part Three | Neusner |

| | | |
|---|---|---|
| 243092 | The Components of the Rabbinic Documents: From the Whole to the Parts, IX. Genesis Rabbah, Part One, Introduction and Chapters One through Twenty-two | Neusner |
| 243093 | The Components of the Rabbinic Documents: From the Whole to the Parts, IX. Genesis Rabbah, Part Two, Chapters Twenty-three through Fifty | Neusner |
| 243094 | The Components of the Rabbinic Documents: From the Whole to the Parts, IX. Genesis Rabbah, Part Three, Chapters Fifty-one through Seventy-five | Neusner |
| 243095 | The Components of the Rabbinic Documents: From the Whole to the Parts, X. Leviticus Rabbah, Part One, Introduction and Parashiyyot One through Seventeen | Neusner |
| 243096 | The Components of the Rabbinic Documents: From the Whole to the Parts, X. Leviticus Rabbah, Part Two, Parashiyyot Eighteen through Thirty-seven | Neusner |
| 243097 | The Components of the Rabbinic Documents: From the Whole to the Parts, X. Leviticus Rabbah, Part Three, Topical and Methodical Outline | Neusner |
| 243098 | The Components of the Rabbinic Documents: From the Whole to the Parts, XI. Pesiqta deRab Kahana, Part One, Introduction and Pisqaot One through Eleven | Neusner |
| 243099 | The Components of the Rabbinic Documents: From the Whole to the Parts, XI. Pesiqta deRab Kahana, Part Two, Pisqaot Twelve through Twenty-eight | Neusner |
| 243100 | The Components of the Rabbinic Documents: From the Whole to the Parts, XI. Pesiqta deRab Kahana, Part Three, A Topical and Methodical Outline | Neusner |
| 243101 | The Components of the Rabbinic Documents: From the Whole to the Parts, IX. Genesis Rabbah, Part Four, Chapters Seventy-six through One Hundred | Neusner |
| 243102 | The Components of the Rabbinic Documents: From the Whole to the Parts, IX. Genesis Rabbah, Part Five, A Methodical and Topical Outline; Bereshit through Vaere, Chapters One through Fifty-seven | Neusner |
| 243103 | The Components of the Rabbinic Documents: From the Whole to the Parts, IX. Genesis Rabbah, Part Six, A Methodical and Topical Outline; Hayye Sarah through Miqqes, Chapters Fifty-eight through One Hundred | Neusner |
| 243104 | The Components of the Rabbinic Documents: From the Whole to the Parts, XII., Sifré to Numbers, Part One, Introduction and Pisqaot One through Seventy-one | Neusner |
| 243105 | The Components of the Rabbinic Documents: From the Whole to the Parts, XII., Sifré to Numbers, Part Two, Pisqaot Seventy-two through One Hundred Twenty-two | Neusner |
| 243106 | The Components of the Rabbinic Documents: From the Whole to the Parts, XII., Sifré to Numbers, Part Three, Pisqaot One Hundred Twenty-three through One Hundred Sixty-one | Neusner |
| 243107 | The Components of the Rabbinic Documents: From the Whole to the Parts, XII., Sifré to Numbers, Part Four, A Topical and Methodical Outline | Neusner |

| | | |
|---|---|---|
| 243108 | The Talmud of the Land of Israel: An Academic Commentary of the Second, Third, and Fourth Divisions, I. Yerushalmi Tractate Berakhot (Based on the Translation by Tzvee Zahavy) | Neusner |
| 243109 | The Talmud of the Land of Israel: An Academic Commentary of the Second, Third, and Fourth Divisions, II. Yerushalmi Tractate Shabbat. A. Chapters One through Ten | Neusner |
| 243110 | The Talmud of the Land of Israel: An Academic Commentary of the Second, Third, and Fourth Divisions, II. Yerushalmi Tractate Shabbat. B. Chapters Eleven through Twenty-Four and The Structure of Yerushalmi Shabbat | Neusner |
| 243111 | The Talmud of the Land of Israel: An Academic Commentary of the Second, Third, and Fourth Divisions, III. Yerushalmi Tractate Erubin | Neusner |
| 243112 | The Talmud of the Land of Israel: An Academic Commentary of the Second, Third, and Fourth Divisions, IV. Yerushalmi Tractate Yoma | Neusner |
| 243113 | The Talmud of the Land of Israel: An Academic Commentary of the Second, Third, and Fourth Divisions, V. Yerushalmi Tractate Pesahim A. Chapters One through Six, Based on the English Translation of Baruch M. Bokser with Lawrence Schiffman | Neusner |
| 243114 | The Talmud of the Land of Israel: An Academic Commentary of the Second, Third, and Fourth Divisions, V. Yerushalmi Tractate Pesahim B. Chapters Seven through Ten and The Structure of Yerushalmi Pesahim, Based on the English Translation of Baruch M. Bokser with Lawrence Schiffman | Neusner |
| 243115 | The Talmud of the Land of Israel: An Academic Commentary of the Second, Third, and Fourth Divisions, VI. Yerushalmi Tractate Sukkah | Neusner |
| 243116 | The Talmud of the Land of Israel: An Academic Commentary of the Second, Third, and Fourth Divisions, VII. Yerushalmi Tractate Besah | Neusner |
| 243117 | The Talmud of the Land of Israel: An Academic Commentary of the Second, Third, and Fourth Divisions, VIII. Yerushalmi Tractate Taanit | Neusner |
| 243118 | The Talmud of the Land of Israel: An Academic Commentary of the Second, Third, and Fourth Divisions, IX. Yerushalmi Tractate Megillah | Neusner |
| 243119 | The Talmud of the Land of Israel: An Academic Commentary of the Second, Third, and Fourth Divisions, X. Yerushalmi Tractate Rosh Hashanah | Neusner |
| 243120 | The Talmud of the Land of Israel: An Academic Commentary of the Second, Third, and Fourth Divisions, XI. Yerushalmi Tractate Hagigah | Neusner |
| 243121 | The Talmud of the Land of Israel: An Academic Commentary of the Second, Third, and Fourth Divisions, XII. Yerushalmi Tractate Moed Qatan | Neusner |
| 243122 | The Talmud of the Land of Israel: An Academic Commentary of the Second, Third, and Fourth Divisions, XIII. Yerushalmi Tractate Yebamot, A. Chapters One through Ten | Neusner |

| | | |
|---|---|---|
| 243123 | The Talmud of the Land of Israel: An Academic Commentary of the Second, Third, and Fourth Divisions, XIII. Yerushalmi Tractate Yebamot, B. Chapters Eleven through Seventeen | Neusner |
| 243124 | The Talmud of the Land of Israel: An Academic Commentary of the Second, Third, and Fourth Divisions, XIV. Yerushalmi Tractate Ketubot | Neusner |
| 243125 | The Talmud of the Land of Israel: An Academic Commentary of the Second, Third, and Fourth Divisions, XV. Yerushalmi Tractate Nedarim | Neusner |
| 243126 | The Talmud of the Land of Israel: An Academic Commentary of the Second, Third, and Fourth Divisions, XVI. Yerushalmi Tractate Nazir | Neusner |
| 243127 | The Talmud of the Land of Israel: An Academic Commentary of the Second, Third, and Fourth Divisions, XVII. Yerushalmi Tractate Gittin | Neusner |
| 243128 | The Talmud of the Land of Israel: An Academic Commentary of the Second, Third, and Fourth Divisions, XVIII. Yerushalmi Tractate Qiddushin | Neusner |
| 243129 | The Talmud of the Land of Israel: An Academic Commentary of the Second, Third, and Fourth Divisions, XIX. Yerushalmi Tractate Sotah | Neusner |
| 243130 | The Talmud of the Land of Israel: An Academic Commentary of the Second, Third, and Fourth Divisions, XX. Yerushalmi Tractate Baba Qamma | Neusner |
| 243131 | The Talmud of the Land of Israel: An Academic Commentary of the Second, Third, and Fourth Divisions, XXI. Yerushalmi Tractate Baba Mesia | Neusner |
| 243132 | The Talmud of the Land of Israel: An Academic Commentary of the Second, Third, and Fourth Divisions, XXII. Yerushalmi Tractate Baba Batra | Neusner |
| 243133 | The Talmud of the Land of Israel: An Academic Commentary of the Second, Third, and Fourth Divisions, XXIII. Yerushalmi Tractate Sanhedrin | Neusner |
| 243134 | The Talmud of the Land of Israel: An Academic Commentary of the Second, Third, and Fourth Divisions, XIV. Yerushalmi Tractate Makkot | Neusner |

## South Florida-Rochester-Saint Louis Studies on Religion and the Social Order

| | | |
|---|---|---|
| 245001 | Faith and Context, Volume 1 | Ong |
| 245002 | Faith and Context, Volume 2 | Ong |
| 245003 | Judaism and Civil Religion | Breslauer |
| 245004 | The Sociology of Andrew M. Greeley | Greeley |
| 245005 | Faith and Context, Volume 3 | Ong |
| 245006 | The Christ of Michelangelo | Dixon |
| 245007 | From Hermeneutics to Ethical Consensus Among Cultures | Bori |
| 245008 | Mordecai Kaplan's Thought in a Postmodern Age | Breslauer |

| | | |
|---|---|---|
| 245009 | No Longer Aliens, No Longer Strangers | Eckardt |
| 245010 | Between Tradition and Culture | Ellenson |
| 245011 | Religion and the Social Order | Neusner |
| 245012 | Christianity and the Stranger | Nichols |
| 245013 | The Polish Challenge | Czosnyka |
| 245014 | Islam and the Question of Minorities | Sonn |
| 245015 | Religion and the Political Order | Neusner |
| 245016 | The Ecology of Religion | Neusner |
| 245017 | The Shaping of an American Islamic Discourse | Waugh/Denny |
| 245018 | The Muslim Brotherhood and the Kings of Jordan, 1945–1993 | Boulby |
| 245019 | Muslims on the Americanization Path | Esposito/Haddad |
| 245020 | Protean Prejudice: Anti-semitism in England's Age of Reason | Glassman |
| 245021 | The Study of Religion: In Retrospect and Prospect | Green |
| 245024 | Jacques Ellul on Religion, Technology and Politics: Conversations with Patrick Troude-Chastenet | France |

## South Florida International Studies in Formative Christianity and Judaism

| | | |
|---|---|---|
| 242501 | The Earliest Christian Mission to 'All Nations' | La Grand |
| 242502 | Judaic Approaches to the Gospels | Chilton |
| 242503 | The "Essence of Christianity" | Forni Rosa |
| 242504 | The Wicked Tenants and Gethsemane | Aus |
| 242505 | A Star Is Rising | Laato |
| 242506 | Romans 9–11: A Reader-Response Analysis | Lodge |
| 242507 | The Good News of Peter's Denial | Borrell |
| 242508 | ΛΟΓΟΙ ΙΗΣΟΥ, Studies in Q | Vassiliadis |
| 242509 | Romans 8:18–30: "Suffering Does Not Thwart the Future Glory" | Gieniusz |

HIEBERT LIBRARY

3 6877 00163 8617

BS
2555.2
.V295
1999

**DATE DUE**

| OC 23 '02 | | | |
|---|---|---|---|
| | | | |
| | | | |
| | | | |
| | | | |
| | | | |
| | | | |
| | | | |
| | | | |
| | | | |
| | | | |
| | | | |
| | | | |
| | | | |
| | | | |
| | | | |

Demco, Inc. 38-293